Teri Pichot, LCSW, MAC, LAC
Marc Coulter, LPC, CAC III

Animal-Assisted
Brief Therapy
A Solution-Focused
Approach

Pre-publication
REVIEWS,
COMMENTARIES,
EVALUATIONS . . .

"**E**very therapist should read this book. Pichot and Coulter not only reveal the transforming ability of the human-animal bond to unlock the healing power in clients' lives, they also provide the vital keys to effective utilization of animal-assisted therapy in the therapeutic setting. The attention to detail for how to implement solution-focused AAT is commendable. This book benefits both the human and animal components of therapy through emphasizing the importance of a balanced partnership between therapist, client, and therapy dog.

The most valuable and informative section is Chapter 3, in which the reader is led on a journey of the 'must-knows' of integrating a therapy dog into one's practice. The transforming ability of a therapy dog partnership comes with tremendous responsibility to ensure the safety, respect, and well-being of the dog, while at the same time understanding how it thinks and what motivates the dog. The realization that this is only one of many applications that can be made to a client's personal relationships is tremendously enlightening and empowering.

For every therapist who wants to explore their hidden potential and creatively challenge traditional treatment intervention. This book is a must-read."

Diana M. McQuarrie
Executive Director,
Denver Pet Partners

More pre-publication
REVIEWS, COMMENTARIES, EVALUATIONS . . .

"*Animal-Assisted Brief Therapy* may be the strongest effort to date to provide a definitive and comprehensive theory base and framework for understanding how animals can be included into a therapeutic setting. In my work as an assistant professor, implementing an academic program and teaching graduate students how to develop the needed skills to incorporate animal-assisted therapy and activities into their practices, we have lacked definitive models and guidelines. We have been awaiting just such a text and look forward to utilizing this book as a required read for students in the animal-assisted social work program at the University of Denver.

It was especially welcome to have the authors highlight the integration of animal-assisted therapy and activities with the progressive model of brief therapy. The book boldly and clearly proposes effective means to integrating these motivational therapeutic approaches, as well as providing the reader an improved understanding of elements of both models. The authors have provided us a carefully laid out discussion of the needed skills and preparation for the successful implementation of a canine therapy program. New practitioners will appreciate the authors' collective experience in navigating the challenges of formalizing a therapeutic canine program in a professional/clinical environment.

Important topics such as credentialing for dog and handler, insurance and liability issues, and developing and maintaining program credibility are clearly defined and addressed in such a complete manner that we no longer have to learn these lessons the hard way. In this book, the authors have provided factual approaches to assessing when to incorporate a therapy dog, the development of treatment plans and objectives, and the strategies and content of these interventions with children, adolescents, and adults. This may be the very first book that has identified the importance of achieving measurable outcomes as part of the animal therapy interventions. No matter how effective we believe these approaches to be, our collective credibility in utilizing them can benefit from the outstanding professionalism encouraged in this book.

This book offers one of the most sensitive and useful explorations into our responsibilities to advocate for our canine colleagues and underlines the point that if pet-assisted therapy is not beneficial to the animal participants, than we have an obligation to our animal relationships to not utilize this approach. This book is an accomplishment on many levels, not the least being the careful effort to provide true and tried approaches from experienced practitioners actively utilizing these ideas in the field."

Philip Tedeschi, LCSW
Assistant Clinical Professor,
Founder/Co-Director of the Institute
for Human-Animal Connection,
Graduate School of Social Work,
University of Denver

More pre-publication
REVIEWS, COMMENTARIES, EVALUATIONS . . .

"Finally, a way of working therapeutically with animals that moves far beyond simply using pets for a 'feel good' experience. This innovative, easy-to-read guide to working in partnership with 'man's best friend' breaks new ground by cleverly integrating AAA/T with brief solution-focused therapy. Utilizing the healing powers of animals, the authors highlight how these animal-enhanced experiences can be used as a gateway to people's strengths, abilities, and preferred identities.

The well-articulated case examples clearly illustrate how to utilize the evocative experience generated by people's interactions with stable, well-trained, dedicated dogs. The book is well organized and introduces the reader to the concept of animal-assisted brief therapy, a realistic understanding of canine culture, how to set up your own successful AAA/T program, and much more. It is both touching and educational. A must-read!"

Jim Duvall, MEd
Director, Brief Therapy Training
Centres–InternationalTM
(a division of Hincks-Dellcrest Centre,
Gail Appel Institute); Senior Editor,
Journal of Systemic Therapies

"This book provides an honest and full-circle approach to the development of AAA/T programs through a solution-focused approach, while taking the animal into account every step of the way. It provides thought-provoking glimpses into a professional and personal relationship between handler and dog. A selfless relationship that is deeply meaningful based on love, respect, hard work, and thorough acceptance. This is truly a relationship that each handler of an AAA/T team shall strive to achieve with their dogs!"

Ashley Foster, BS
Owner, Complete K-9
Dog Training and Consultation

"This book is a useful introduction to both solution-focused and animal-assisted therapies. Both the therapist and nonprofessional will find that the many examples and vignettes bring this approach to therapy vividly to life. The appendices list helpful resources and guidelines. This is an excellent sourcebook for practitioners, animal lovers, and the general public."

Gail F. Melson, PhD
Professor Emerita,
Purdue University,
West Lafayette, IN

"Pichot and Coulter have creatively combined two effective models of healing and caring into a revolutionary therapeutic approach that truly is larger than the sum of its parts. Compellingly useful for anyone in the helping professions, *Animal-Assisted Brief Therapy* will not only enable therapists and their clients to discover effective solutions, but a new view of humanity as well."

Charlie Johnson, MSW
Founder, Solutionmind.com;
Co-author, *Recrafting a Life:*
Solutions for Chronic Pain and Illness

More pre-publication
REVIEWS, COMMENTARIES, EVALUATIONS . . .

"Using their extensive experience with 'Rocky' as well as the professional literature about both SFBT and AAA/T, the authors give us a thoughtful discussion of how animals can further the work of therapy. Their book is thorough and thoughtful and gives the clear message that animal-assisted therapy is much more than simply taking your dog to work with you. Pichot and Coulter demonstrate how, when implemented carefully, AAT can positively affect the crucial but intangible aspects of therapy—helping clients feel safe in the session, stimulating interaction, reducing the power differential between us and our clients. For those considering developing an AAT program, Pichot and Coulter provide clear guidance on how to integrate AAT into an agency—from how to deal with issues specific to the actual therapeutic work to how to negotiate agency policy and staff concerns. For those already providing AAT, the book offers a theoretical perspective for the work in solution-focused brief therapy that capitalizes on the resources that therapy animals have to offer. All in all, this is a wonderful resource."

Eric E. McCollum, PhD
Marriage and Family Therapy
Program, Virginia Tech

"This thoughtful and inspiring book provides detailed and practical guidelines for doing therapy assisted by an animal. The basics of solution-focused therapy are briefly but adequately explained. The discussion of pet psychology and what the authors call 'canine culture' is a joy to read. It will be relished by anyone who likes dogs. The authors offer detailed advice on how to set up successful treatment plans and protocols with a wide range of clients and in various settings. Written in a clear and precise, but also warm and moving, style, this book is the perfect companion for anyone who wishes to tap the resources pets can offer in doing effective psychotherapy."

Luc Isebaert, MD
Psychiatrist and Psychotherapist;
Former Head, Department
of Psychiatry and Psychosomatics,
St. John's Hospital, Bruges, Belgium;
President, Bruges Group
of training institutes

Animal-Assisted Brief Therapy
A Solution-Focused Approach

Brief Therapy Series
Yvonne M. Dolan
Editor

Animal-Assisted Brief Therapy: A Solution-Focused Approach by Teri Pichot and Marc Coulter

More Than Miracles: The State of the Art of Solution-Focused Brief Therapy by Steve de Shazer, Yvonne Dolan, Harry Korman, Eric McCollum, Terry Trepper, and Insoo Kim Berg

Other Titles of Related Interest:

Becoming a Solution Detective: Identifying Your Clients' Strengths in Practical Brief Therapy by John Sharry and Brendan Madden

Brief Psychotherapy with the Latino Immigrant Client by Marlene D. de Rios

Case Book of Brief Psychotherapy with College Students edited by Stewart E. Cooper, James Archer Jr., and Leighton C. Whitaker

Comparative Approaches in Brief Dynamic Psychotherapy edited by William Borden

Education and Training in Solution-Focused Brief Therapy edited by Thorana S. Nelson

Handbook of Solution-Focused Brief Therapy: Clinical Applications edited by Thorana S. Nelson

Solution-Focused Brief Therapy: Its Effective Use in Agency Settings by Teri Pichot and Yvonne M. Dolan

Animal-Assisted Brief Therapy
A Solution-Focused Approach

Teri Pichot, LCSW, MAC, LAC
Marc Coulter, LPC, CAC III

Routledge
Taylor & Francis Group
New York   London

Routledge is an imprint of the
Taylor & Francis Group, an informa business

PUBLISHER'S NOTE
The development, preparation, and publication of this work has been undertaken with great care. However, the Publisher, employees, editors, and agents of The Haworth Press are not responsible for any errors contained herein or for consequences that may ensue from use of materials or information contained in this work. The Haworth Press is committed to the dissemination of ideas and information according to the highest standards of intellectual freedom and the free exchange of ideas. Statements made and opinions expressed in this publication do not necessarily reflect the views of the Publisher, Directors, management, or staff of The Haworth Press, Inc., or an endorsement by them.

Identities and circumstances of individuals discussed in this book have been changed to protect confidentiality.

Cover design by Marylouise E. Doyle.

Beagle photographs by Patrick Hayes II, www.patrickhayesart.com.
Photograph of Teri Pichot's dog, Rocky, taken by Kodi Bryant.

Library of Congress Cataloging-in-Publication Data

Pichot, Teri.
Animal-assisted brief therapy : a solution-focused approach / Teri Pichot, Marc Coulter.
    p. cm.
Includes bibliographical references and index.
ISBN-13: 978-0-7890-2981-2 (hard : alk. paper)
ISBN-10: 0-7890-2981-2 (hard : alk. paper)
ISBN-13: 978-0-7890-2982-9 (soft : alk. paper)
ISBN-10: 0-7890-2982-0 (soft : alk. paper)
    1. Pets—Therapeutic use. 2. Animals—Therapeutic use. 3. Solution-focused brief therapy.
I. Coulter, Marc. II. Title.

RM931.A65P53 2006
615.8'515—dc22

                       2006006410

To all the pets throughout our lives
who taught us the amazing power
of the human-animal bond.

ABOUT THE AUTHORS

Teri Pichot, LCSW, MAC, LAC, began her career as a psychotherapist more than 15 years ago. She has worked extensively with individuals, couples, and families distressed by issues such as substance abuse and domestic violence. She is a Delta Society Pet Partner with her canine companions, Rockefeller and Jasper, and she enjoys partnering with them to provide animal-assisted interventions to her clients. She has designed and implemented innovative programs that utilize solution-focused therapy (with and without therapy dogs) with both adults and adolescents. She is currently Program Manager of the Substance Abuse Counseling Program at the Jefferson County Department of Health and Environment in addition to maintaining a private practice in the Denver area. She has published numerous journal articles, and enjoys providing training on solution-focused therapy and its implementation with "challenging" populations.

Marc Coulter, LPC, NCAC I, CAC III, is a senior counselor at the Substance Abuse Counseling Program (SACP) at the Jefferson County Department of Health and Environment. He has contributed significantly to the success of the unique solution- focused brief counseling model, which is currently used at the agency. He is a Licensed Professional Counselor and an Addiction Counselor Level III. He is a member of the Delta Society and has worked extensively with the pet partner team of Teri Pichot and her canine companion, Rockefeller, in utilizing animal-assisted interventions with clients. He assists in training on solution-focused brief therapy, as well as utilizing animal-assisted interventions on both local and national levels. His counseling background includes providing HIV testing and counseling and harm reduction interventions.

CONTENTS

Foreword

I have long known that animals could be therapeutic. During my thirty-year career as a psychotherapist, I have specialized in working with people who have suffered trauma. Because my office adjoined my home, the family pets (cats and dogs) often functioned as receptionists and occasionally even co-therapists. All my pets have been former strays or "rescue" animals. They have been friendly but usually a bit reticent in approaching the psychotherapy clients in my waiting area. For example, my cats would sit quietly in the corner near the newcomer as he or she waited, but they would not approach unless invited. The dogs would do the same. However, for some reason both my dogs and cats would always escort clients down the hall to my office and leave them at the door.

When the session was over, one of my pets would escort the person or, in some cases, several persons, to the front door. They did this quietly, typically without making a sound. If one of my clients reached down to pet the dog or cat, the animals would nuzzle in to prolong the contact. Otherwise they would remain somewhat aloof, but definitely present as they accompanied the guest to the door. Many times, after the first session, my clients asked if one of my pets could sit in on the session. Even more often, my clients spontaneously told me how spending time with animals had proven helpful at various times in their lives.

Many people told me that it was comforting to be able to hold or touch an affectionate animal while thinking about difficult, complicated issues or problems. Some said that being with their pet or even in the presence of wild animals in a nature preserve had somehow made loss and grief more bearable, and had lessened post-traumatic stress symptoms following natural disasters. A number of people told me that they thought better, more clearly, or effectively when they were touching an animal or near an animal, and a few even described how love of an animal had helped them survive the ravages of addiction and suicidal depression.

As a solution-focused therapist, I recognize the importance of identifying and replicating the things that strengthen, support, and help people live rewarding, healthy lives. Most of the people who seek help from caregivers are experiencing or have experienced some difficulty in life, and often this has resulted in some personal suffering or even trauma. Reflecting on this history can be painful, and focusing on the future is sometimes rather scary because of the anticipation of more difficulties, or fear of failure, or even more trauma. The presence of an animal almost immediately and inevitably orients one's attention to the present. Most people's senses become attuned to the comfort and furry reassurance that is potentially available.

Many years ago, I was working with a man who had suffered many traumas. He always stopped and petted my dog before coming into my office. One morning, as he sat in my office, he asked if I would bring my dog in before we started. When my dog came in, the man began to cry. The dog rested his head on the man's lap while the man sobbed and sobbed for several minutes. After the man finished crying, he wiped his eyes with his hands and my dog gently licked the tears off his fingers. Then, taking a deep breath, the man looked up at me and said, "Okay, now I am able to talk." He explained that his lover had been brutally assaulted the night before. It was as if the dog's presence not only comforted him in his pain, but also somehow helped him find the courage to confront what he needed to in order to go on. It seemed to me that my dog had provided a beneficial therapeutic experience that would have been otherwise unavailable.

Many years have passed, and although the advent of trained, credentialed therapy dogs has made therapeutic experiences involving animals far less unique, and more reliably available to those who can best benefit, I believe that trained therapy animals are capable of bridging the gap between humans in ways that cannot be reduced to words or simply explained. Because they convey comfort and affection wordlessly, animals can respond therapeutically to a wide variety of complex emotions and situations without risk of misunderstanding or trivialization. They can convey encouragement, support, empathy, affection, and even humor, and they can elicit it in their human counterparts. This book is a wonderful resource for helping professionals, caregivers, and administrators who wish to optimize therapeutic re-sources by incorporating animal-assisted therapy into their work or workplace. It is also an inspiring and uplifting read for anyone who cares deeply about people and the animals who help them heal and create better lives.

Yvonne Dolan
President, Solution-Focused
Brief Therapy Association

Acknowledgments

So many people deserve a special "thank you" for their part in this project. First and foremost we would like to thank the clients at Jefferson County Department of Health and Environment for all they have taught us through this journey of implementing our animal-assisted activities/therapy program. Although book learning is invaluable, it is the hands-on learning that plays the most important role in solidifying that knowledge and in honing our skills and understanding. Second, special thanks to our administrators, Dr. Mark Johnson and Elise Lubell, who once again demonstrated an incredible ability to critically evaluate and embrace new ideas. Their willingness to open their hearts and minds to integrating the power of the human-animal bond into public health continues to show their dedication to both innovation and forward thinking. Their ongoing, courageous professional status makes it a joy to work at this agency.

We would also like to thank all the employees at Jefferson County Department of Health and Environment who embraced Rocky from the moment he set paws in the agency. We never could have imagined the degree to which he and this program have been accepted. Without their compassion toward animals and understanding of the positive impact of the program on both staff and clients, this program could not have succeeded. Nancy Braden and Susan Trimmer have played a significant part in the nuts and bolts of informing the public about this program through their computer skills and public relations work. We could not have done it without them. A special thank you to Susan for all her hard work on the figures and photos for this book. Her attention to detail and expertise were invaluable. We would especially like to thank the Substance Abuse Counseling Program team: Calyn Crow, Carole Elia, Lisa Gray, Bobbi Kraft, Karen Nielsen, Amanda Fitzsimons, and Diane Strouse. Their enthusiasm right from the start for the animal program has been refreshing, and their genuine acceptance of Rocky as a co-worker has been a key factor in the program's success. A special "thank you" to Calyn for all her work throughout the writing of this book. Her feedback on the manuscript has been a godsend! It is truly an honor to work with such a wonderful group of peers.

We would also like to thank Yvonne Dolan for believing in this project and for supporting us every step of the way. She is truly an inspiration, and it has been wonderful to work with her on this project. Last, we would like to thank the Substance Abuse Counseling Program's Advisory Board members: William Cloud, Dr. Michael Faragher, Dr. Vel Garner, Charlie Johnson, Dr. Ruby Martinez, Dr. Scott DeMuro, Philip Tedeschi, Jonathan Heitsmith, David Blair, Dr. Tracy Todd, and Scott Storey. Their dedication to provide ideas and guidance on behalf of substance-abusing clients in Colorado and volunteer their time to ensure that the full continuum of alternatives is available to clients is truly appreciated.

I (TP) would like to personally thank Patti Yoensky, Diana McQuarrie, Ashley Foster, and Mark Hochstedler for their individual roles in the training and credentialing of Rocky. Patti was Rocky's first teacher, and was instrumental in teaching not only Rocky, but also me, about the basics of good dog behavior. We are both wiser (and better behaved) because of her. Diana first introduced me to the benefits of the Delta Society, and she painstakingly reviewed every word in this manuscript, gave advice throughout the implementation of the program, and lent her expertise about AAA/T to this project. Her knowledge about and dedication to the human-animal bond are truly an inspiration. Ashley is Rocky's ongoing professional consultant and advocate, and she serves the all-important role of helping to troubleshoot day-to-day issues in the workplace to ensure Rocky's well-being and solid manners. Her compassion for dogs and her knowledge and dedication to therapy dogs' mental well-being have inspired me to never stop learning and trying to understand how I can best partner with my dog. Every working dog deserves to have an "Ashley" in his or her life. Mark Hochstedler is my best friend and husband. Despite his long hours and hectic schedule, he always makes the time to help with Rocky's training and to reinforce and support the newest thing I decide to do. He serves as Rocky's chief photographer, business card designer, dog walker, and general dog chauffeur. I know I don't say it enough . . . thank you.

Any acknowledgment section I write would not be complete without a specific mention of gratitude to Insoo Kim Berg and Steve de Shazer. Their way of thinking and viewing clients and the world has forever touched my life, and has become a way of being for which I will always be grateful. Although they both chuckled when I first mentioned integrating a therapy dog into the approach they developed, they were supportive and encouraging right from the start. They listened with characteristic curiosity, and both seemed to quickly embrace the power of using animals to uncover differences and exceptions and to engage clients of all ages. Last, a special thank you to Charlie Johnson; my friend and mentor. His support and enthusiasm remains an energizing force in my professional life.

I (MC) would like to thank the many friends and family members who have been a part of my life and helped support and guide me on my journey. Your faith in me when I doubt myself means more to me than I can ever express. To my parents who continue to provide a nurturing environment for both me and a menagerie of furry critters. For my mom who taught me what it means to be compassionate to both people and animals, and for my dad who taught me the importance of spending time outdoors surrounded by the magnificence of nature. I am grateful for my colleagues and the clients of the Jefferson County Department of Health and Environment who have helped foster my curiosity and for their patience with my constant questions. A special acknowledgment to Teri Pichot for opening new doors of possibility in my life and for constantly encouraging me to live my miracle. You have all changed my life.

Photo by Mark Hochstedler. Used with permission.

Introduction

One of my first childhood memories is riding home in the back seat of my parents' car after picking up my first dog. She was a black toy poodle named J. J. (Her official name was Poodle Town's Black Jade Princess, but that was far too complex for a two-year-old. So, J. J. it was.) I was so excited! J. J. and I were best friends throughout my childhood. We spent countless hours playing together in our California backyard, and she patiently allowed me to dress her in doll clothes and push her down the street in my doll carriage. She was my best friend, and she always seemed to understand when no one else could. I had no idea how much J. J. would change my life. She unleashed my love for dogs and showed me how powerful the human-animal bond could be.

I loved dogs, and enjoyed reading about them as a child. My first "research" paper (in eighth grade) was about Seeing Eye dogs. I was fascinated with the idea that a dog could go everywhere with a person and take a role so vital in someone's life. I decided that someday I wanted to raise Seeing Eye puppies to help with this important mission. Unfortunately, as my mother quickly pointed out, J. J. was completely untrained and was an outdoor dog, and although I made some periodic attempts to teach J. J. some tricks, I quickly gave up. I didn't know how to help her learn. As I grew up, I spent less and less time with J. J. The years of adolescence provided little time to be outside with her. Although our time spent together dwindled, my love of dogs continued. I decided that as an adult I would get a dog that lived indoors to prevent having to choose between time with my canine friend and indoor activities.

That dog turned out to be a pocket-sized Chihuahua terrier named Snokie. He was adorable! He soon became my buddy, and I treated him like a little person with fur. He slept in the bed with me and sat on the couch. People food was of course shared with my furry friend. After a few years, a Shetland sheepdog named Pepsi Cola joined our family and enjoyed the same privileges. Although friends and family deemed my pets to be on the spoiled side, I couldn't see it. Snokie and Pepsi filled a special place in my heart. Those two dogs became an enormous support system during the death of my daughter, a divorce, medical problems, and other life tragedies. They were even my study partners throughout college as I earned my master of social work degree. These years reinforced to me the healing power of animals. There was just something about seeing how happy they always were to see me when I came home, how they never seemed to mind my bad moods, and how easily they could turn my tears into laughter.

As my professional life blossomed, my pets remained important, yet separate from work. I took a job as a clinical and administrative supervisor at a county-based substance abuse treatment program. We built a strong clinical team that was based on an innovative treatment approach first developed in Milwaukee by Insoo Kim Berg and Steve de Shazer called solution-focused brief therapy (de Shazer, 1985). The results with clients were amazing! Gone were the days of power struggles and burnout. This approach valued who the clients are, and made no effort to change their way of viewing the world. My role was to learn to really hear them; to respect them. It was through this respect that I could learn to hear what they wanted to be different and discover clues of how that could come to be. It was revolutionary!

As my professional life fell into place, Snokie and Pepsi eventually succumbed to old age. I came to see how incredibly generous my canine friends had been with me as I learned the lessons of early adulthood. I now saw how selfish I had been with them. They were always there for me, yet I had never taken the time to learn how to be there for them; to learn their culture (it never even occurred to me they had a culture separate from mine). I promised myself that my next dog would go to puppy school. That dog was a sweet-natured sable and white collie named Rockefeller (Rocky to his friends and family).

Our first day in puppy school was an eye opener. I listened as the instructor started the lesson by saying, "Now remember. Dogs are not just people with fur!" I soon realized that my way of thinking was going to change, and that Rocky was not the primary one who* was go-

---

*Although grammatically animals are referred to as "that," we have purposefully chosen to disregard this rule throughout this book and refer to animals as "who" due to their central role in our lives and in the purpose of animal-assisted solution-focused therapy.

ing to get an education at puppy school. Class was about learning how change works for dogs and about building a working relationship so that Rocky and I could communicate effectively. He already knew how to sit, lay down, etc. I just had to discover a way to communicate with him about these already known positions. Suddenly it all made sense to me why I could never seem to train my animals. My focus had been all wrong! I wanted to learn more. I signed up for every class the dog school offered. Rocky and I practiced faithfully every day, and we both learned. In doing so, a sense of accomplishment and pride was clear upon both of our faces, and a strong bond developed. His quiet whine and look was now a way to communicate with me, to which I understood and respectfully responded. And, my hand signals and quiet commands were clear communications to him, which he quickly responded to as well.

As I learned more about how dogs learn, I realized the striking similarities with my professional work. Similar to my work with clients, I was not to be the expert, but a partner in the change process. Although I was to be looked to by Rocky as the "leader of the pack" (like a client looks to a therapist to be able to help), I was to be an expert on the process, not about Rocky's culture and how he thought. He remained the expert there. I learned how he thought by taking the generic knowledge I learned in class and watching him and how he responded to the world (since he couldn't tell me directly). I was amazed to discover that the very philosophy of change that I found so effective when working with my clients, also applied with my canine friend. I learned that the most effective relationship came from valuing how my pet thought and viewed the world, not from insisting that he saw it my way. By using this as a starting point and the foundation of our relationship (similar to working with clients), amazing results became possible. I saw Rocky's motivation to work and learn.

As Rocky and I spent time in the community to provide the needed socialization, we were regularly approached by strangers. If we passed a seemingly grumpy person, her or she would see Rocky and smile, changing his or her mood. Children approached us asking if they could pet Rocky, and their parents frequently initiated conversation about how Rocky was trained or about his good behavior. I was struck that my answers to these strangers were oftentimes the very answers to questions that I wished clients at our substance abuse treatment program would ask us about how change worked! The mood around Rocky was always light and playful, yet meaningful conversation with strangers was oftentimes at the heart of these interactions.

These interactions had a profound affect on me, and I could not help but wonder if others might respond similarly. The agency where I worked was full of stressed and angry clients who are told they needed to change and who were seeking services at someone else's request. I wondered if our clients would respond the same way as these strangers. Could Rocky find a smile within them and lighten the agency's mood? In addition, our agency had many children in the hallways and waiting rooms. Parenting was an issue we faced every day, and parents frequently became defensive when staff tried to initiate conversation about their children's behavior. Could Rocky's presence facilitate a willingness on the part of parents and children to approach us with questions? Could he assist us in creating an opportunity to teach parents and children alike? It was an idea so full of possibility that the obstacles involved in obtaining permission to allow a dog into a county health department seemed well worth the effort.

Although there was significant literature about the effectiveness of using therapy dogs in a variety of settings, I could find nothing on how therapy dogs have been used by psychotherapists using solution-focused therapy. In addition, nothing had been written about using a therapy dog in substance abuse treatment or in a county health department. It was soon clear that we were charting new territory. I began discussing my plan with my colleagues and was both pleasantly surprised and perplexed by their responses. The majority of my colleagues voiced support immediately, underscoring the therapeutic value of animals. Many confided that they had used their own pets during therapy sessions in the past and had seen a marked difference in their clients as a result. However, none had worked with specially trained or credentialed animals or seemed to be aware of the potential risk factors involved in using an untrained household pet in a professional setting. Although the benefit of using animals was readily accepted, the level of professionalism which I envisioned for my work with Rocky had been unheard of until now within my professional circle.

One of my colleagues, however, had a markedly negative reaction about my plan to use Rocky with clients. He accused me of pursuing this because I liked animals rather than because it was in the best interest of my clients. Stunned due to the level of respect I have for this colleague, I asked him to explain and learned that his only experience of using animals with clients was that of a previous officemate who brought her dog to work. The animal was untrained, intrusive to others, and the owner's interventions lacked purposefulness. In this context, my colleague's skepticism suddenly made sense. Once I explained the level of training Rocky would receive, the national credentialing requirements, and the plan to only use him with clients specifically identified as appropriate for this intervention, his attitude shifted, and he became very supportive. This informal polling of my peers provided valuable and necessary insight into the level of education needed within our profession in order to ensure that therapy animals can be used safely and credibly and allow us to reap the benefits promised by the research.

After months of research, writing proposals, crafting policies and procedures, and working diligently to obtain the necessary national credentials (for both myself and for Rocky), we were successful: Rocky became an official employee of the Jefferson County Department of Health and Environment! The impact on clients and staff has been incredible! Within a few short weeks, Rocky's presence created opportunities with staff and clients that had previously seemed unattainable. Parents welcomed staff interaction with their families; providing opportunities for Rocky's accompanying therapists to effectively intervene with the clients' children and offer impromptu parenting lessons. Perhaps most significantly, previously hostile and uncooperative parents whose children had been removed from their custody by Social Services due to abuse and neglect, demonstrated compassion and caring with Rocky (even kissing him gingerly on his nose). This provided the therapists with valuable evidence of the clients' ability to bond and of their ability to potentially respond compassionately to their own children. It also provided valuable information previously unavailable in our therapeutic setting. Observing these changes has been magical.

As we have delved into the world of animal-assisted activities and therapy (AAA/T), we have learned so much! We have discovered that AAA/T (using animal-related interventions with clients and including a specially trained animal in the therapy work with clients to create change) and solution-focused therapy can indeed be complimentary and that AAA/T can assist therapists in overcoming significant therapeutic challenges. Despite the considerable advantages, incorporating animals into the psychotherapy setting while complying with professional standards and minimizing liability can initially be an overwhelming task. In order to lessen that burden, in this book we will pass on the lessons that we have learned. We hope that this will encourage other therapists to join us on the richly rewarding and satisfying path. Animals and humans have an amazing bond, and we would be remiss to not use this bond when appropriate to help our clients when it might be the very thing that could make a difference in their lives. Those of you who know the power of a wet, cold nose, a loving look that melts your heart, or a wagging tail that makes you smile, you can readily imagine the potential of uncovering that power to heal the pain that often floods our clients. For others, this will be a new discovery. In either case, we invite you to settle into a comfortable chair, kick off your shoes, and read about a world in which nature joins hands with behavioral science, uniting to create miracles.

WHAT TO EXPECT FROM THIS BOOK

This book provides an overview of animal-assisted activities/therapy and demonstrates how we incorporate our animal-assisted activities/therapy program with solution-focused treatment at our agency. We offer practical and specific information about the elements necessary to consider before embarking upon a journey to utilize animals in therapy sessions. Although this book reflects our own agency setting, the information presented will be helpful for anyone considering implementing AAA/T. The concepts and information provided will be helpful for therapists regardless of whether they are in private practice, working in an agency setting, or simply curious about whether their pet might be appropriate to incorporate into their therapy/volunteer work.

Chapter 1—The Basics of Animal-Assisted Activities/Therapy (AAA/T)—provides an overview of both animal-assisted activities and animal-assisted therapy. It also provides information on the harmonious relationship between the values of AAA/T and solution-focused therapy.

Chapter 2—The Solution-Focused Basics—provides a blueprint of solution-focused therapy and a review of the principles and interventions typically used in this approach.

Chapter 3—What Every Therapist Needs to Know About Dogs Before Partnering with One in AAA/T—explores the common myths about dogs, and provides basic information that every therapist should know before entering into a co-therapy partnership with them. We examine the canine culture and explore how this differs from some of the popular notions human society teaches us about animals.

Chapter 4—How to Create a Successful AAA/T Program for Your Setting—focuses on the planning phase of implementing an animal-assisted activities/therapy program and clearly delineates the common threats to credibility and potential liability. It also provides ideas on how to address these areas according to national standards in order to ensure a program's success.

Chapter 5—Using AAA in Solution-Focused Treatment Settings—offers a hands-on approach to solution-focused therapy while partnering with animals in real-life treatment settings.

Chapter 6—Using a Therapy Dog in Solution-Focused Therapy Treatment Sessions—gives clear guidelines for determining when including a therapy dog in a treatment session will be most useful, writing treatment plans incorporating a therapy dog as a purposeful intervention tool, and structuring a treatment session once the dog is in the room.

Chapter 7—Applying AAA/T to Special Populations—illustrates the importance of examining how various client populations can be uniquely impacted by or benefit from animal-assisted activities and therapy (AAA/T) in order to fully appreciate the power of AAA/T. Included are sections about working with children, adolescents, adults, and substance-abusing clients, as well as a discussion of cultural considerations.

Chapter 8—Using Animal-Assisted Activities with Employees and Agencies—explores the impact of the presence of a therapy dog on the handler and the professionals both within the agency and the surrounding community and explores how the benefits of AAA can be utilized purposefully to transform an agency setting.

Photo by Teri Pichot.

Chapter 1

The Basics of Animal-Assisted Activities/Therapy (AAA/T)

No person is too old or ugly or poor or disabled to win the love of a pet—they love us uncritically and without reserve.

Elizabeth Marshall Thomas

While many therapists intuitively recognize the healing power of animals, there is solid evidence to support it as well. Animals' healing properties have been well researched and used for decades. This chapter will provide an overview of the history, research, and current developments in the field of AAA/T.

A BRIEF HISTORY OF AAA/T

Throughout history, many types of domesticated animals have played significant therapeutic roles. While horses were used in the 1700s to assist in the therapy of a variety of diseases (Beck & Katcher, 1996, p. 132), the first documented case of animal-assisted therapy appears in 1792 at the York Retreat in England (founded by the Society of Friends). Using rabbits, chickens, and other farm animals, William Tuke, a Quaker merchant, noted that animals would "enhance the humanity of the emotionally ill" (Beck & Katcher, 1996, p. 132). This was probably no surprise. Later, Florence Nightingale is credited as the first known clinician to study animals in health care. She observed that small companion animals were beneficial to her chronically ill patients (Nightingale, 1860). Throughout history animals have been observed to improve motivation, self-control, and responsibility, as well as numerous other mental and physical benefits (Beck & Katcher, 1996; Friedmann et al., 1980; Sussman, 1985). One of the first formal research studies followed ninety-two outpatients from a cardiac care unit. They found that patients who were pet owners lived longer than those who did not own pets (Friedmann et al., 1980). Further research confirmed that animals have the ability to reduce stress in humans (McNicholas & Collis, 1995; Serpell, 1996; Siegel, 1990).

Today, domestic animals are routinely used in a variety of settings including schools, hospitals, nursing homes, mental health units, physician offices, prisons, and businesses. Therapeutic equine riding programs are becoming more common, as horses are used to improve the physical and emotional health of children and adults alike in the field of hippotherapy. Dogs are frequent helpers to physical therapists with their patients. Fish are often found in doctors' offices to decrease patient anxiety, and cats, rabbits, and dogs are becoming more frequent visitors to the elderly in nursing homes. Therapy dogs are becoming more common in the role as hospital visitors as professionals better understand and appreciate the healing powers of the presence of animals. Llamas, dolphins, and cows are even mentioned throughout the literature as playing a valuable role in the field of AAA/T.

The type of animal and the settings in which the animal can make a positive difference are virtually limitless. For simplicity, and to remain within the scope of our personal knowledge, this book will focus only on the therapeutic use of dogs in mental and public health settings. We hope that this book will serve as a jumping point for your imagination, and we encourage you to refer to the reference section for additional sources on how to use this foundational information with a variety of other animals.

WHY USE ANIMALS?

Physical Benefits

A child's first pet is frequently a fish. Fish have relatively short life spans, and are far less of a responsibility than a dog. Parents often view a fish as an excellent way to begin to teach the lessons of responsibility, as the child learns the importance of feeding, cleaning the bowl, etc. However, few people put much thought into the health benefits of fish or why one frequently finds an aquarium in waiting rooms in physician offices. Although aquariums have the potential to increase the amount of work required by the staff (people are often unaware of the amount of work the care of a large aquarium takes), the addition of an "aquarium in waiting rooms, treatment rooms, and community areas within institutions has great potential for decreasing anxiety and concomitant physiological arousal" (Sussman, 1985, p. 199). This positive benefit on staff and patients makes the work to maintain an aquarium a good investment. Since a decrease in anxiety and physiological arousal are frequently observed in humans when animals are present, one commonly researched aspect of this benefit on health is the impact on blood pressure. One study measured the impact of the presence of a dog on the blood pressure of twenty-six male and female children (average age was twelve years old). It demonstrated that the blood pressure of the children was significantly lower when the dog was present. An important component of this research was that the children did not interact with this dog during the study. The dog's very presence in the room with the children resulted in the health benefit. The researchers concluded that the dog's presence changed the children's perception of the setting, thereby resulting in decreased anxiety and lowered blood pressure (Friedmann et al., 1983).

If the mere presence of fish and a dog can have that much impact on those around them, imagine the power of an animal that interacts with clients, for the power of touch only further enhances the health benefits. When an animal is present, people are frequently seen smiling and inviting the animal to touch them by offering an outstretched hand. There is the desire by many to interact. This touch is known to decrease an individual's "anxiety and physiological arousal and can have important health effects" (Sussman, 1985, p. 199). Not only can petting a dog lower a person's blood pressure, it has been known to ease the pain of arthritis (Davis, 2002).

Although many of the health benefits have been documented in research, others remain anecdotal due to the difficulty of measuring and reproducing the exact cause of the health change. These accounts frequently lack the rigorous testing that research provides, but they include testimony from medical professionals that there is no other known explanation for the health improvements. They are found throughout the literature, and are frequently told as firsthand accounts by those who work or volunteer with their animal partner. They serve to demonstrate the strong connection between one's physical and mental well-being. Such accounts include patients awakening out of a coma by a therapy dog's touch as well as other unexplained sudden improvements in otherwise terminal conditions (Crawford & Pomerinke, 2003).

Mental Health Benefits

The majority of people own pets not for the physical benefits, but for the social and mental health benefits. Of those, companionship is the most researched aspect. Owning a pet leads to "decreased loneliness and increased psychological and physiological health" (Sussman, 1985, p. 198). Sussman goes on to state that "pets can decrease owners' depression, anxiety, and sympathetic nervous system arousal" (p. 199). People have a special kind of relationship with animals that can rarely be found with human companions. Animals have a way of accepting without judgment; they don't condition their love and affection, and they are able to quickly forgive injustice. These animal traits make relationships with animals less threatening than those with people (Sussman, 1985). In a world in which human interaction can at times be stressful, demanding, and riddled with misunderstandings, animals have the ability to give humans an emotional break. They have the ability to just "be." They seek companionship, yet are not emotionally demanding. Their desire to fall asleep next to their owners, notice when situations are distressing, and respond with affection, can serve as a source of comfort and companionship. In addition, the responsibility of owning a pet can promote good health by giving a sense of responsibility, purpose, and self-worth. These can be extremely valuable benefits for the elderly or those who find themselves in the position of having to redefine their purpose in life.

In children, the benefits include an important role in the development of such vital characteristics as responsibility, competence, self-esteem, trust, cause and effect, and feelings of empathy. Children frequently view a family pet as a peer and as having a common status within the family system (Sussman, 1985). This role benefits the child by allowing the pet to not only be a playmate, but a confidant as well (frequently sharing secrets and dreams that are not told to adults). The pet provides a safe relationship in which imagination can flourish and social skills can be developed and practiced. In addition, pets are frequently children's first experience with death and loss. Although this can present a challenging teaching experience for the parents, the loss of a pet provides them with a wonderful opportunity to teach children about the cycle of life, the role of grief, and how to begin to confront the concept of mortality.

Because of the rich learning environment that animals offer for both educational and social development, schools systems frequently incorporate animals into class settings through the use of class pets (usually small, low-maintenance pets such as rabbits, fish, etc.). Teachers have learned that many of the benefits of pet ownership are transferable to those who are only able to visit with a pet at school. This allows the professionals to purposefully use the benefits of pet ownership to assist and teach those who do not have a pet of their own. In addition, these class pets provide a more structured opportunity for object lessons that can be readily controlled and initiated by the professional. It is this important tenet, that many of the benefits of pet ownership can be reaped by those who can only visit for a short period with a pet, that is at the foundation of AAA/T.

THE USE OF ANIMALS IN PROFESSIONAL SETTINGS

There are two distinct ways that animals are used in professional settings. We will explore these two ways in depth in this section. However, as in any profession, strict standards and ethical guidelines exist, and therapists who use animals should be aware of and abide by these standards. Regardless of how the animal is being used, the following standards* are considered to be necessary for good practice:

1. No person (client, staff, visitor) shall be forced to have contact with an animal.
2. A facility shall have written policies and procedures in place before introducing an animal.
3. Animals and handlers shall be screened before participation in a program.

---

*Reprinted courtesy of Delta Society®.

4. Clients will be screened for contraindications before an animal is introduced.
5. The rights of those who wish to have no contact with an animal shall always be respected.
6. No client or visitor is ever left alone with an animal.
7. At all times the rights of the animals shall be respected and ensured. This includes humane treatment, protection from undue stress, and availability of water and exercise areas. (Delta Society, 1997, introduction p. 2)

In addition, the following code of ethics* is in place for personnel who engage in AAA/T:

1. Animal-Assisted Activities and Animal-Assisted Therapy Personnel will perform duties commensurate with their position and training.
2. Animal-Assisted Activities and Animal-Assisted Therapy Personnel will abide by the professional ethics of their respective professions and organizations.
3. Animal-Assisted Activities and Animal-Assisted Therapy Personnel will demonstrate a belief and attitude of reverence for all life.
4. Animal-Assisted Activities and Animal-Assisted Therapy Personnel will, at all times, treat all, the animals, the people, and the environment, with respect, dignity, and sensitivity, maintaining the quality of life and experience for all involved.
5. Animal-Assisted Activities and Animal-Assisted Therapy Personnel will be informed and educated on the aspects and issues related to Animal Assisted Activities and Therapy.
6. Animal-Assisted Activities and Animal-Assisted Therapy Personnel will demonstrate commitment, responsibility, and honesty in all phases of their activities.
7. Animal-Assisted Activities and Animal-Assisted Therapy Personnel will be responsible for complying with local, state, and federal laws and Delta Society Policies governing Animal-Assisted Activities and Animal-Assisted Therapy.
8. Each individual and organization will establish or adopt written guidelines to assure a quality program. All programs need to be

---

*Reprinted courtesy of Delta Society®.

continuously evaluated and, when appropriate, improved to assure quality standards and service. (Delta Society, 1996, p. vii)

Animals can be used in two distinctly different ways in professional settings. They are animal-assisted activities and animal-assisted therapy. The following sections explain the differences between these approaches.

Animal-Assisted Activities (AAA)

The following is the formal definition of AAA*:

> Activities that involve animals visiting people. The same activity can be repeated with different people, unlike a therapy program that is tailored to a particular person or medical condition. AAA provide opportunities for motivational, educational, and/or recreational benefits to enhance quality of life. AAA are delivered in a variety of environments by a specially trained professional, paraprofessional, and/or volunteer in association with animals that meet specific criteria. (Delta Society, 1997, p. 79)

AAA is a broad category of activities and is frequently described as a "meet and greet" type of interaction that can be repeated from individual to individual with no specific treatment goal for the individual clients. A common form of this type of activities is when dog and handler teams visit with patients in hospitals or nursing homes. The animal-handler team moves from patient to patient, allowing the opportunity for each patient to meet the animal, and to spend a few minutes interacting. The interaction can take as long as is desired. In this type of interaction, the facility has prescreened the patients for appropriateness of AAA, and has usually informed the handler of who would like visits. Interactions are spontaneous in nature.

Although an expected benefit exists for the individual clients who are receiving a visit during AAA, no treatment plans have been formulated and change is not prescribed nor documented. While the handler and animal must have completed some type of formalized behavioral and health screening to evaluate the team's safety and skill, the handler is frequently a volunteer working with his or her animal

---

*Reprinted courtesy of Delta Society®.

due to the lack of specific professional training that is required for this type of interaction. (However, a professional can serve as the handler for AAA as well.) Although no specific goals exist for the individual clients, there are specific goals and expected benefits for the general environment when using AAA. Common environmental goals are as follows:

1. Change the power differential between professionals and clients.
2. Increase the general comfort level of clients.
3. Encourage clients to focus on a positive activity.
4. Assist clients in focusing attention on an external source.

Change the power differential between professionals and clients.

When an animal is present, otherwise assumed boundaries between people tend to become less observed. People tend to feel more comfortable making casual conversation with a stranger who is walking a dog. Even people who normally rigidly keep to themselves and don't talk to strangers in public settings, are more likely to smile and say hello to a stranger walking a dog. The research supports that the "presence of a pet attracts attention to the person, predisposes the observer to respond positively to him or her, and then provides an occasion for a safe and neutral comment" (Sussman, 1985, pp. 16-17). Even gender does not seem to be a factor in the phenomenon. Sussman goes on to state that both men and women are received as more approachable when with a pet. In addition, they are much more likely to be greeted, engaged in longer conversations, smiled at, etc., when with a pet. This can serve a valuable role for therapists.

When an animal is used in AAA, clients who would normally not interact become more talkative and initiate contact. When a therapist uses AAA, it can serve as a "social lubricant" (Fine, 2000, p. 181). The therapist can either be a handler and use an animal partner in an AAA fashion to encourage clients to feel more comfortable talking to him or her, or the therapist can use a volunteer handler-animal team to work within common areas or waiting rooms to get light conversation going. In either fashion, clients have started to talk and become more comfortable interacting with each other and with professionals. This conversation can then be channeled in a purposeful direction at a later time.

Last, effective handlers tend to squat by their animal partner or sit on the floor during interactions with clients. This position is important to support the animal as well as to ensure safety during the interactions. This change in position results in a more relaxed environment than the traditional stance. This more informal position is extremely powerful when the therapist is also in the role as the animal's handler. The clients then benefit from the more casual conversation and position prior to formal work beginning.

Increase the general comfort level of clients.

Clients frequently feel uncomfortable in new settings or due to the circumstances in which they find themselves. Because of the social lubricant factor that AAA provides, clients soon find themselves chatting comfortably with previous strangers about neutral subjects such as current or previous pets, animal-related television commercials or movies, etc. These conversations often result in happy memories or funny stories which lead to smiles, laughter, and other light conversation. Even clients who are not directly involved in the animal interaction frequently have difficulty holding back a smile as they watch the visiting animal perform tricks, or they see a toddler squeal with delight at a dog's wet nose or soft fur. Staff and clients frequently laugh together and share lighthearted experiences, thereby lessening the discomfort and apprehension the clients once held. The environment can not help but be transformed.

Encourage clients to focus on a positive activity.

As the animal-related activities unfold in the environment, clients' attention is focused on a pleasant activity. Clients who were initially angry about having to wait, those who have to deal with a cranky child, or those who are having a bad day, now find themselves focused on something more positive; whether it is an animal-related story or simply observing the animal interacting with others. It catches clients' attention and redirects that attention to something more positive. It is very powerful to witness an angry client sit in a waiting room (withdrawn or glaring at staff) as an animal-handler team enters the area. The expression on the client's face quickly changes from anger to curiosity. Frequently the client soon engages in interacting with the animal-handler team and those around the client would never know he or she was previously upset. This brings us to our fourth environmental goal.

Assist clients in focusing attention on an external source.

Understandably so, our clients are frequently absorbed in their own problems. These problems may be causing them emotional or physical distress, and are thereby demanding all of their attention. Unfortunately, many of our clients' problems only worsen with continued attention (i.e., worry, anxiety). Combine this with the discomfort that clients frequently feel about coming to talk to a stranger about these problems. This can make our waiting rooms and common areas heavy and depressing areas to visit. This is precisely where AAA can be just the approach that is needed. When an animal-handler team enters such an area, attention is drawn immediately from the clients to the animal. The animal distracts the clients from needless worry by providing an external focus. This, combined with the other previously discussed environmental goals, provides an excellent way to shift the focus and pleasantly pass the time until it is time to work with the professional to address the client's need. This shift in focus frequently provides an immediate relief from low-level worry, anxiety, and depression; thereby allowing the client to have a more productive emotional outlook for the upcoming session.

AAA programs can be designed with specially trained, internal staff and their pets (in a resident handler/dog model such as we use in our program) or with volunteers who visit at designated times with their pets. Regardless of which model is employed, the marked changes to the environment that AAA produces impact not only the clients, but the staff as well. These environmental goals are frequently achieved in everyone. As Sussman (1985) writes, "The presence of pets can lead to significant improvement in staff morale, which can eventually improve staff-patient relations and care" (p. 199).

Animal-Assisted Therapy (AAT)

The following is the formal definition of AAT*:

> AAT involves a health or human service professional who uses an animal as part of his/her job. Specific goals for each client

---

*Reprinted courtesy of Delta Society®.

have been identified by the professional, and progress is measured and recorded. AAT is a goal-directed intervention in which an animal meeting specific criteria is an integral part of the treatment process. AAT is delivered and/or directed by a health or human service provider working within the scope of his/her profession. AAT is designed to promote improvement in human physical, social, emotional, and/or cognitive functioning. AAT is provided in a variety of settings and may be group or individual in nature. The process is documented and evaluated. (Delta Society, 1996, p. 79)

AAT is used in health care by physical, occupational, and speech therapists for a variety of goals. For example, a speech therapist might use a dog to encourage a child to increase vocalization or enunciation. The child might be asked to give the dog commands, such as "sit" or "down." The dog rewards the child's vocalizations by complying with the request. At the beginning stages of this goal, while the child's enunciation is poor and the dog might not understand the command, the handler might stand behind the child facing the dog and give the hand signal for the command that the child has given to encourage the child's efforts. This assistance by the handler would only be done upon direction from the speech therapist, when he or she has determined that this type of encouragement would be therapeutic for the child.

An occupational therapist might use a dog to increase a patient's fine motor skills. For example, the patient might be encouraged to brush the dog's coat as the dog lies patiently on the floor. This task requires that the patient hold onto the brush and control his or her arm movements. The dog reinforces the patient's efforts through the dog's presence and enjoyment of the activity. The patient can take periodic breaks to pet the dog (which also requires arm and hand control). Other therapeutic activities might include holding the dog's leash to walk him around the room, assisting in food/water preparation, or throwing a toy for the dog to retrieve. All of these activities could be part of a treatment plan for increasing use of affected extremities, crossing midline, increasing fine/gross motor skills, increasing strength and endurance, etc. The use of a dog in these exercises significantly increases the patient's enjoyment and thereby increases motivation and effort.

Although used less widely until now, mental health therapists can also benefit from the assistance of a therapy dog. For example, a dog might be used to assist with a child who has difficulty with empathy. In this case, it might be most helpful for there to be a separate therapist and handler to maintain greater control over the situation. (This is a very helpful strategy any time a client might have quick, unpredictable movements.) The therapist can work closely with the child to talk about the dog's feelings, discuss how the dog might like to be treated, practice some appropriate petting, and explore the dog's response to the child's interaction, while the handler is present to move the dog as appropriate to ensure the dog remains safe while the child learns. If the parent is present, this can afford a wonderful opportunity for the therapist to respectfully demonstrate how the parent can teach empathy to the child by using the dog. The therapist can then explore with the parent other real-life situations in which she or he can use to teach the child empathy in a safe fashion.

In addition, therapy dogs can be incorporated into mental health treatment plans to increase self-esteem, self-confidence, self-control, increase interaction, brighten mood, address grief and loss, improve reality orientation, encourage eye contact and verbalization, improve ability to express thoughts and feelings, improve cooperation, etc. For example, a child who is having difficulty with self-esteem and therefore initiates minimal interaction with those around him or her might benefit from interactions with a therapy dog due to the unconditional love most animals exude. The therapist could speak for the therapy animal during the session, giving words to the animal's interactions such as, "He really likes you. He wants you to pet him." Not only do most children find a dog's request for attention irresistible, this helps the client to understand the animal's intentions and serves as an invitation for further therapeutic conversation. AAT is best thought of as another tool that the therapist can use to design effective treatment plans for clients. It is limited only by the therapist's imagination and the therapy dog and handler's skills.

It is important to mention that not every dog is appropriate for every situation or treatment plan. A therapist must be attentive to and respect a dog's comfort level and ability in order to ensure safety for everyone involved. In addition, a therapist must carefully consider if it is best to design the intervention with a separate handler to work with the dog or if the therapist has the ability and attention with the given client to effectively attend to both the dog and the client (a much more challenging and not always possible task). Similar to every other therapist intervention, each situation is unique and must be individually evaluated and designed. Although it can be tempting for a therapist to bring his or her therapy dog to work to be a part of the day's agenda, it is crucial that the therapist carefully evaluate each client and session the dog attends as well as the clinical appropriateness of the dog being a part of that intervention. A therapy dog should not be present simply because it is convenient for the therapist or because it "won't hurt," just as a therapist should not use any other therapeutic tool without purposefulness and design.

COMMON VALUES BETWEEN AAA/T AND SOLUTION-FOCUSED THERAPY (SFT)

Any time a therapist combines two fields of discipline, it is wise to take a few moments to ensure that the core values of the fields are compatible. Overlooking this crucial step can lead to incongruence in one's work and a negative fallout for the clients. In this section we will briefly explore the commonalities between the values of solution-focused therapy and AAA/T. We identified the following common values:

1. Respect for life and change
2. Respect for culture and everyone's unique way of viewing the world
3. Belief in hearing and respecting the wisdom of those with whom we are working
4. Belief that the interaction should always be purposeful and with the end result in mind
5. Belief that partnership is the most effective strategy
6. Belief that small steps can make a big difference

Respect for Life and Change

As solution-focused therapists, respect for life and change is at our core. Without this respect, there would be no point in working for change with clients who have many times already lost hope that this change is even possible. It is our belief that all life is worthwhile that propels us forward to be curious about what change a client desires (albeit dependent on a miracle). It is this respect for life that allows us to see possibility when clients describe the toughest circumstances. It is this same belief that makes us curious what difference a dog could make in a client's life. Dogs are amazing creatures, and the changes in strangers and passersby that are frequently observed during day-to-day activities cannot help but make one curious and tap into the respect for life and change.

Respect for Culture and Everyone's Unique Way of Viewing the World

SF therapists believe that every client is unique. It would be erroneous for us to assume anything about a client based on his or her culture, gender, etc. We must listen carefully and ask respectful, well-worded questions to really understand the heart of another human being. Furthermore, we must wish to understand and be curious about what we will learn as a result. It is only through this listening and curiosity that we can understand the client's desires, hopes, and solutions. In working with animals, it is important to remember that each animal is unique. Dogs have a culture, a way of thinking and behaving, and a way of communicating that are uniquely theirs. In addition, each dog communicates in his or her own way low-level warning signs that something needs to be changed. It is not only disrespectful to put our way of thinking onto them, but it is unsafe for clients. Unless we really understand and respect the animal's unique way of interacting and communicating, we may miss early warning signals of discomfort in a situation. When this happens the dog then needs to communicate progressively "louder" in an effort to better communicate to us. If the signals are still ignored they may ultimately communicate in the only other way available to them: with their teeth.

Belief in Hearing and Respecting the Wisdom of Those with Whom We Are Working

SF therapists believe that the clients are the experts on themselves. While the therapist remains the expert on the change process and on asking excellent questions to facilitate change, the therapist can never know what is best for the client. The belief in the client as expert results in a stance of curiosity rather than censor when clients do unexpected things. Because she or he trusts the client's wisdom, the therapist explores unanticipated changes in behaviors or perceptions in the favorable context of the client's desired solution.

Over and over again we have observed and heard stories of therapy dogs communicating things to their handlers that the handlers would have otherwise missed. It would be unwise for those communications to go unnoticed. For example, a dog may suddenly refuse to lie down in a group of children due to the handler consistently missing that the children frequently step on his tail. By exploring the possible reason for the apparent disobedience, the handler learns to better protect the dog's tail from children's feet. Once the dog feels assured that the handler will protect his tail, the dog is able to relax and obey with confidence.

Belief That the Interaction Should Always Be Purposeful and with the End Result in Mind

Solution-focused therapy is very purposeful in all interventions. The therapist begins by assisting the client in clearly describing and defining the details of the desired outcome (through the use of the miracle question). It is through this clear description of the desired outcome that all work takes place. Scales serve the purpose of continuously evaluating the client's progress toward the goal, while leaving room for the goal to be modified as needed throughout. Similarly, AAA and AAT must have clearly defined outcomes, whether it be for the environment or for the individual clients. While AAT has much more defined treatment plans that are continuously monitored and recorded, AAA also has general goals and is not done without thought or careful reevaluation to ensure that the desired outcomes are met. Policies and procedures are required to ensure purposefulness and to design a program that best meets the needs of the clients.

Belief That Partnership Is the Most Effective Strategy

SF therapists hold a strong belief that their role is to work with clients to assist the client in creating change. The therapist is in a partnership role rather than an expert role. Through questions, the therapist assists the client to determine what outcome is desired, what change strategies have been most effective, and what changes would bring the desired outcome in this situation. The therapist never pushes from behind, nor leads from ahead. I often think of the analogy of a tour guide walking beside a client down a trail, asking the client lots of questions to assist the client in taking desired paths as he or she comes to forks in the road. The therapist could never make good decisions for the client since only the client holds the answers. However, the client makes better decisions when gently challenged by the therapist's questions. In working with a therapy dog, the dog is viewed as a partner; no more or less important than the human partner. The dog is able to make changes in the environment and clients that the handler could never do, and the dog could never make the changes without the training and opportunities that the handler provides. It is truly a partnership in which the abilities of both are enhanced by the presence of the other.

Belief That Small Steps Can Make a Big Difference

SF therapists believe that no step is too small, and that it is the culmination of all of the client's steps that results in the client's goal. In fact, it is often because clients overlook the small steps they have already taken that they lose hope and forget the wealth of knowledge that they already have. Once they remember and give themselves credit for these small steps, they regain their footing and continue toward their solutions. Similarly, it is the small things that occur during an AAA/T interaction that make incredible differences in clients' lives; the change in the environment when a client simply sees a dog walk by, a touch by a soft muzzle, the wag of a tail. All of these things lift spirits, bring a smile, change a client's outlook, and give hope.

SUMMARY

Animals have an amazing impact on humans. The connection between people and animals is powerful when used in the helping professions. Clients often gain motivation, hope, or joy from animals in the face of incredible life obstacles. When used in a purposeful way within the scope of AAA/T, therapists and agencies can benefit from this human-animal bond while maintaining credibility within the community and within their profession. Chapter 4 describes many of the hurdles professionals face when implementing AAA/T programs and explains ways to overcome these. But first we will provide an overview of SFT in the next chapter.

Photo by Mark Hochstedler. Used with permission.

Chapter 2

The Solution-Focused Basics

What if you slept? And what if, in your sleep you dreamed? And what if, in your dream you went to heaven and there plucked a strange and beautiful flower? And what if, when you awoke, you had the flower in your hand?

Samuel Taylor Coleridge

We hope that Chapter 1 has whetted your appetite to learn more about AAA and AAAT. Before we go further however, we want to acquaint you with the approach behind the interventions described in the subsequent chapters of this book. This chapter provides an overview of solution-focused therapy (SFT) which was created in the late 1960s by Insoo Kim Berg and Steve de Shazer. Their writings (Berg 1994, 1995; de Shazer, 1985, 1988, 1991, 1994; DeJong & Berg 2002; Miller & Berg, 1995; Miller & de Shazer, 1998) were instrumental to our understanding of this approach and continue to be among our favorite professional texts. This overview will be helpful for readers unfamiliar with SFT, and will serve as a refresher for those already knowledgeable about the approach. By the end of this chapter you will have acquired the basic knowledge needed to utilize solution-focused therapy whether or not you are including animals in the therapy session.

INTRODUCTION

Many differences exist between traditional problem-focused approaches and solution-focused therapy. Perhaps most significant are the focus of the therapist and the purpose behind the therapeutic questions. Traditionally, therapists focus on problems, seeking to understand their origins and consequently identify the most appropriate solutions. Similar to a medical model in which a physician determines a diagnosis of a patient's disease and then treats based upon the diagnosis (DeJong & Berg, 2002), therapists are trained to ask questions about the problem and attempt to get to the root of the problem. SF clinicians acknowledge that problems exist, but spend the majority of the session time exploring and discussing a time in the future when the problem has disappeared. Solution-focused therapy postulates that regardless of a client's history, clients have the tools to create a desirable future, and it is understood that solutions are not necessarily related to the problems that bring the clients to treatment. Solution-focused therapists help their clients envision a time when the problem is reduced or no longer exists. These tenets are instrumental in helping clients develop solutions.

A couple of years ago, while just beginning the process of learning SFT, I (MC) came across a cartoon in a local paper of a kitten stuck in the top of a tree. This image has stuck with me and helps me to remember the basics of SFT. Imagine a tiny, blue-eyed Siamese kitten stranded forlornly at the top of a large oak tree. Cold, hungry, scared, and afraid to make a move, the poor kitty is crying out for help. Does it really help for us to talk about the many reasons the kitty may have gotten up the tree, or to spend time analyzing what a horrible situation the poor kitty is in? We could spend hours talking about the current situation and how bleak it is while the kitten starves, freezes, or both. We could spend a lot of time analyzing how the kitty could have done things differently and asking why he let himself get into this predicament, but by then the cat may have frozen to death. Isn't it more helpful for us to aid the kitty in getting down the tree? After all, we are the ones not stuck in the tree; we are not the ones in crisis. Granted it would be wise to later look back from a place where the solution is reality, and determine how to avoid this situation in the future. Right now, though, the kitty needs a solution, and he needs it quick. Like the kitty, clients need to have hope that solutions are possible and that they won't forever be stuck up in that tree. They are in a much more effective position to explore ways to prevent a future problem from the safety of a place in which the problem no longer exists.

PROBLEM SOLVING
VERSUS SOLUTION BUILDING

As a therapist trained in problem solving, it would be natural to spend countless hours trying to problem solve with the clients represented by our fictitious kitty. For example, if we were to problem-solve with the kitty, we might spend a lot of time talking about the problem of being up in a tree. Of course, we would naturally ask the kitty what the problem is, and how does he know it's a problem? Do other people, his owners perhaps, think that this is a problem? How long has he been stuck there? When did he first get stuck? How many times has this happened before? We would also want to know what kind of problems the kitty is having as a result of this getting stuck up a tree. We might go on to spend more time speculating about the underlying cause of the problem. Perhaps the kitty really wants attention, or perhaps if the kitty weren't so afraid of dogs he wouldn't be in this current situation. We might also consult with colleagues about the deep-seated root of the problem. With all of this information, we may go on to prescribe a course of treatment for the problem. We could talk about the many ways in which the kitty could get out of his situation. We might explore ways in which the kitty could become desensitized to dogs and possible relaxation techniques that have been effective for other felines in similar situations. All of these lines of conversation would possibly increase the kitty's understanding of the problem and might result in some insight into the origins of the problem. The kitty most likely would even gain some skills for future use. However, one might wonder if the kitty would find these new skills a good fit for who the kitty really is and therefore how likely the kitty might be to use these skills in the future. How tempting it is to think that because we have seen other cats in similar situations that we might best understand the most effective approach for the kitty in front of us. In adopting this stance of knowing, the professional might very well be correct; however, the professional might also have a very good solution, but one that is just not a good fit for this particular kitty.

In contrast, when using a solution-focused approach, we spend our time building solutions and seeking to understand who the client is, how the client sees the world, and therefore what the client views as the most appropriate solution. Using our example of the kitty in the tree, we would first ask him how he wants his life to be different as a result of our help. We begin with the end of the story at a place in which the problem is resolved, and work backward from there. This helps the clients pinpoint exactly what it is they want to be different in their lives. In our example, the kitty might say he wants to get out of the tree, or that he just wants to be more comfortable while he's there. When using SFT we ask our clients questions to help them identify what their lives will be like once the problem is resolved and what difference this will make for them and those who are close to them. This places the responsibility of identifying and evaluating possible solutions back on the clients rather than having the therapist prescribe a solution for them.

As part of focusing on what life will be like when the clients' problems are resolved, we help clients create a very detailed description of their solutions. These precise details help clients experience their solutions, and therefore make it more realistic. We want the clients to be able to fully imagine themselves in a place in which the problem is resolved and imagine what it will be like when they are able to reap the benefits of their hard work. This not only helps clients to identify solid, realistic solutions, but also helps them to see that effective solutions are a tangible possibility. This will in turn instill a sense of hope that soon the solution will be reality. With this hope, clients become more motivated to work toward that future that they have envisioned. In addition, the identified solutions are highly likely to be continued after treatment concludes since the solution was identified by the client, and the client has determined that the solution is indeed compatible with his or her culture and individual life factors. For example, if the kitty wants out of the tree, we would have him imagine what his life will be like once this has happened. Is the kitty basking in the warm midday sun? Is he playing with a friend or chasing butterflies in the garden? How much confidence does he have that he can prevent this from ever happening again? Will he have a stronger support system to help him from getting stuck in the future? We want to know what his solution looks like and what difference it will make to him when he is unstuck. Our job is to help him explore his life without the problem, and to help him make this solution a reality.

GUIDING PHILOSOPHY AND PRINCIPLES OF SFT

Like having a blueprint when constructing a house, understanding the guiding philosophy of SFT is imperative. Without this guiding philosophy, solution-focused interventions could easily be combined with other approaches and no longer be solution focused. For many therapists and clients, using solution-focused techniques while operating from a problem-focused approach is not problematic and is often very useful. However, using the solution-focused interventions without fully incorporating the solution-focused approach is limiting and lacks the richness that is possible when using the full approach as designed. Pichot and Dolan (2003) note that there are three distinct stages when incorporating solution-focused therapy into a new environment.

1. Incorporating solution-focused interventions into a problem-focused philosophy
2. Incorporating both the SF interventions and philosophy in the work with clients while remaining problem focused in interactions with others outside of the counseling sessions
3. Incorporating both the SF interventions and philosophy in both the work with clients as well as in interactions with others outside of the counseling sessions (p. 11)

When learning SFT, professionals inevitably come to a place with the approach that they must decide how much of it resonates with their own understanding and beliefs about how people change. This will determine how much the professional decides to integrate this approach into his or her clinical work. Regardless of the level of integrating SFT that is desired, it is important to have a solid understanding of the basic principles.

Basic Principles

The basic principles of solution-focused therapy are identified as follows:

- If it's not broke, don't fix it.
- If it's not working, do something different.

- If something is working, do more of it. Focus on what's working.
- Small steps can lead to big changes.
- The solutions are not necessarily related to the problems.
- No problem is constant; exceptions always exist.
- The future is created and negotiable. (Pichot & Dolan, 2003, p. 13)

These basic principles guide our solution-focused therapy sessions. While some of these principles share commonality with other approaches, they are unique in their combination, in their future-focused stance, and in how they are used with the solution-focused techniques we will soon describe. It is these principles that form a framework and therapeutic stance, and they help the therapist create a powerful environment in which clients are able to make changes. We will explore these principles in more detail in Chapter 5 during our discussion of animal-assisted activities in a solution-focused treatment setting. In addition to these principles, five key elements of the philosophy warrant specific mention.

The answers are not within the problem.

One of the important elements that makes solution-focused therapy unique is the clinician's focus during the session. In solution-focused therapy, the focus is always toward what life will be like once the problem is resolved. Therefore, the actual "problem" is rarely the topic of conversation. This paradigm shift to being curious about and directing the majority of clinical questions toward an exploration of the solution can be quite challenging given the traditional training and emphasis on problem exploration of most clinicians. However it is imperative to really understand that when a solution-focused therapist works from a place in which the problem is resolved, the problem does not go ignored; the solution-focused therapist acknowledges and accepts that the problem does exist. To not do so would be insensitive to the very real consequences of the problem, which are causing pain and other negative effects in the client's life. Until the client believes the therapist understands and appreciates the impact of the problem, it will be difficult to move beyond the problem to explore the solution. While we know that validating the problem is very important, we find that it does not need to be time consuming. The therapist is able to quickly transition from the presenting complaints to solution building. Returning to the kitten-in-the-tree analogy, although we appreciate the reality of the kitten being stuck, it would be wrong to focus solely on that; the kitty is in crisis and needs help. The best way to help the kitty get unstuck is not to spend our time stuck in the tree with the kitty dwelling on the problem and losing hope, but to help the kitty move in his mind to a time when he is no longer stuck in crisis. This allows the kitty (or perhaps more significant, the client represented by the kitten!) to build hope that change is possible and to explore solutions that he personally envisions as effective and culturally sound. We help our clients to look past the problem, see that a solution exists, and help them to see a reality for themselves in which the problem is resolved. Solution-focused therapists remain empathetic, and make sure to acknowledge to the client that they are hearing the impact the problem has had on the client's life, therefore providing the client the courage and freedom to accept the invitation to move to a place in which the problem no longer exists.

Helping the client focus on a time in which the problem no longer exists is the hallmark of SFT and where the power of this approach lies. Each client has his or her own concept of how he or she wants his or her future to be when the problem is no longer there, it is our job to help uncover this and help to make it a reality.

What one focuses on gets bigger.

Whatever we choose to focus our attention upon tends to become bigger. For example, we've all had bad days in which seemingly everything goes wrong. It's raining out, the alarm doesn't go off, we get cut off in traffic, co-workers are critical, etc. Sooner or later someone eventually asks how the day is going. Trusting that this person is someone who really wants to know, you might go into great detail about all of the incidents that led up to having a bad day: the alarm, the rain, the traffic, the bad drivers. Pretty soon you notice that your heart rate is going up, and you are getting anxious as you review all of the problems you've had throughout the day. You again feel the tension that you felt when that man in the red convertible zipped right in front of you only to slam on his brakes.

This very same principle can be used to create a positive change during a therapy session. For example, imagine what would happen if a solution-focused therapist were to say to that same person having a bad day, "Wow, you've had such a rough time today. I'm impressed that despite all of these bad things that have happened to you today, you've made it this far without completely losing it. What was it about you that helped you get through this bad day?" Imagine the different answers that the listener might hear. We've had clients say such things as, "Well, I'm not a quitter," "I'm a strong person," "I know things will get better," "I've had a lot of support," or "I guess it really wasn't that bad. I would have completely lost it before, but I'm much more patient now." The person's emotional state during the conversation would be quite different as well. By the end of the conversation, the person would likely feel much better and maybe even experience a sense of pride in how he or she handles difficult days. By inviting the person to shift his or her attention to his or her effective problem-solving skills, the difficult circumstances are all but forgotten while the individual's coping skills are explored.

This is a common shift that we typically invite our clients to take in a solution-focused session; to shift gently and respectfully from the difficult circumstances to how they are able to cope with what is happening. This reminds us of a client who complained that he was so overwhelmed by the burdens in his life that he felt as if he was spending all of his time "putting out fires." Needing a way to effectively assist him I decided to utilize the "fire" language he had already used. It was at a time in which there were many wildfires burning in the mountain areas in Colorado, so wildfires were in the news and on many residents' minds. I asked him what percentage of his own "fires" had been contained. He answered that a surprising (to me anyway) 80 percent had been contained. From the initial conversation and his apparent frustration, I would have guessed that he might have answered 10 percent at the very most. So I asked what let him know that there was 80 percent containment, what he was doing to ensure the fires that were already contained did not flare up again, who was on the front line with him fighting these fires, and who he had as reinforcement. All of these questions together effectively changed the focus of our session and resulted in a useful conversation about his coping strategies, support, and plans to make and maintain future changes. It would have been easy, given my problem-focused training, to focus on his initial feelings of being overwhelmed and spend the session exploring these. However, a completely different atmosphere resulted from basing the selection of questions from a place in which the problem was resolved. By using an analogy that by its very nature acknowledged the potential threat and devastation that the problems were causing, the client was then able to shift and explore the most meaningful part of the analogy; that of containment and prevention. Once the client's focus shifted to noticing which parts of the problem had been contained, he gained hope and momentum, encouraged by the work he had already done and the resources he had on hand to finish the job.

People want to get better and have the resources to do so.

A central tenet of SFT is that it is the clients who are the experts on their lives and what is best for them, not the therapists. While therapists play a very important role in the change process, they are the experts on how change occurs and on asking questions to create that change. It is through a partnership of these two different kinds of experts that SFT occurs. Clients solve problems every day. It is only a select few of these problems that bring them into therapy, needing assistance. However, clients frequently lose sight of these successes when faced with the challenges of the current, seemingly overwhelming problem. They need assistance in remembering that they do know how to find their own solutions, for they may not have ever thought about or been asked about the tools they already have that help them get through. The solution-focused therapist is the expert on listening to the clients and asking questions that help them discover their own solutions. It is through this listening and trusting that the clients truly hold their own answers that the therapist is able to assist the clients in envisioning how life will be once the problem is resolved and then help them to identify the steps to make their solutions a reality.

One of our clients told us that he was struggling to remain substance free and finding it difficult to cope with the thoughts and urges to use. He confided that he didn't know how to stay substance free. We began by acknowledging how difficult stopping substance use can be, and then we asked him to notice any times in his life when he was able to cope effectively with the thoughts and urges to use the drug. To his (and our) subsequent surprise, he discovered that he sometimes would have a craving but that it would go away if he got busy working in his garage or doing something with his family. In SFT we call these discoveries "exceptions." (We will discuss these in more detail later in this chapter.) As we continued to follow the exceptions down this conversational path, he reported that he liked to make things for his family and friends with his woodworking tools in his garage. He noticed that while he would sometimes have thoughts of using, he would never act upon them when he was busy working. He discovered that the urges came on stronger and were harder to ignore when he wasn't busy. When our client said this out loud, he realized that he had found a potential solution to his problem. Through this conversation he realized or perhaps remembered that he was able to cope much better with his drug cravings when he was busy than when he was bored. As our conversation neared an end, we complimented him, telling him how impressed we were that he had figured this out on his own. He smiled and looked stunned for a moment and replied, "I guess I do have the answers myself." He then reported that he was going to stay busy this coming weekend by making a wooden wall hanging with the words, "I have the answers."

People have good reasons for what they do.

When a therapist remains genuinely curious about clients and is able to set aside preconceived notions of who they are and why they do what they do, surprising things happen. This is an extremely difficult skill to perfect, but one that is well worth the effort as the next case suggests. Our agency receives many referrals from Child Protective Services and often these clients' children have been removed from the home due to horrific conditions and circumstances. One such case was a mother and father who had used duct tape on their adolescent daughter's hands and feet to restrain her in bed. Obviously, this was an extreme situation, and Child Protective Services needed to intervene. How easy it would have been to have simply focused on the facts of the case and not have been curious as to the motivation and possible attempt at a solution that led these parents to such desperate measures. When we met these parents we were curious as to who they were as people and how they wanted their relationship with their daughter to be. We discovered that these were loving, and compassionate parents who, above all, wanted to keep their daughter safe. In a desperate act to keep their daughter away from the dangerous people with whom she had been spending time, they resorted to what they thought was the only way to keep her at home, where they could protect her. They explained that their daughter was involved with very dangerous people and that they had done what they thought was the only thing they could to ensure her safety. Granted, this reasoning by no means justified their actions, and they chose a very poor method to keep their daughter safe at home. However, by listening to what was really important to these parents, we could view the parents as kind and loving people rather than uncaring, abusive monsters. We could see them as loving parents who lacked skills to parent an adolescent. We were able to work successfully with them to find alternative methods to help them ensure their daughter's safety. Understanding that these parents loved their daughter so much that they were willing to go to extreme measures to keep her safe, we could recognize that they had a good motive for what they did, but an extremely poor method of implementing their choice to keep her safe. They were doing the wrong thing but for the right reasons.

It's best to remain neutral. (Don't believe or disbelieve.)

It is human nature to have an opinion. There is something comforting about "knowing," one way or the other if something is true. As therapists it is natural to want to believe our clients. Unfortunately, many therapists, jaded by years of believing followed by disappointment when clients' half truths and lies were exposed, have become convinced that clients can't be believed. This is not only painful for therapists, but can be frustrating and hurtful for clients who are genuinely telling the truth. In SFT, the therapist sets this entire struggle aside. Opinions such as right versus wrong or truth versus lie are not a part of this approach. This is not meant to imply there is no such thing as "truths" or "lies," but rather that it is the client and his or her system that evaluates the facts and makes this determination, not the therapist. The therapist's role is to remain neutral and to ask the questions so that the client and those who are in the client's life can accurately evaluate the merit and effectiveness of each potential action. Similarly, it is the client and his or her system that determines the changes that are necessary to resolve the problem. Therefore, the solution-focused therapist must come to each session with a clean slate and without an agenda so that he or she can really hear the client. He or she should assume nothing and let the client set the agenda for each session. Because many things can happen between sessions, we should not assume that what was important to a client last session will necessarily be important to him or her in a following session. Change happens constantly and even overnight a client can make major changes or make an important decision. In other words, we walk beside the clients rather than taking a leadership stance, and focus on learning what is important to them that day. Part of this involves asking the client what important others from his or her system (e.g., caseworker, probation officer, parent) would say is important or how they would interpret an action that the client plans to take. This helps to ensure that planned changes are systemically ecological and will truly help the client achieve the desired end result. This naturally results in the client challenging his or her own thinking and actions from the perspective of people important to him, thus allowing the therapist to remain neutral.

We must keep our own agenda out of the counseling session in order to remain neutral. For example, if a client discloses that abstaining from drugs or alcohol is not important to her, we go on to ask her what *is* important. She may, for example, respond by saying that her children have been taken from her by Child Protective Services due to substance use, and that she is attempting to regain custody. We then ask how we can help her with that. A frequent response to this question is that the client needs to prove to her caseworker that she is not abusing substances. In this case, we ask her what her caseworker would need to see to be convinced she does not have a problem with substances. Rather than forming an opinion about whether the client has a problem with substances and focusing on that, we encourage her to imagine a time in the future when she is able to prove this to her caseworker, and then we join her in exploring what real-life decisions she would have necessarily made to achieve this goal.

Over the years, we have seen many clients who despite positive urine drug tests protest that they have not used substances. Although the urine tests speak for themselves, it is not our "job" to convince them that they have indeed used substances, and it would not be effective to even try. In fact, if we did form an opinion it would negatively taint our view of the client and prevent us from really hearing the client and being curious about his or her goals. We might become so caught up in confronting a possible lie, that we would stop actually hearing important things the client is telling us and miss hearing details that are crucial to solution building. Instead, we simply report to the client that this is what the lab result states. We then ask the client what needs to happen now that this new information has been presented, and what they need as a result of the information. We make it our job to gather the information, such as the urine screen result and the client's report of not using the drug in question, and then share this information with the relevant parties in the client's system, such as the referral source. We think this is sufficiently important to bear repeating: It would be a waste of time for us to convince clients that they have used substances when they are stated that they did not. More often than not, the clients subsequently confide to us that they did in fact use the drug, but that they were not ready to admit it to themselves. In the interim, rather than wasting time arguing and confronting, we can still do effective work with a client by focusing on how the positive urine screen result impacts their overall goal.

INTERVENTIONS

Six key interventions are commonly used in solution-focused therapy. They are:

1. miracle question,
2. scaling,
3. relationship questions,
4. exception questions,
5. compliments, and
6. difference questions.

The miracle question is the foundation of all SFT, for it assists the client in imagining how life will be once the problem is resolved (Miller & de Shazer, 1998). The remaining five forms of interventions are then built upon the miracle question and interwoven throughout the sessions to assist the clients to develop a clear picture of what life will be like once the problem is resolved and then to work toward that end. The following sections explore each intervention in more depth.

Miracle Question

One of the most effective ways in which we help clients get a vivid picture of a place in which the problem is resolved, and therefore their solution, is to ask what is called the miracle question. The miracle question is described as follows:

> I am going to ask you a rather strange question. [pause] The strange question is this: [pause] After we talk, you will go back to your work (home, school) and you will do whatever you need to do the rest of today, such as taking care of the children, cooking dinner, watching TV, giving the children a bath, and so on. It will become time to go to bed. Everybody in your household is quiet, and you are sleeping in peace. In the middle of the night, a miracle happens *and the problem that prompted you to talk to me today is solved!* But because this happens while you are sleeping, you have no way of knowing that there was an overnight miracle that solved the problem. [pause] So, when you wake up tomorrow morning, what might be the small change that will make you say to yourself, "Wow, something must have happened—the problem is gone!"? (Berg & Dolan, 2001, p. 7)

There are five elements of the miracle question that must be in place in order for it to be most effective (Pichot & Dolan, 2003). If one of the elements is missing, the miracle question loses some of its power and may result in a novice therapist believing that the miracle question is not effective.

A Significant Change

The first element is introducing the concept of a significant change occurring in a client's life that would not otherwise take place. This is introduced with the preface "a miracle happens and the problem is solved," which invites the client to suspend disbelief and to begin to imagine what might have been a previously unimaginable change can now be explored.

Miracle

The second element that needs to be in place is ensuring that both the client and the therapist understand what the miracle is. Each client's miracle is different, but the common denominator for all is that the problem that brought him or her to treatment is resolved. It is the responsibility of the therapist to be sure that he or she understands the issue before asking the miracle question or else run the risk of asking about a miracle that is unimportant to a client.

Immediacy

The third element is immediacy. The miracle happens when a client goes to sleep tonight and wakes up tomorrow morning, thus creating the possibility of the miracle happening at any moment. It creates an air of expectancy and excitement; that change could be underfoot right now and one might miss it if not hypervigilant to change. In addition, the connection is made to an everyday, common occurrence: sleep. This creates a natural reminder each day of the intervention and invites the client to begin to look for miracles each and every morning. This also helps the client to notice the small changes that are currently happening in his or her life that he or she may have previously overlooked that are aspects of the miracle.

Surprise

The fourth element is surprise. The clients are unaware that the miracle has happened when they wake up in the morning, therefore they will be looking for clues that indicate something is different in their lives. Without this element, clients would not hunt as carefully and would not explore every aspect of the morning, looking for clues of the miracle.

Signs and Details of the Miracle

This leads us to the fifth element that needs to be in place, that is looking for signs or details that the miracle has occurred. The client is asked to notice the small details in his or her life on the miracle morning that let him or her know something is just a little bit different than the night before. This is also a great opportunity for the therapist to ask relational questions about what other people, such as a partner, child, or co-worker will notice about the client after the miracle occurs.

When asked purposefully and effectively, the miracle question not only helps the client realize that change is possible, it helps provide significant details of the benefits of achieving his or her miracle and the difference it will make in his or her life. Listening carefully to the client's response to the miracle question allows the therapist to momentarily view the solutions through the client's eyes. This ensures that the treatment goal is culturally sensitive and more likely to be embraced by the client (Pichot & Dolan, 2003). Because the clients create their own miracle vision of life in which the problem is resolved, they remain the experts on their own lives. Once the client describes the miracle, solution-focused therapists ask questions that identify times in which aspects of their miracle are already happening to some extent in the client's everyday life. This helps to ground the miracle in reality and help the clients to experience concretely that their miracle is not just a pipe dream.

Scaling

Scales are one of those tools that are found in many different theories and approaches. They are useful for measuring otherwise vague concepts. However, scales are used uniquely in the SFT approach in two important ways. The first is that scales are only used to measure aspects that are desirable. Although scales are traditionally used in other approaches for measuring pain or depression, a solution-focused therapist would only use scales to explore desired traits, behaviors, or skills such as confidence or ability to cope. Second, solution-focused scaling typically has a client place himself or herself on a scale from 1 to 10 or from 0 to 10, where 10 is the desired outcome and 1 or 0 is the opposite. This encourages clients to move up the scale and maintains the focus on desired elements (remember the principle that whatever one focuses on gets bigger).

In SFT, scales can be very useful in assisting the therapist and client in identifying aspects of the client's miracle that are already taking place. Scales are a tool that can help clients identify their own assessment of things such as progress, motivation, hopefulness, and confidence (Berg & Reuss, 1998). Just as a physician uses different scales during an office visit (a weight scale, a blood pressure monitor, a thermometer, or even a pain scale to rate the amount of pain a person is experiencing) the solution-focused therapist uses different scales to obtain various information. When using scales, both ends of the scale must be purposefully defined by the therapist depending upon what it is he or she is trying to assess, and the client must understand the definition of each end of the scale (Pichot & Dolan, 2003). Using our example of the kitty in the tree, we could have him scale his confidence in getting out of the situation, or have him scale his hope of getting out, or even his investment or willingness to change his situation. Scaling is a useful technique for making complex aspects of the client's life more concrete and accessible to the therapist and client. They have great versatility, and they can be used to access the client's perception of almost anything (DeJong & Berg, 2002).

Relationship Questions

Relationship questions are used in solution building to invite clients to create a description and meaning from interactional events (DeJong and Berg, 2002). All clients have relationships with others in their lives. These relationships may be of the client's choosing, or they could be relationships that are forced upon them such as with probation officers or Child Protective Services caseworkers. Most of the clients at our agency have external referral sources requiring that they comply with treatment recommendations, and most clients would prefer that these referral sources not be involved in their lives. However, having these referral sources in their lives is the client's reality, and we ask questions that help them cope with and incorporate the consequences of their reality. The following interaction describes how we might ask relationship questions to a client:

CLIENT (C): I'm done. I don't need any more treatment.

THERAPIST (T): Really, great! What lets you know you're done?

C: Well, I've reached my goal—I don't use drugs and I've got a job and a place to live.

T: Sounds like you're noticing some really positive changes in your life.

C: Oh yeah.

T: What do you think your caseworker or probation officer would say about you being done?

C: I dunno. I don't talk to them very much.

T: Hmm, well, you have spent a lot of time with your caseworker during your visits with your daughter, what do you suppose she would say about you being done?

C: Last time I talked to her, she said that she thought I was doing really good. She said that she heard I have a place to live now, and that I have a job. So I guess she knows I'm doing good.

T: Wow, so even your caseworker, who you said you don't talk to very much, is noticing some positive changes?!

C: Yeah, I guess so.

T: Who else in your life is noticing these changes in your life?

C: My daughter.

T: Really?! What is she noticing?

By asking relationship questions to this client, he now has to really think about what is different in his life, not only from his perspective but from important others as well. In addition, he now has to explore the impact of these changes on his long-term goals and on those who matter to the client. By asking the client to step outside of himself, relationship questions have the ability to increase empathy and objectivity.

Exception Questions

Because no problem exists constantly, it is important to spend time exploring the times when a problem doesn't exist. I'm reminded of a story in which a client came to her solution-focused therapist complaining about being depressed since childhood. The therapist asked how she knew she was depressed if it had been that way for so long, maybe this was just her normal state. She insisted that this was not the case because there were times when things were better. "Aha," said the clinician, "tell me about these times." Obviously exceptions abound, and it's the job of a solution-focused therapist to notice when the client talks about these exceptions and to then further explore them. Going back to our kitty who is now out of the tree, we might ask about the times when he has been frightened by an approaching dog, but then found alternatives to racing up a tree. Or perhaps there were times in the kitty's past when he has been in the tree but was able to get right out. Again, the problem-focused therapist might spend most of the therapeutic time on our kitty being "stuck." The solution-focused therapist seeks to help the client notice the times when he or she is not stuck. We would ask kitty to identify times when his life mimics the vision of a solution he has for himself. We help him identify when his life has resembled or resembles the solution, even if it is in small pieces of the larger solution.

This will assist kitty in seeing that he has the power over these exceptions and can therefore make these exceptions happen more often; thereby creating a solution. So, for example, if the kitty has determined that he wants out of the tree, but lacks the courage to get himself out of the situation, we may ask about times when the kitty was courageous in the past. If he lacks decision-making skills, we would ask him about the times in his life when he was able to make decisions. Has the kitty been stuck in a tree before? If so, how did he manage to get out? This empowers our clients to realize that they already possess the skills needed to obtain their solution. This can often be difficult for clients to remember especially in the midst of a crisis. We notice that as we work with clients, and help guide them through this self-discovery, a visible change comes over them. We frequently notice a relaxed posture, a thoughtfulness, and oftentimes a smile as they discover that they posses the skills to create change, and that they have used these skills countless times previously in their life.

Compliments

As we mentioned previously, clients have the skills to cope with many situations, however these frequently go unrecognized. Compliments serve to highlight these unnoticed skills and to underscore the usefulness of behaviors or skills that the clients possess. Compliments are derived from what the client communicates through words or process, and are often used to reinforce in the client's mind what the clients have already established as being important to them. Here is an example:

CLIENT (C): I finally told my daughter that she couldn't go out last weekend.

THERAPIST (T): Really? Tell me what happened.

C: Well, she came home two hours after her curfew and I told her that she couldn't go out the rest of the weekend. It was really hard though, I don't like being the bad guy.

T: So, even though it was really hard, you stuck to your limits.

C: Yeah, she wasn't too happy, but I knew I had to do it. She was starting to really get out of control.

T: How impressive! You knew you had to do it despite risking being the bad guy. You've just touched on one of the most important lessons a parent can learn—setting boundaries with your children.

C: Yeah, I think I know it's for the best.

T: What a great skill to have, doing what's best for your children!

Solution-focused therapists compliment only the behaviors that the clients recognize themselves as being useful toward helping them reach their goals. The use of compliments therefore remains client driven as the therapist validates and acknowledges those behaviors that are working for the client.

Difference Questions

One of the ways to increase the richness and meaningfulness of a therapy session is to ask difference questions. Difference questions are simply any question that explores what difference any past, current, or potential change has or might make on the client or those in the client's life. The following example is an interaction demonstrating the power of difference questions.

CLIENT (C) (while exploring the miracle): As I get up, I'm not feeling rushed. I feel like I can take my time and really focus on what I need to do for the day.

THERAPIST (T): Wow! And what difference does it make to you when you're focused?

C: I'm able to get the things done that I need to get done instead of waiting for someone else to do them for me.

T: Really, so you're getting things done?

C: Yeah.

T: What difference does it make for your son when you're focused, and able to get things done?

C: Um, I guess he is able to get the things done that he needs to.

T: So when you're focused, your son is able to be focused too.

C: Uh-huh.

T: What difference does it make to your son when he is able to be focused?

C: He is able to do better in school, and hopefully graduate.

T: Wow! That is a big difference! What difference does it make to you if your son is able to do well in school and graduate?

C: Well, I probably would be relieved that I did a good job in raising him.

T: So you will be proud not only of your son, but proud of yourself as well.

C: Yeah!

Difference questions help identify the impact potential changes may make on a client's life or can enhance awareness or deepen meaning of goals. This often will result in increased motivation to make additional changes and increased hope that change is possible (Pichot & Dolan, 2003).

BENEFITS TO THERAPISTS USING SFT

At our agency, we have incorporated the solution-focused approach not only into the work we do with our clients, but into our daily interactions with each other as well. Although neither of these changes happened overnight, those who have witnessed the changes at the agency over time have noticed a remarkable difference. We know that utilizing solution-focused therapy has an impact on our clients, and we have been rewarded by seeing a shift in our clients within a very short period of time after coming to our agency. Our clients are usually involved in a system that is designed to form opinions about them, whether it be the courts or child protection. When the clients enter our agency, they typically expect to find that same judgment from a substance abuse treatment provider, and this results in the clients having their guard up, ready to defend themselves. However, because they are greeted in a nonjudgmental way and because we very quickly ask questions to help us understand what's important to them, they end up feeling heard and are more cooperative. Clients may expect us to place labels upon them such as "alcoholic" or "drug addict" and are usually surprised when they are greeted in a way that focuses upon what they are doing that is working. We have heard such comments as: "You are the first person who didn't look down at me," or "I thought you were going to be like the rest of them." It's comments like these that give energy to our staff and help keep our morale high.

Staff turnover is extremely low, which is unusual for a substance abuse counseling agency. We get excited along with our clients as we talk about the goals they are setting for themselves and the steps they are taking to reach their goals. As a staff we set our own goals for our agency, and we look at our individual professional goals as well. In doing so, we are able to incorporate individual goals with team goals. One of the ways we do this is by partnering with community agencies at which our interests lie. For example, we have a staff member who is more interested in working with the adolescent population and therefore partners with the school system. Another staff member is interested in the judicial system and works closely with the local diversion and probation departments. Yet another staff member is interested in the politics that go along with a community agency and spends time at more administrative meetings. And of course this book would not be written if it were not for one staff member's interest in incorporating animal-assisted therapy into our agency.

Needless to say, morale is high, and those who visit the agency notice the playful attitude and respect we have for each other. We are direct with each other, and don't spend time complaining about circumstances or other annoyances. When there is a problem, it gets addressed, and we continue to move forward toward our ideal work environment. According to Pichot and Dolan (2003), "the potential and the impact of this approach are endless, and . . . [the] understanding of solution-focused therapy would be best viewed as a journey rather than a destination" (p. 5).

SUMMARY

Because solution-focused therapy is the foundation for all of the work we do, it naturally applies to our use of AAA/T, and a strong understanding of this approach, the guiding principles, and the interventions is necessary to really understand our subsequent chapters. Working in partnership with our therapy dog, we assist clients in resolving problems not through traditional problem exploration, but by challenging them and others to explore a place in which the problem is resolved; a place in which miracles are a reality. The next chapter will explore the basics of canine behavior relative to therapy work.

Photo by Mark Hochstedler. Used with permission.

Chapter 3

What Every Therapist Needs to Know About Dogs Before Partnering with One in AAA/T

> In order to really enjoy a dog, one doesn't merely try to train him to be semihuman. The point of it is to open oneself to the possibility to becoming partly a dog.
>
> Edward Hoagland,
> American novelist

Creating an effective animal-assisted activities or therapy program for an agency or within a private practice can be a challenging endeavor. However, before one can begin to create a program and use a therapy dog safely and effectively within a therapeutic setting, it is vital that therapists really understand how dogs think and what motivates them. Without this, therapists risk over- or underestimating their canine partner's ability, thereby creating a potentially dangerous situation for clients. This chapter explores the common myths about dogs, and provides basic information that every therapist should know about dogs before entering into a partnership with them as cotherapists.

UNDERSTANDING CANINE CULTURE

I grew up loving animals; especially dogs. One of my favorite animal stars was Lassie, followed by Benji at a close second. Both dogs were incredible as they problem solved, were best buddies to their child co-stars, saved lives, put others' needs before their own, etc. It seemed there was nothing that these canine heroes could not do! How could anyone not want a dog like that? Walt Disney furthered this idea of the thinking, reasoning, moral-guided dog as Goofy, Pluto, and other Disney characters instructed viewers on the dangers of road rage and other community issues. They talked and sang their way into America's hearts. As childhood fades everyone realizes that dogs can't sing and that the level of intelligence that was portrayed on the big screen was exaggerated, but there can't help but be a subtle, lasting effect. Even though we know that dogs aren't capable of the level of fictitious escapades that are so entertaining in books, television, and movies, it is often left to the imagination to decide how much they really do understand and how they process information. In many ways the movies and stories that made us all love dogs so much did our canine friends an injustice. They created a myth that dogs were somehow semihuman in their desires, thinking, and moral structure; people with fur if you will. It is now common to believe that dogs are capable of feeling low-level remorse and even planning revenge (e.g., urinating on the floor out of anger at being left by their owners).

Jean Donaldson (1996) summarized the consequences of our humanization of animals best when she stated, "As soon as you bestow intelligence and morality, you bestow the responsibility that goes along with them" (p. 13). Once we believe that dogs urinate in the house or chew our favorite items deliberately, they are now deserving of punishment, for they should be held responsible. Unfortunately, we often overestimate our canine friends' abilities and set them up for failure. In America we love our pets, and we tend to spoil them. However, our ideas of spoiling them frequently entails giving them things and privileges according to human thinking and desires. As a society these same "spoiled" pets are frequently neglected in the way that matters the most; understanding their culture and what makes them tick.

This trend of humanizing dogs is especially dangerous for therapists who would like to use a dog with clients. One of the most important factors necessary to ensure safety when working with a dog is an accurate and thorough understanding of how the dog responds, what motivates him, as well as what is most likely to spook and comfort him. Because of this it is crucial to have a clear understanding about canine culture. According to Donaldson (1996), here are the top ten things we know about real dogs:

1. It's all chew toys to them (no concept of artifacts, tokens or symbols)
2. Amoral (no right vs. wrong, only safe vs. dangerous)
3. Self-interested (no desire to please)
4. Lemon-brains (i.e., small & relatively unconvoluted brains which learn only through operant and classical conditioning)
5. Predators (search, chase, grab & hold, dissect, chew all strongly wired)
6. Highly social (bond strongly & don't cope well with isolation)
7. Finite socialization period (fight or flee anything they're not socialized to)
8. Opportunistic and keen scavengers (if it's edible, eat it, NOW)
9. Resolve conflicts through ritualized aggression (never write letters to editor, never sue)
10. Well-developed olfactory system (p. 20)

Although all ten factors are important for a dog owner to really understand and embrace, seven are especially important for therapists who work with therapy dogs to fully grasp.

Amoral (No Right versus Wrong; Only Safe versus Dangerous)

As therapists we are suckers for the idea that a dog can personify the qualities of a therapist. Animals are frequently portrayed in this manner (i.e., good judge of character, sensitive to people's feelings, knowing when someone needs help). Now we are not implying that dogs are not highly in tune to human beings, for we do know that "dogs are highly sensitive to human emotions and are equally perceptive to reading our body language" (Monks of New Skete, 2002, p. 98). However it is important to make the distinction between in tune and able to read people versus able to make a moral judgment. Dogs constantly evaluate the environment to ensure that things are "safe" from their perspective. A professional would be remiss to trust a dog unsupervised with anyone, for a dog can interpret a situation far differently than a human would in a matter of seconds. I have heard dog owners mistakenly say, "Oh don't worry. My dog is great with kids!" While that may be true, a wise owner still watches over the situation carefully to ensure that the children are socialized to dogs and that the dog is interpreting the situation as "safe." The most dangerous situations are those in which the handler believed the dog was automatically safe and therefore lowered his or her guard. For example, I view my own therapy dog, Rocky, as excellent with children. However, I am continuously surprised when well-meaning therapists and co-workers have encouraged me to allow Rocky to "play" with an employee's small toddler without close supervision during business meetings. Rocky has no concept of right versus wrong and without guidance, he could quickly misinterpret a toddler's pulling of his hair or ear, and without intervention, the situation could escalate to the point of compromised safety. While he is usually very patient, without close supervision, his communication of any discomfort and need for assistance would go unnoticed, forcing him to communicate in a more forceful manner. Rocky has no concept that biting or growling at a child is "wrong." However, he does know that I (TP) am there to assist him in changing the environment to increase his safety when he gives me a certain look or moves closer to me to communicate his discomfort. It is my role as his handler to quickly notice his communications and make changes in his environment to increase his feeling of safety.

Self-Interested (No Desire to Please)

This concept is by far the most difficult for many dog lovers, for the myth that dogs love to please their owners runs deep. Donaldson (1996) goes so far to say that after all her years of experience with dogs, "I'm still waiting to meet the desire to please dog. If it shows up, I'll send it for psychotherapy" (p. 16). Dogs are motivated by many things, and one of the first steps to successful training is to learn what motivates that particular dog. However, dogs are only motivated by things that they perceive to be of an interest or benefit to them (food, play, access to the outdoors, etc.). Praise can be a weak to moderate motivator for some dogs, however it is usually because it has been paired with a primary reinforcer such as food, not because the dog cares that the owner is happy. The praise is then interpreted by the dog as a sign he is on the right track and is more likely to get something of interest to him (Donaldson, 1996).

The desire-to-please myth has been confused with the very real concept of loyalty and dedication that dogs can develop to their handler when the handler assumes an attitude of respect toward the dog. "Such an attitude on the part of the caretaker frees the dog to respond with a natural willingness and over time nurtures a profound level of loyalty and dedication" (Monks of New Skete, 2002, p. 96). The dog trusts the handler to care for and protect him, therefore a natural partnership and mutuality can develop. The dog has learned that good things consistently happen as a result of being with and obeying his handler. However, it is important to really understand that the dog is not obeying because he knows it "pleases" the human. Human love stems from the ability and desire to care for and put another's needs before one's own. Dogs, although strongly bonded, can not make this moral decision to "sacrifice" for the sake of a loved one. Although dogs have been known to do some heroic things, it is not realistic to assume that the dog made a conscious decision to put the needs of others before his own. Such a decision would require the ability to weigh the pros and cons of an action in moralistic terms, which dogs cannot do.

One example of where this canine trait might come into play in work with clients is on those occasions when the dog shows little to no interest in a specific client, who would like to have a visit. Although it would be wonderful if therapy dogs could read the emotional needs of clients and consistently respond in an empathic way to meet the clients' needs, that just simply does not always occur. Dogs (like people) don't like everyone. However, dogs lack the people-pleasing quality of feigning interest that humans have learned. Dogs don't have a sense of fairness or a sense of obligation to ensure that each person in a room gets equal visitation time. They are attracted to the individuals who are interesting to them and are very good at assessing who likes them. They are genuine and live in the moment. They have no concept of what would make the client feel happy; only whether there is anything about the person that interests them. This is where the handler's people skills (to cover for the dog when needed) and ability to interest the dog come in handy. The handler's ability to understand and appreciate the dog's motivation and the ability to compensate for the dog's inabilities highlight the true sense of team-work that is the hallmark of AAA/T.

Lemon-Brains (i.e., Small and Relatively Unconvoluted Brains Which Learn Only Through Operant and Classical Conditioning)

Dogs (not unlike humans) naturally and constantly offer behaviors as an experiment to determine which ones work. The definition of "work" to a dog means that the behavior resulted in the dog getting something that is of value to him (e.g., attention, food, let outside, access to other dogs, play). Simply put, dogs continue the behaviors that work, and discontinue the behaviors that don't. The key to controlling dog behavior is to remain vigilant of the dog's behavior and consistently manipulate the consequences of his actions (Donaldson, 1996). In addition, it is most effective to teach the dog what you want, rather than what you don't want. By ignoring the negative behavior or by teaching the dog an incompatible behavior, the negative behavior disappears. This requires discipline on the part of the handler not to succumb to the cute antics of the pet, and give in "just this once." For example, rather than trying to teach a dog not to beg at the table for food (a very natural and rewarding thing for a dog to do, especially should the dog succeed in obtaining a morsel of food in the process), instead reward the dog for lying quietly during meal times. The dog cannot lie quietly and beg at the same time, and he soon learns that he is more likely to get a big treat for lying down during meals than hovering around the table.

Reading the available dog training literature can be a frustrating and confusing process. There are many different schools of thought about the best ways to train a dog. Even within the field of dog training itself there is controversy, with many traditional training methods now justifiably viewed by some as abusive and inhumane (Clothier, 2002; Donaldson, 1996). We find ear pinching, leash jerking, electrical shock, choking, dragging, and other methods meant to inflict pain to the dog as a method of instruction very disturbing to say the least. Kinder and gentler methods are now advocated by many professional trainers. It is now recognized that a large majority of dogs respond very well to positive reinforcement alone, therefore popularizing training methods such as Clicker Training (Donaldson, 1996; Pryor, 1999; Tillman, 2000; Wilkes, 1995).

Unfortunately, we were disturbed to find that many texts (including some authors we have otherwise quoted for their advocacy of relationships with canines) still include sections on discipline that advocate physical force as a means to correct a dog who is misbehaving. While admittedly we are therapists by trade and are not professional dog trainers, we unequivocally take the stance that any training method that uses physical force or pain as an aversive technique is not appropriate for training a potential therapy dog or any dog, for that matter. As we will explain in Chapters 5 and 6, the training and other factors of a therapy dog's life are frequently used to create therapeutic parallels for parenting and other behavioral changes. The use of inhumane or abusive tactics when training the dog would not only be ethically questionable and incompatible with solution-focused therapy, but would render this intervention impossible and inappropriate. Unfortunately, we have discovered that while many trainers hold themselves out to only use humane and positive approaches, some revert back to physical coercion for difficult behavioral problems (Clothier, 2002). The most important elements to consider when selecting the training method for a potential therapy dog is to ensure that the training methods are both humane and are such that enhance the human-animal relationship. Many traditional training methods use negative reinforcement or punishment as primary training methods, which can damage the relationship and result in obedience out of fear. We urge readers to carefully select trainers based on a similar commitment to humane and positive treatment no matter how difficult the canine behavioral problem may be to resolve. Although this kind of training may be difficult to locate, it is well worth the effort for both the dog and the relationship between the handler and canine.

Regardless of the obedience level of your dog, we would recommend participation in a formal obedience class led by an experienced trainer. Participation in such a class with your dog is for much more than simply teaching the dog good manners. It is through such a class that you as the handler will learn how dogs think, will receive valuable professional feedback about your relationship with your dog, and will receive valuable assessment information from a professional about your dog's personality, temperament, strengths, and weaknesses. All of these factors are invaluable in ensuring a successful human-animal partnership.

It is especially important to note that the "principal role in obedience training is to give feedback" (Donaldson, 1996, p. 168) to the dog about his behavior as opposed to giving commands. Participation in professional training allows the handler to observe the precision and level of feedback that professional trainers give to dogs during training. A research study showed that trainers give considerably more information/feedback to a dog that they are handling (approximately every six seconds) as opposed to owners (every twenty seconds) (Donaldson, 1996). This increased flow of information allows the dog to know what behaviors will most likely result in reward, and what behaviors can be discontinued. The most effective form of feedback includes both a reward for good behavior as well as a no-reward mark. This is often a vocal cue to the dog such as "wrong" or a low-pitched grunt that communicates to the dog that he is in danger of losing a future reward if he continues that behavioral path. Once the dog is familiar with the no-reward mark, the dog will stop all behavior upon hearing the cue and look to the handler for a command for the desired behavior. This requires considerable discipline on the part of the handler to be able to rapidly shift from reward (higher pitched, happy vocal tones) to no-reward (low-pitched, serious vocal tones) feedback within a matter of seconds to give immediate information to the dog about the desired behavior. This does not leave room for the emotional-laden intonations that plague human interactions, which simply leave dogs confused.

These concepts are especially important in work with therapy dogs, for human-animal teams are frequently confronted with unusual and new situations. Trainers frequently encourage handlers to "talk the animal through" new situations. While the dog has minimal to no understanding of the words that the handler is saying, the dog understands the constant stream of high-pitched or calming tones (meaning all is well, and continue with current behavior) versus low-pitched, staccato tones (meaning stop immediately). In my work with Rocky, I frequently chatter quietly to him as we walk the hallways (e.g., "That's right. You are doing good. Hey, look! There is your friend, Heidi. She looks busy today. Come on; we better keep going. We will come back later. Let's go!"). Those who are not familiar with this form of "jolly talk" (Davis, 2002, p. 106) could easily think that I erroneously think Rocky can understand. I know that he has no idea of what I am saying. I talk to him in this way because I would simply feel foolish chattering away without forming logical and complete sentences that make sense to humans who might overhear. By engaging in jolly talk with Rocky, I let him know that all of the other distractions (children running by, odd noises and smells) can be ignored, and that he should pay attention to my voice. Should he become distracted and pull in a direction to investigate something unhelpful, my jolly talk quickly but quietly stops, I give a quick, low grunt or a command he understands, and then resume the jolly talk once his behavior returns to what is desired.

Dogs are predators (search, chase, grab and hold, dissect, chew all strongly wired).

When working with a dog around clients, it is very important to understand the breed of dog and the inherent traits that might become triggered by various client activities. For example, Rocky is a rough-coat collie, which is a herding dog. There are certain traits and resulting behaviors in him as a herding dog that I have ultimately learned to predict and avoid. Rocky naturally wants to bark and chase when he sees a client (or anything else for that matter) running. Since Rocky is always on a leash when working with clients, he is not in danger of chasing. However, the occasional bark has happened when this instinctual drive has been triggered. Because of this, it is important that I notice the running first, and give a command that is incompatible with the undesired behavior (e.g., "quiet"). In addition, we have posted signs requesting that clients refrain from running while indoors. Because of Rocky's chase/herding instincts, it would be unsafe to use him in any intervention in which he was off leash, or in which a child was intentionally running.

Each breed has its inbred traits, and understanding both the breed and the individual dog is necessary. However, to maintain safety, it is vital to ensure that the cause of the behavior is clearly understood and that undesirable behavior is not hastily attributed to the dog's breed without considering other causes such as the dog's attempt to communicate lack of perceived safety or comfort. This is where a good relationship with a professional trainer, who is very familiar with the particular dog, is vital. The trainer can provide objective information about the cause of the behavior, assess the safety of continuing to work with the dog in that work environment, and provide tips to minimize the potentially negative impact of the dog's breed in the workplace.

Dogs have a finite socialization period (fight or flee anything they're not socialized to).

Contrary to what is frequently portrayed on television or in the movies, dogs don't instinctually like to be handled and are not eager to explore new and different situations or objects. They could not survive in the wild if they were prone to constantly investigate the unknown. Dogs must be purposefully socialized at a very young age in order to teach them to behave tolerantly. In addition, a dog's socialization must be diligently maintained throughout his life. As puppies, dogs are much more curious as compared to their adult counterparts, and most experts estimate that there is a "socialization window" that closes between three and five months depending on the breed and individual temperament (Donaldson, 1996, p. 61). During this window, puppies are curious and open to readily explore new situations, people, and objects with minimal hesitation. As the puppy grows older, his natural instincts develop to protect him from the unknown, and fear or apprehension replaces curiosity in order to ensure survival. As an adult, a dog that encounters something to which he has not been socialized will frequently respond with caution or aggression until it has been established that the new object is not threatening.

For therapy dogs, this socialization period is of utmost importance, for therapy dogs are exposed to new people and situations on a daily basis. People will touch the dog in ways that he might not expect (rough pats, or even mild hair or tail pulling), others will utilize wheelchairs and other walking equipment. Some will wear hats or flowing clothing, while others speak different languages and dialects; all are part of a therapy dog's day. People love to get up close and personal with therapy dogs, so this type of day-to-day interaction must be part of the socialization. Therapy dogs must learn to safely tolerate children's faces close to theirs, their paws being held or petted, their tails being flopped around in a jump-rope fashion, and an occasional tight hug around their middle or head. All have to be interpreted by the dog as safe.

However, it is imperative that handlers really understand that it is impossible to socialize a dog to all possible situations, people, and objects. There will inevitably be times in which a therapy dog encounters the unfamiliar. In these situations the handler needs to be aware of the potential danger that the dog may interpret the situation as threatening and thereby resort to fight or flight mentality. (It is most effective when the handler can identify the potentially new object prior to the dog reacting.) In these situations, the handler needs to continuously evaluate the dog's comfort level, use his or her voice to assist the dog in feeling more comfortable, and then remove the dog if needed.

For example, one day when Rocky and I were working in the agency's clinic waiting room, I noticed a woman sitting in an electronic scooter talking on the telephone. Although the scooter was not in motion and Rocky did not seem to notice, I immediately remembered that Rocky had barked and backed away from the last (and only) moving scooter he had ever encountered. (Although Rocky trained around wheelchairs, we did not have an opportunity to work around the more expensive electric scooter models, and they are rarely seen in outpatient or community settings.) Not wanting to take the risk of Rocky feeling uncomfortable or spooking in public, I quickly repositioned us so the scooter was not in his line of sight. We finished visiting with the children in the waiting room, and then took an alternative route to exit the waiting room that would avoid him having to walk near the scooter. Although Rocky did notice the scooter at one point and gave me a sign of nervousness (a slightly lowered head, ears laid back, looking at me as he leaned into me), this extra measure of caution prevented any noticeable signs of apprehension by others in the workplace. Although we were successful in the workplace in this situation, I continue to seek out training opportunities outside of the workplace in which to expose Rocky to electric scooters to increase his comfort level. Training and exposure to new situations are a constant for therapy dogs, but the work setting and with actual clients are not the appropriate setting for this form of active training. Clients frequently come to us in a vulnerable state and can have unpredictable behaviors. In order to ensure safety for our clients, we must only use a therapy dog in settings in which we know the dog is sufficiently trained and safe. The dog's behavior must be predictable in order to effectively work with clients whose behavior may not be. Failure to do so would potentially increase risk to clients. Clients come to us for services, and we must be careful to only use interventions that we know are effective and safe.

It is also important that handlers be willing to put people's feelings secondary to their canine partner's comfort. Failure to do so may result in an unsafe situation. For example, should the woman in the electric scooter whom Rocky and I encountered that day have requested a visit from Rocky, I would have had to decline. Rocky had effectively communicated to me that he was not comfortable, and I already had a previous encounter with a moving scooter while on a walk at a park in which Rocky had responded with fear. It would not be safe to put a client in that situation when I knew my dog was not sufficiently socialized for that situation.

My best response would be to apologetically explain that Rocky was not familiar with such a modern scooter and could not yet work safely around it to visit. I would further explain that I plan to work with Rocky to train him around this kind of equipment in the future to prevent this limitation. During this interaction with the woman I would observe how Rocky was responding from the safe distance. If he was alert, comfortable, and curious (by observing his head, ear, body, and tail positions) I would advance to allow Rocky the opportunity to safely explore (even allowing Rocky contact with the woman if he initiated it). However, if he was fearful or anxious we would stand our ground and speak with the client from the safe distance. Although the woman would be disappointed that a visit was not possible, safety must come first.

Dogs are opportunistic and keen scavengers. (*If it's edible, eat it,* now.)

It will probably come as no surprise that dogs love to eat anything! In addition, they explore their surroundings through their nose and mouth. This characteristic can have a significant impact on a therapy dog's work. Although therapy dogs are well trained and are perceived as "great" dogs, they are still dogs. To forget this risks the dog's safety. Dogs are able to detect the presence of objects of interest quite rapidly through their keen sense of smell. For example, a small, dropped tablet of medication can be quickly snatched from the floor by a canine's tongue if the handler is distracted and inattentive, resulting in illness and even death for the dog. AAA/T work requires that the handler be simultaneously attentive to many levels of distractions; people, environment, objects, situations, interactions, as well as the dog's response and comfort level. In addition, by bringing a dog into a treatment environment, we are typically introducing a dog into an environment that dogs infrequently visit, and are therefore not dog proofed. Consequently, there is an inherent danger of the therapy dog finding objects that are poisonous or choking hazards. The handler must repeatedly scan the floor to ensure there are no dangerous objects, instruct the dog to leave unsafe objects, and be prepared to remove any objects from the environment that might serve as distractions or pose a safety risk. In addition, it would be considered unprofessional and obviously in "bad form" for a therapy dog to be allowed to randomly take objects or go through a trash can, regardless of the safety element! In addition to scanning for hazards, the handlers should be aware of changes in the dog's behavior that might indicate that an interesting smell has been detected, for cleaning products, insecticide sprayed in corners of a room, and mouse traps, are all invisible, but potentially dangerous to a dog. While allowing a dog to contentedly lick the carpet at home may very well be safe, in the workplace it might expose the dog to toxic chemicals.

People like to connect with therapy dogs, and they frequently think of food as a way to do this: offering pieces of their sandwich or snack. Although their intentions are good, the resulting begging and unknown food content consumed by the dog are undesirable. Therefore, the handler must have clear guidelines before encountering these situations. I find that clients and staff are very understanding when I tell them that Rocky does not eat any "people food." Staff members have responded by asking if they could bring him some dog treats, which I have allowed under the condition that they limit the treat to one small treat, which he earns with a trick. This has had a positive benefit of teaching staff how to interact with Rocky and gives them something to look forward to during each visit, as he performs tricks and is greeted with praise, clapping, and cheers from the staff during his visits. Although the agency is rather large, staff members have been very respectful of the importance of watching Rocky's weight and not overfeeding him (however, I would intervene if necessary).

Although we do not like to think of our clients as ever wanting to harm our dogs, it must nevertheless be considered a possibility, and therefore allowing a client to bring or offer food from an unknown source is always risky and not recommended. A safer option is to carry small treats that clients can give the dog with the handler's permission. This can serve as an educational tool about the importance of good nutrition (by mentioning the importance of watching what the dog eats, how much, etc.), while ensuring safety.

For example, I sometimes ask a shy child if he or she would like to give Rocky a treat as a way to structure a visit and help the child gain courage to interact. This frequently results in the child laughing and petting Rocky once the child sees that Rocky is safe. However, it is wise to always teach the child to give treats with an open hand, palm up. This allows the dog to lick the treat from the hand and avoid the appearance of having to use teeth to get the treat. Dry treats can also be helpful, since they stick to the dog's wet tongue, encouraging gentle access. However, it should never appear that a therapy dog is reliant on treats for good behavior. Treats should be used purposefully, and a therapy dog should be constantly observed obeying and being polite even when treats are not being offered.

Resolve Conflicts Through Ritualized Aggression

It is all too easy to take the safety of dogs and their predictability for granted. Even though we hear of dog bites on the news, those situations are frequently dismissed as anomalies unique to that particular dog. It is assumed that the dog was flawed rather than the owner missing a series of subtle communications that were offered by the dog prior to the problem. When a dog owner fails to respect, ignores, or responds inappropriately to the animal's attempts to signal distress or discomfort, these signals escalate to the most obvious form, that of aggression. Significantly, "almost all owners of dogs who inflict serious bites seemingly 'without provocation' believed their own dog to be safe the day before or the minute before the dog bit for the first time" (Donaldson, 1996, p. 57). The most dangerous dogs are those who are viewed by the owners as being the kind of dog who will "never bite," for there is no such dog. Every dog, regardless of breed, temperament, or training, has the potential to bite if aggression is ultimately needed in order to communicate.

Every dog has a first method of defense when spooked; either flight or fight. If that first method of defense fails, he will resort to the alternate method. Rocky, for example, uses flight as his first line of defense when something frightens him. First he stops or backs up (preparing to flee). If I fail to notice these signs, he proceeds to look at me and move closer, seemingly as if to ask, "I'm not sure about that, are you seeing it too? Are you going to take care of it, or do I need to take action?" If these communications are unheeded, he may bark or forcefully pull away to retreat. Usually these levels of escalation are gradual and pronounced, giving me time to increase his comfort level. However, there was a rare occasion when Rocky was very young, when he became extremely fearful and escalated quickly to this higher level of barking and pulling away before I could calm him. You can imagine the danger if Rocky's first level of defense was aggression. Although I have never seen Rocky switch to use his second line of defense, fight, I bear in mind that it is always a possibility, and therefore it is imperative that I notice and intervene at the earlier levels while he remains in flight mode.

When thinking about what escalates a dog to bite or show aggression, it is helpful to assess unique risk factors. All dogs have things that antagonize them, and these vary from dog to dog. These might include but are not limited to being petted on the top of the head, categories of people to whom the dog is not socialized, people or things rushing toward the dog, moving a food object, being crowded, loud noises, etc. If a dog is presented with only one of these things, he may be able to cope. However, if several antagonistic things occur simultaneously, the dog may be pushed over his threshold and respond with aggression (Donaldson, 1996, p. 91). By clearly understanding the individual dog's annoyance factors, vulnerabilities, and fears, his threshold for responding to these individually or in combination, the dog's pattern or progression from flight (first line of defense) to fight (second line) can be predicted more reliably, allowing the handler to make the adjustments needed to ensure safety. If the handler lacks this necessary knowledge, the dog can best be described as a time bomb at the mercy of the environment.

THE ROLES OF RELATIONSHIP AND RESPECT

This brings us to the importance of relationship when working with dogs in the workplace. Therapy dogs and their handlers are typically described as "teams." In fact, their certification/credentials are given to the "team," rather than the individuals. This reflects the fact that it is a partnership in the truest sense of the word. The therapy dog enhances the therapist's ability and opens doors to interactions with clients that the therapist could not otherwise easily achieve. These might include casual conversation with an uncomfortable client, introducing otherwise avoided topics such as nutrition or parenting, or simply providing a context to express compassion for a living thing. Dogs have the ability to mirror "us back to ourselves in unmistakable ways that, if we are open, foster true understanding and change" (Monks of New Skete, 2003). This greater understanding and change is of course, what psychotherapy is all about, and it is this ability to connect with clients in this special and powerful way that makes dogs so useful for therapists. Without the therapy dog, therapists would need in many situations to be far more intrusive in order to offer the assistance or get necessary information from their clients.

Obviously the sort of teamwork described earlier is not something that can be solely limited to the workplace or turned on or off at whim. This is precisely why therapy dogs are owned by their handlers. The resulting bond between the human and dog team members has sometimes been described as a "deep spiritual connection" (Monks of New Skete, 2002, p. 98). This requires much more than simply allowing a well-behaved family pet into the work place, for the therapist must really know and understand the dog in order for the partnership to exist. And it works both ways. Both dog and human must know how the other will respond. Since dogs communicate through their body language (Coren, 2000; Dibra, 1999) rather than talking about what they are thinking and feeling, their human partners must become familiar with their communication patterns through careful and repeated observation. Carefully observing a dog is analogous to listening to a person. As Davis (2002) states, "The dog can't tell you what has happened; you have to know. This essential part of handling a therapy dog makes it a twenty-four-hour-a-day responsibility" (p. 151).

The relationship between the handler and the dog results in a sense of mutual trust. The dog not only trusts the human to notice and meet his needs, but the human also learns to trust the dog's judgment. Dogs will at times exhibit "intelligent disobedience" (Davis, 2002). This is when a dog deliberately disobeys a command because the dog has information that the handler lacks. For example, the dog might break from command in order to maintain safety. For example, Rocky has been trained to trust that I will not step on him when I walk closely around him or even step over him when he is lying down. I have trained him in this way so he and I are always both clear about whose responsibility it is to ensure safety when we are in close proximity. He is to trust me explicitly unless I command him to move. The "move" command lets him know it is now his job to adjust to me. Rocky has learned to expect that staff members and clients know this and will always be careful not to step on him. However, there have been occasions with clients when Rocky has quickly moved out of the way, and I learned afterward that someone accidentally stepped on him. By moving, Rocky lets me know that person doesn't know the rules and is not watching out for him. By trusting that Rocky knows something I missed and is signaling that more caution is needed, I then interpret his breaking from the "down-stay" command as a form of communication rather than disobedience. I then reassure him that I'll watch more carefully, and he resumes the trusting stance. Situations like this are where it is crucial that the handler understand how the dog responds, so that the dog's communications are accurately interpreted.

Therapy dogs are constantly being watched by people in the workplace, partially because people love dogs, and partially because working dogs are different and at times not understood. Many people have never seen a well-behaved dog before and only associate dogs with those in their neighborhoods who are unkempt and unruly. This frequently sparks conversation and provides a context to interact with clients. This high level of visibility brings not only opportunity however, but responsibility as well. Every interaction between dog and handler should be purposeful and assumed to be observed. Notably, "People tend to treat your dog the way you treat it. Your kindness toward the dog becomes a model for them" (Davis, 2002, p. 161) and an opportunity to use their observations in a therapeutic way at a later time.

Last, similar to SF work with clients, handlers' behavior should reflect faith in the dogs' abilities, as evidenced by constantly seeking the best from their dogs. Although dogs clearly have a different culture and way of viewing and interacting with the world than humans, they have amazing potential for learning, communication, and partnership. "Many owners who think their dogs are stupid have not given them enough attention or encouragement to communicate" (Davis, 2002, p. 81). Despite the high level of training and expectations we have for our dogs, we recognize that we never reach our dogs' full potential, and this provides a wonderful analogy for our clients. By trusting in a therapy dog's abilities to learn and communicate we remind ourselves of the importance of trusting in our clients' abilities as well. And, when our clients inevitably comment on the high level of respect, communication, and obedience obvious in the interaction between handler and therapy dog, it provides a wonderful opportunity for us to address and explore untapped potential and abilities they may have overlooked in themselves.

SUMMARY

Before a therapist can effectively develop a successful AAA/T program or utilize a therapy dog in a private practice setting, he or she must fully understand and appreciate the dog's unique culture, methods of communication, and way of interacting with the world. Once this is in place, the therapist can join in partnership with the therapy dog to change the work environment and positively impact clients. It is only after the therapist is fully cognizant of the actual abilities and potential of a therapy dog that he or she can design and implement an animal-assisted activities/therapy program that is both effective for clients and credible within the community. The next chapter will address the many factors that must be considered, as well as possible solutions, when designing a program and developing the necessary policies and procedures to use a therapy dog with clients.

Photo by Mark Hochstedler. Used with permission.

Chapter 4

How to Create a Successful AAA/T Program for Your Setting

Obstacles are what you see when you take your eyes off the miracle.*

Brian Tracy

With a solid understanding of the canine culture described in the last chapter, the necessary foundation is now in place for you to design and implement an effective AAA/T program. Although many therapists have skipped this planning phase without incident, we do not recommend this. In this age of evidence-based treatment and ever increasing accountability, planning is an important way to avert legal or credibility problems before they happen. Although the tasks of design and implementation may seem daunting at first glimpse, the benefits will outweigh the potential struggles. In this chapter we will clearly delineate the common threats to credibility and potential liability and provide ideas on how to address these areas according to national standards.

BASIC CONCERNS

When the use of a therapy dog is proposed, initial concerns are typically voiced by those involved. These might include, for example, agency administrators, co-workers, licensing bodies, payment or re-

---

*We substituted the word "miracle" for Brian's original word "goal."

ferral sources, community members, or even clients themselves. These concerns typically reflect the following issues:

- The credibility of using a dog in a professional setting
- The dog's behavior
- Cleanliness
- Allergies
- Phobias
- Insurance and protection from liability
- The environmental structure
- The dog's needs

Three Models of AAA/T

Before addressing each of these areas of concern in more detail, we will describe the three primary models for AAA/T (animal-assisted activities/therapy) programs. The first is a visiting dog model, the second is a resident handler/dog model, and the third is the resident animal model. In the visiting dog model, therapy dog-handler teams are trained and credentialed volunteers from an external organization and are not employed by the agency. The teams are scheduled at pre-determined times to either work with clients independently according to agency policies and procedures performing AAA or to work in collaboration with agency staff to perform AAT. (It is important to note that in this model agency staff must be present for the visiting team to conduct any therapy, or AAT work.) The therapy dog-handler teams are present for only short periods of time during the day or week. In this model the teams work only a few hours at a time and multiple teams may regularly visit the agency and become well-known to the staff and clients. Dog-handler teams are well matched to the clientele and their designated roles within the agency. The visiting dog teams play an important role for both the clients and the employees.

In the resident handler/dog model, the specially trained therapy dog is owned and handled by an agency employee. The dog may be present at the agency for long periods of time, accompanying his handler for an entire shift. The employee/handler must organize to make AAA/T activities available to clients while protecting the dog from overwork, taking into consideration how many client hours are appropriate for the dog and when the dog needs to rest. The employee must juggle the roles of agency staff member and dog guardian, for the dog never works without the handler present in this model. Dogs in this model frequently work one to two full days per week, taking the other days off to rest. In this setting, the dog becomes part of the staff and is integrated into the agency's day-to-day activities. The dog-handler team is frequently on call throughout the day to work with clients as needed, and clients may ultimately view the therapy dog as just another employee who is involved in their care.

The third model is the resident animal model. Although this model is beyond the scope of this book since it does not include an active handler, we felt it important for the reader to be aware of its existence. In this model the resident animal literally lives at the facility. This model is commonly used in nursing homes and other residential facilities. In this model the animal is frequently given free rein of the facility, working without a handler. The benefits of having an animal in a facility are plentiful, and this has led to an increased popularity of this model. Although it can be tempting to include an animal in a facility without much thought or preparation, it is however imperative that safety, hygiene, animal care, liability, and all of the other factors we will discuss in this chapter be well thought out and documented in policy and procedure prior to implementing a program based on this model design as well. This is important, for animals who are working without the direct observation and care of a handler can be at particular risk from clients and work-related stress, thereby the risk for heightening potential accidents and injuries.

Now let's return our focus to the first two models; those that involve a handler and are most appropriate when using a practical clinical approach such as solution-focused therapy. Both of these models have their unique benefits and challenges for both the dog-handler team as well as the clients. Let's take a closer look at how these can be effectively addressed regardless of which AAA/T model is employed.

The Credibility of Using a Dog in a Professional Setting

Credibility is crucial for professionals. Regardless of your decision to use a visiting or resident handler/dog design, without credibility, referrals, payment, and reputation are at risk. There is often a fine line between being perceived as foolhardy or as innovative. Frequently the determining factors are one's credibility and reputation for having sound thinking behind one's action. One of the most effective ways to establish professional credibility when using an innovative intervention is to refer to national standards and accepted practice as precedence. It is best to utilize all current and available research and knowledge to bridge the gap between accepted approaches and innovations one wishes to introduce.

The use of a therapy dog is no different in this regard. When well-meaning professionals have not taken this more credible path despite the merit of their innovative approach, it has only added fuel to the fire for critics, who can often cite many examples of therapists using their family pet without addressing legitimate safety concerns or demonstrating purposeful intervention. Ironically, it is the mistakes in any profession that typically gain notoriety, while the successes frequently occur without fanfare.

Fortunately, there are now very clear and established standards, ethical guidelines, and credentials in place for the clinical use of therapy dogs. The most effective and efficient way to gain credibility is to simply cite these standards and practice according to them. This is an eminently sensible idea because in the case of a mishap, these are the standards to which professionals would be held.

Three national organizations in the United States are known for their credentialing of therapy dog teams: Delta Society, Therapy Dogs Incorporated, and Therapy Dogs International. These organizations have set educational and testing standards for both human and canine team members that must be met prior to receiving certification. These typically include an education class for the handler and a behavioral screen, a temperament screen, and a health screen for the dog. (Please refer to Appendix A for a complete description of these three organizations, including credentialing requirements and standards.) In addition, some state or local organizations are well known and accepted for their professional standards. We advise steering clear, however, of organizations that do not appear to be well organized or that are lax about providing some form of behavioral, temperament, or health screening for therapy dogs.

It is prudent to research and become affiliated with the most well-known and most widely respected organization in your community. For example, at the time of this writing the most widely accepted organization in our area is the Denver chapter of the Delta Society (Denver Pet Partners), so those are the standards and guidelines we use at our agency. Rocky and I are credentialed as Delta Society Pet Partners and abide by their guidelines for all client interactions. For instance, Delta Society requires that therapy dogs be on a leash at all times when with clients. Although other organizations do not require this, Rocky always works on leash. Should a mishap occur, Rocky and I would be held to Delta Society standards in determining if we practiced responsibly, therefore following all of Delta Society's standards for good practice is necessary.

The best organization with which to affiliate may vary depending on geographical location. Regardless of which organization you choose, make it a point to have clear reasons why that particular organization's standards are most appropriate for the work you plan to do. Credentialing standards vary from least to most restrictive. Although it can be tempting to adopt the most lenient standards to give maximum flexibility, in the case of litigation therapists are most likely to be held accountable to the most widely recognized standards within that community. Typically these are the national or international standards.

Hospitals are frequently a good source of information about community resources for therapy dogs because they frequently work with national organizations or local volunteer groups and welcome therapy dog teams to visit with patients.

Once you select an established organization, adopt these standards for working with clients, and obtain credentialing, many benefits become available. The first is the credibility associated with the organization. These credentials and this organization name now demonstrate a level of competence for both you and your therapy dog. Educating others about the training and testing requirements of this organization increases awareness of the professionalism inherent in AAA/T. Brochures can be obtained from these organizations which you can make available in the waiting rooms or during presentations thereby lending further credibility to your work. Your interventions and use of AAA/T are thereby framed in the context of a much larger, standardized field. Clients, referral and payment sources, and community members are now more likely to view your work with a therapy dog as a viable and recognized clinical tool instead of thinking of it simply as a way for you to bring your pet to work.

A second benefit is that large organizations frequently have regular meetings, Web sites, and other forms of communication that can be valuable in providing updates, additional education, support, and resources. For example, the Delta Society publishes a quarterly magazine, *Interactions*. Not only can these magazines provide helpful information to professionals, but copies can also be placed in waiting rooms to provide additional credibility, awareness, and information about the international field of AAA/T.

It is important to remember that as therapists we are experts in human behavior. Although many of us have had animals all of our lives, using them in the workplace requires a different set of knowledge and skills. Giving yourself access to a group of people who have significant experience in animal behavior and the therapeutic use of animals (regardless of their professional training), is not only good practice, but an ethical must whenever possible. Because association with these larger organizations requires us to withstand well-intentioned scrutiny from AAA/T experts, we are thereby challenged to develop well-thought-out explanations for our interventions and program design. This keeps us in the ideal position of accountability, learning, and curiosity.

The Dog's Behavior

A well-trained dog is a must in a professional setting. The presence of a dog attracts attention, making the dog's behavior even more pivotal in maintaining credibility. Many people's only exposure to dogs has been to their neighbor's unkempt and poorly behaved pets. Jumping, barking, nipping, marking, and rough play are common fears of those who initially encounter a dog. A therapy dog must immediately demonstrate something different by being under control at all times and unobtrusive. Furthermore, the dog-handler team must consistently demonstrate an ability to be respectful and meet the needs of the clients and agency. For example, to demonstrate Rocky's good manners as he enters a building, I ask him to sit politely and wait as I open the door to the building. I then quietly give the command for him to walk beside me as we enter the building. I frequently give quiet directional commands ("left" or "right") as we enter the designated area. This demonstrates to those watching that this is a very well-behaved dog that should not be feared.

Although therapy dogs do not have to complete formalized obedience classes, a standardized level of obedience is expected. The American Kennel Club has a standardized test called the Canine Good Citizen test that has been adopted by many national organizations as the expected level of obedience. As part of this test, dogs are required to demonstrate the ability to sit, lay down, stay, and come to the handler on command as well as demonstrate appropriate behavior while being handled, being ignored, being petted, walking on a leash, passing another dog, walking through a crowd, encountering a loud noise, etc. All of these skills are part of a therapy dog's day.

In addition to this initial training and testing, some form of periodic continuing education for the dog is helpful to serve as a refresher for his obedience skills. This helps to hone his obedience skills and assist the handler and dog in strengthening their ability to work effectively as a team. This continuing education may be in the form of a formal obedience class or some more recreational class that includes a high level of communication such as agility.

Once the dog is trained and working as a therapy dog, it is tempting to become complacent. However, just as it is ethically necessary for therapists to maintain a relationship with someone from whom they can get clinical supervision when needed, it is necessary to maintain a relationship with an animal behavior expert from whom one can seek consultation as new behaviors occur. Therapy dogs are constantly exposed to new situations and people, and they use behavior to communicate their needs and discomforts. Although it is necessary that a handler knows his or her canine partner well, it is nevertheless easy to misinterpret new behavior. It is imperative that we maintain a relationship with an animal behavior expert who has the dog's best interest at heart and who has no incentive to maintain the dog in the workplace if it is contraindicated. This is important even when utilizing a visiting dog model, for it is ultimately the therapist's responsibility to ensure safety when working with his or her clients.

Having an animal expert periodically evaluate the program design and observe the interactions among the dogs, handlers, and clients is a nice way to ensure that the handlers are in tune with their canine partners and maintaining a safe environment for the clients. Using volunteer teams affiliated with a reputable therapy dog organization provides an added level of safety because the teams are credentialed and regularly reevaluated by animal experts.

Naturally when using a resident handler/dog model, it is a good idea to maintain a close relationship with an individual animal behaviorist who knows your dog. The animal expert's knowledge of your dog's personality, as well as his strengths and weaknesses provides a means to readily evaluate new behavior. Special considerations apply when using the resident handler/dog model due to the increased time that the therapy dog is in the facility. Due to this increased time, dogs frequently become much more comfortable in the setting and can begin to display some more familial behaviors in the workplace. When this occurs it is important that these behaviors are verified with an animal behaviorist to ensure that they are not indicators of animal distress.

For example, as the canine member of a resident handler/dog team, Rocky is provided with "down time" while in my office. He has his own bed, toys, and water and spends many hours each workday lounging while I work on the computer or do various other tasks. I use a baby gate at the office entrance to allow my door to be left open while eliminating any fear of Rocky wandering out of the office. Staff members can then step over or remove the baby gate to enter my office. After a few weeks at his new job, Rocky began to occasionally bark (two or three quick midrange barks) when a non-staff member unexpectedly came up to the gate and interacted with me. He also would occasionally give a few quick midrange barks when he saw someone in the hallways late in the evening when the other staff and clients were in group sessions. Concerned that perhaps Rocky was distressed or uncomfortable with some aspect of his new job, I quickly e-mailed his trainer, Patti, and asked for her opinion. She responded that it sounded like Rocky was "guarding" and offering an alert-type bark notifying me of the presence of someone. She went on to explain that it was an ingrained behavior, and that the only hope of change was to anticipate the situation/person before Rocky did. She gave me specific ideas on how to communicate to Rocky that I saw the person and that he did not need to inform me. The incidents soon began to decrease, confirming that it was normal canine behavior.

Despite a therapy dog's high level of training and continuing education, it is very common for questions to arise concerning how the dog will respond should the handler be threatened by a client in some way. Dogs are accurately portrayed as being very protective of their owners, and those around the dog frequently assume that the dog will become aggressive to protect the handler should a client become hostile. Should a therapy dog display aggression in such a situation, the dog would then become part of the problem in an already potentially dangerous situation. Several points should be emphasized when such a situation arises. The first is that prevention is an important element. Visiting volunteers and their therapy dogs should be trained to quickly recognize when a situation is escalating and to then leave the situation, allowing staff to manage the escalating client. Resident handlers and their dogs should also be skilled at recognizing signs of potential trouble and have a clear plan on how to remove the dog from the situation. This may include taking the dog to a safe location (i.e., an office) so that the handler can safely return and care for the client. An employee should not be expected to effectively handle the dog and therapeutically intervene with an escalated client simultaneously.

For example, one evening one of our therapists asked me to intervene with an upset mother and her teenage son. The mother had brought the son (a current client) to our agency and stated that we needed to take him since she could no longer control his behavior. Rocky was working with me that day, and the mother had met him many times before. I knew that she enjoyed Rocky's company, so I was not concerned working with the mother as Rocky accompanied me. As I entered the room, I asked permission to bring Rocky along, and she quickly granted the request, indicating a visit would be welcome. I could tell immediately that the mother was tense and upset, and Rocky responded to the emotional tension by wagging his tail in recognition and approaching the mother to snuggle during the conversation. The mother appeared to relax as she softly petted Rocky. As the conversation began and the mother's story began to unfold, she began to express her anger about her son's behavior. She raised her voice, stomped her feet, and the tears began to flow. Rocky offered his head for petting in an attempt to comfort her, but the mother's mood had clearly shifted, and she said, "Not now, Rocky." I quickly asked Rocky to return to my side, and I asked the mother to excuse Rocky and me for a moment. I then made arrangements for Rocky to stay in a therapist's office with her as she continued her work on the computer (this was a therapist Rocky knew and loved and an office he was familiar with). Knowing that Rocky was safe and well cared for in a manner that was consistent with our agency's policy and procedures, I returned to the mother without my canine partner and continued to address the difficult family situation. This allowed me to focus on the mother's needs while knowing that my therapy dog's needs were being met. Not taking the time to remove Rocky would have been disrespectful to the client's message that the dog was distracting and no longer welcome and would have risked Rocky misinterpreting the mother's angry words and behaviors.

This brings us to our second point. Skillfully handling the dog must be the handler's top priority. This may require that the handler calmly call for another staff member's assistance while he or she leaves the situation with the dog. The keys to safety in such situations with a therapy dog are a solid relationship between the handler and the dog, close observation of the dog's response to the situation by the handler, and good communication by the handler to the dog that assures the dog that the handler has the situation under control and that the handler will protect the dog. "The handler must protect the dog so that the dog won't decide to take responsibility for the situation" (Davis, 2002, p. 203). Dogs become aggressive and protect the handler when they have not been convinced that the handler is truly the "alpha" (Beck & Katcher, 1996, p. 177) or leader or because they do not believe this leader will protect them (the dog and handler). This may occur because the dog sees a situation that the handler missed or because of poor communication by the handler to the dog. Therefore quick recognition, preventive action, and good communication of the plan to the dog are the necessary steps to maintain safety when clients escalate during a visit or therapy session.

Third, dogs are highly sensitive to potentially dangerous situations. However, they always warn and give behavioral indicators before becoming aggressive, making it imperative that the handler notice and respond to the body language of the dog at all times in an AAA/T setting. Because the dog may very well notice a potential problem before his human partner, it is critical that the handler trust the dog's instincts and take action, for it may signal impending trouble. An inexperienced handler is at an elevated risk of missing the subtle signs that his or her dog gives due to the complexity of handling a dog as well as interacting with clients, agency staff, etc. Some of these signs may include raised hackles, dilated pupils, a wrinkled nose, slightly curled lips, or a change in body, ear, or tail positions (Coren, 2000). With experience the handler is better able to constantly monitor the dog's behavior to assess his mood while skillfully interacting with clients and others in the environment. This comes with time and practice, and this ability significantly increases the handler's ability to prevent problems.

A nice example of this protective quality in therapy dogs occurred with my friend, Diana, and her therapy dog, Gypsy. One afternoon they were at home relaxing with friends and family. Diana's friends had brought their newly adopted shepherd/rottweiler mix with them on this visit, and after ensuring that the family dogs (including Gypsy) interacted well with her friends' new dog, they settled in to enjoy each other's company. As usual, Gypsy never left Diana's side. Diana sat on the floor, happily interacting with the canine members of the group when they approached, when suddenly Gypsy got up and stood between Diana and her friends' dog as he came close to Diana's face. Although the dog appeared friendly, Gypsy let out a low warning growl to the dog sending a very clear message that he was to back away from Diana immediately. The dog complied, and the exchange between the dogs was over. Diana was surprised since she had never seen this behavior from Gypsy, who was always very quiet and easy going. Diana later learned that her friends' dog had once seriously bit a woman in the face when he was at face level, and that the bite had occurred seemingly without provocation. Gypsy had sensed the danger, noticed that Diana was oblivious to the threat, and had taken action to protect her partner. Had Diana been working with clients with Gypsy rather than lounging with friends, she most likely would have been much more attentive and responsive to the earlier behavioral indicators from Gypsy that preceded the warning growl.

The fourth point is that there is occasionally a benefit to clients believing that a therapy dog might protect his handler. Although it is important that co-workers and other agency staff thoroughly understand the safety factors, and while we would never recommend encouraging a misperception about therapy dogs to clients, clients' beliefs that a dog might become protective in a dangerous situation can at times be helpful in encouraging clients who might otherwise act out to remain more in control in the dog's presence. This client awareness of cause and effect followed by a deliberate increase in self-control on the part of a client can be a valuable lesson for a therapist to explore with the client in a therapeutic setting.

Cleanliness

Cleanliness is a valid concern when developing an AAA/T program. Not only are clearly defined areas for elimination and protocols defining who is responsible for and how the waste is disposed of vital, but issues of cleanliness and a clear delineation of responsibility indoors are crucial as well. Regardless of the decision to use a visiting or a resident handler/dog team, the handler typically remains the sole person responsible for maintaining the cleanliness on behalf of the animal. Ensuring that plastic bags to collect any waste are always close at hand is considered to be part of responsible pet ownership. Therapy dogs should be provided with ample time outdoors prior to beginning their work and at set increments throughout their workday to avoid any chance of accident. In addition, handlers are expected to have a good working relationship with their canine partner so that any request to go outdoors for elimination is quickly noticed and addressed. One way to better understand the dog's communications is to know the dog's routine elimination schedule, and to use this knowledge to interpret the dog's communications. For example, Rocky's request to go outdoors to eliminate can sound very similar to his communication that he is bored and would like to go do something different. When he makes a request while at work and I know that he has not already eliminated according to his normal schedule, I am much more likely to quickly stop what I am doing and take him outdoors. However, when I have determined it is not likely that he needs to eliminate and that he is bored, I gently ask him to give me a moment and then take him back to my office to take a break. I have found that Rocky is generally very good at accepting my decision and that he will persist in his request when I have misread his communications.

On occasion, therapy dogs (like any other professional) may become ill while at work. Should this occur, the dog should be immediately taken home until he regains full health. Therapy dogs should not be expected to work when they are not up to par. Despite the best preventive measures, vomiting in the workplace can occur, and having a plan of action is wise. For example, during a meeting at work one day Rocky became restless and whined while looking at me in earnest. I was unsure what was troubling him. After taking him outside to no avail, I suddenly recognized the unmistakable sound of the churnings of a dog in the beginning stages of vomiting. Despite my feelings of embarrassment and concern due to the public setting and the newness of the AAA/T program, I quickly dropped to the floor to help my partner. I reached for a trash can and gently held Rocky's head over the waste receptacle. Once he was finished, I excused us and made arrangements for my husband to pick up Rocky and take him home. I later learned that Rocky's ability to vomit into a trash can on command actually served to further impress agency staff with his good manners and cleanliness and to endear him to the agency. Staff members were later heard saying, "Wow! I can't even get my child to do that!"

Therapy dogs should be thoroughly groomed according to that breed's standards (coat, ears, eyes, nails, teeth) prior to each workday/visit. Adequate time should be scheduled prior to taking the animal into a professional setting to ensure that he is completely clean and well groomed. The handler's knowledge and ability to comply with accepted grooming standards is commonly part of national therapy dog organization testing, and these organizations can be a good source of information about accepted standards. In addition, professional groomers and veterinarians can be additional sources for information about accepted grooming standards. Specially made canine snow boots can use used to keep the therapy dog's feet clean and dry when having to walk through inclement conditions prior to entering the building. In addition, canine wet wipes are available for a quick clean up as needed throughout the day.

Visiting standards and protocols should be clearly established that will also ensure agency cleanliness. Therapy dogs are frequently expected to stay off furniture both to ensure client safety from jumping animals and to minimize the spread of pet hair and dander. Large dogs can easily visit while sitting on the ground, but small dogs (twenty pounds or less) may require being held by the handler or a designated towel or mat on which the dog can sit may need to be placed on a chair beside a client so that the client can reach the animal to visit.

Last, special considerations should be made for the canine members of resident handler/dog teams to ensure that they have adequate personal space in the workplace and that this space is well kept and clean. If the building uses a cleaning staff, they should be alerted to the dog's presence and the need to provide additional vacuuming/sweeping in the areas in which the dog spends excessive time to keep the area free from pet hair and dander. The handler should ensure that the dog's water dish and other items are maintained and present a clean and well-kept air. Personal items such as a brush or comb, a towel, and a lint roller can be handy for a quick clean up for both the dog and the personal space. Most important, one must keep in mind that the level of necessary cleanliness is elevated when in the workplace due to the need to maintain credibility. While at home a few hairs on furniture or dirty paws from being out in the rain are frequently considered commonplace; in a professional setting, they must be kept up.

Allergies

In an outpatient environment in which the therapy dog is well groomed and cleanliness standards are closely followed, allergies will be minimal, for the primary causes of allergies (dander and saliva) are well controlled. Clients who receive services in an outpatient setting are considered to be stable, meaning that they are able to routinely adapt to the allergens that are commonly found in day-to-day environments (dogs being one of those common allergens). In addition, the amount of contact that clients have with a therapy dog can be easily varied according to each client's needs. By ensuring that therapy dogs are not allowed to touch a client without the client's permission and by asking each client if he or she would like the dog to approach prior to coming in close proximity, any allergic reaction can be minimized and oftentimes prevented, for it is primarily by touching that a client with allergies in an outpatient setting would experience any noticeable reaction from a well-groomed therapy dog. It is this requirement of permission before contact that places control back in the client's hand and provides the best possible protection from any unwanted reaction. Handlers can also encourage clients to wash their hands or provide a hand sanitizer after a visit which will further minimize any reaction to dander or salvia. When using a resident handler/dog team, it is prudent to keep clients away from the animal's sleeping area, for this area will have the most hair and dander, making it an elevated trigger for allergies. Visiting should be done in common areas that are well cleaned and in which the dog only visits. Additional steps can be put into place to prevent problems from allergies. Clients can be screened for allergies upon admission and notices (see Figure 4.1) can be posted informing clients of the presence of a

Rockefeller "Rocky," CGC
Therapy Dog

Meet our newest employee, Rocky the Therapy Dog. Rocky has recently joined our team here at the Jefferson County Department of Health and Environment, Substance Abuse Counseling Program, so you may see him walking the halls with his handler, Teri Pichot, LCSW, MAC, LAC. Rocky has trained for over nine months to prepare for his role as a therapy dog, and he has passed national behavioral and medical testing to ensure that he will be an asset to our team. Please feel free to ask Teri any questions you have about Rocky's role here at the Health Department. If you would like to meet Rocky, please ask any staff member to direct you to the Substance Abuse Counseling Program, and their staff will see if Rocky is available. If your child would like to say "hello," please accompany your child so that we can make sure he/she has your permission.

FIGURE 4.1. Poster of Rocky (Photo by Mark Hochstedler. Used with permission.)

therapy dog. Both of these measures allow clients the opportunity to discuss concerns with staff prior to encountering the therapy dog. Regardless of the efforts taken, a clear plan should be in place to ensure that clients who do not want contact with a therapy dog or whose allergies would be triggered despite the protective efforts are provided services without the dog present.

When working in a residential or inpatient setting, all clients should be screened for possible allergies and for the appropriateness for working with a therapy dog. When severe allergies or respiratory conditions exist, a medical professional should make the final determination that a client's condition would not be exacerbated by a visit from a therapy dog.

Phobias

It is important to stress that the purpose of using a therapy dog is not to resolve clients' fears and phobias of dogs. If a client is afraid of dogs, AAA/T is not the appropriate intervention (Delta Society, 2003). Therefore necessary steps need to be put in place to ensure that clients are comfortable around dog prior to exposing them to dogs in a clinical setting. The protective factors put in place to protect clients from allergic reactions also frequently protect clients who have dog phobias. Since dogs are considered to be commonplace in day-to-day environments, clients who receive services on an outpatient basis most often have the necessary coping skills to manage any fear of dogs. Most people smile or give some type of nonverbal sign of comfort when they see a therapy dog in the workplace. The efforts taken when entering a building to demonstrate that the dog is well behaved and controlled quickly eliminate most fears. By being aware of people's reactions to seeing the therapy dog, the handler can quickly determine when someone is startled or uncomfortable. This is true even for clients who do not speak the same language as the handler. When this occurs it is imperative that the handler is in tune and respectful, quickly moving the dog out of the way or even out of the line of sight. This combination of watching clients' nonverbal cues and always asking permission before allowing the dog to approach anyone allows the handler to avoid the majority of problems caused by phobias.

In addition, it can be helpful to screen all clients at admission for dog phobias and post signs (see Figure 4.1) informing clients of the presence of a therapy dog so no one is surprised if the dog and handler walk around a corner. Most clients with dog phobias have encountered an unruly or aggressive dog in the past. We have found that even clients who initially state that they are afraid of dogs are eager to interact with our therapy dog once they understand his level of training, guidelines, and purpose. When clients initially indicate upon admission that they are afraid of dogs, the therapist explains Rocky's role and asks if they would like to see a picture of him. (Seeing a picture is frequently helpful since clients often have a fear that initiated with one breed of dog. Once they see that Rocky does not look like the offending dog, they are less fearful.) If they are interested, we offer a photo album that shows him at work and in other settings. We can even schedule an introduction meeting with Rocky should the client state that he or she would like to meet him. To date we have not encountered a client who is afraid of Rocky after we have taken these steps. However, it is imperative that no client is ever encouraged or asked to interact with a therapy dog against his or her wishes.

Insurance and Protection from Liability

This was by far the most challenging obstacle I encountered when I first started working with my therapy dog. The more I researched this issue, the more I learned that professionals often take significant and frequently unknown risks in this area. Professionals whom I spoke with many times assumed they had coverage for their work with their therapy dog, without insisting that this coverage was put in writing. I soon discovered that as I pushed my own insurance carriers for statements in writing, I encountered loopholes in the most commonly assumed insurance coverage methods that left me vulnerable and uninsured. This ambiguity opens professionals up for risk and headache should an incident occur. No one likes to think that their dog will ever injure anyone. Our dogs are very well trained, and are not aggressive. However, it only takes one small misunderstanding (e.g., an unsteady toddler falls over as a dog walks by) to result in a lawsuit and threat of significant legal and financial hardship. Five primary avenues for insurance coverage for therapy dogs are: the governing therapy dog organization's liability policy, the agency's liability policy, the handler's professional liability policy, the handler's homeowner's policy, and the handler's umbrella insurance policy. We strongly suggest that regardless of the type of coverage you determine covers your work with a therapy dog, that you have a statement to this effect in writing from your carrier prior to working with clients.

The Governing Therapy Dog Organization's Liability Policy

Many national therapy dog organizations provide a liability policy for animal-handler teams who are credentialed by that organization, who are abiding by their guidelines, and who are volunteering in the community. This is the best source of coverage for agencies that are using the visiting dog model. By working closely with the therapy dog organization when designing the program, the agency ensures that they have considered the most important elements and that the organization will stand behind the visiting animal-handler teams should an incident occur. This partnership (between the therapy dog organization and the agency) and the insurance coverage should be written into the governing policies and procedures for the AAA/T program. However, most therapy dog organizations' liability coverage will not cover the animal-handler team if they are working under a resident handler/dog model (for they are no longer volunteering, and the work is part of the handler's employment). In addition, most policies of this kind will not cover a paid professional providing AAA/T in a private practice setting. Therefore alternative coverage must be secured.

The Agency's Liability Policy

Every agency must have a liability insurance policy that protects clients against injury that occurs on the property. This is the most logical policy to explore when using a resident handler/dog model, since the dog is used as a tool that an employee is utilizing with clients on behalf of the agency. Our therapy dog, Rocky, is covered under this method for his work at our agency. Prior to Rocky coming to the agency I received written verification from our Risk Management Department that our agency's policy would cover him in case of a mishap. As his handler, I keep a copy of that statement at home and at work. In addition, that agreement of coverage is included in our agency's policy and procedure that delineates our AAA/T program.

The Handler's Professional Liability Policy

Professionals commonly obtain professional liability insurance to protect them from lawsuits by clients. When professionals decide to incorporate a therapy dog into their work, the dog becomes another tool available for use by the professional with clients. Although it seems logical that professional liability policies should cover the credentialed dog when used in this fashion, we have yet to see a professional policy that includes therapy dogs. In addition to my work at the agency, I see clients independently in my private practice. When I contacted my own professional liability insurance and inquired about my coverage when using Rocky, I was told that my clinical decisions when using AAT as a therapist were protected and covered under the policy, but that any injury that the dog caused would not be covered. As you can imagine, this leaves a significant gap in coverage if I were to depend on this coverage as my primary method of protection. Although this does provide some coverage, this method can often only be used in combination with other policies to ensure full coverage. It is prudent to carefully explore your professional liability policy and obtain a statement of coverage in writing prior depending on this method of coverage.

The Handler's Home Owner's Policy

Most home owners' policies routinely include coverage for any injuries caused by the owner's pets. This was the most common method of coverage that professionals used to cover their work with therapy dogs that we discovered when researching insurance coverage. However, we did not find a single professional who took the additional step of asking for a statement in writing from their insurance provider that their pet is covered when working as a therapy dog. Many professionals seemed surprised that we would even ask them if they had obtained a statement about coverage for therapy dogs. However, when I contacted my own home owner's insurance company (a very large and well-known company in the United States), I quickly learned that they had no policy about family pets who work as therapy dogs and therefore, they quickly stated that therapy dogs are excluded. After nine months of pushing the subject with my insurance representative, threatening to change insurance carriers, and arguing the merits, I obtained a statement in writing from the company stating that they would cover my dog even if I took him to work. They still are not willing to put in writing that he is covered when working as a therapy dog. This experience provided valuable information about how challenging it might be to utilize a home owner's policy should an incident occur with a client during an AAA/T session. Under the stress of a client injury, the nine months of haggling with the insurance company may not be possible. Home owner insurance companies may likely try to claim that the dog was "working" and therefore should be covered under the professional's liability coverage. For professionals who own homes this is a good source of possible coverage, however we would recommend that you fight to get a statement in writing and that you do not rely too heavily on this avenue due to the high likelihood of challenge during the very time coverage is needed the most. Unfortunately, for the many professionals who do not own homes, this source is of no use.

The Handler's Umbrella Insurance Policy

Most insurance companies provide additional insurance to cover a variety of conditions not covered by other policies. They are frequently called "umbrella policies." Should the other sources of coverage not be adequate, the best bet is to have an honest conversation with your insurance provider and secure a policy that states in writing that it will cover any injury caused by a therapy dog while with clients. For professionals who do not own homes, this kind of policy is prudent to provide coverage for the dog while on walks and in the community even when not working with clients.

The Environmental Structure

Having a clear plan for how the therapy handler-dog will be incorporated into the professional setting is critical. For a visiting dog model, this should include issues such as how therapy teams will be screened and selected to ensure a good match and professionalism, how client confidentiality will be protected, who will receive visits, where the visits will occur, if agency staff will be present during the visits, how documentation of the visits will be kept, etc. All of these decisions should be clearly indicated in an agency policy and procedure that is available to all agency staff and visiting handlers. In addition the agency's activity level and amount of staff involvement need to be assessed to determine the most appropriate skill and temperament rating that the therapy dog team should have to ensure a positive and safe experience for clients, staff members, and the team.

Ensuring That Clients/Staff Who Don't Want Contact with the Dog Don't Have Contact

When using a resident handler/dog model, additional issues need to be addressed. When incorporating a therapy dog into a professional setting, it is important to respect client and staff wishes and to remember that not everyone likes dogs nor desires to be around them. This issue is heightened when a dog is part of the environment for long periods of time as in the resident handler/dog model. Consideration must be made to ensure that clients and staff who do not prefer contact with the therapy dog have adequate access to the handler when the dog is not present. This will be done very differently depending on the agency's job description for the handler. For example, my job description is Program Manager. I do not have regular, scheduled contact with agency clients, but I do have regular, scheduled contact with agency staff members whom I supervise. Before Rocky started his job at the Health Department, I asked my staff if anyone had any concerns about having a therapy dog around or if Rocky's presence would decrease their comfort level interacting with me. They assured me that this would not be an issue. Should it have been an issue for any of my direct subordinates, I would not have been able to be a handler in the workplace, for my first responsibility to the agency is to remain available to my subordinates. Should a therapist at our agency desire to be a handler, we would need to consider his or her role with clients and how clients who do not prefer to be around a therapy dog could still have full access to his or her services. For example, clients could be informed when they schedule an initial appointment by phone that this therapist works with a therapy dog. They could then be asked if they would like to meet with the therapist on a day that the therapist has the dog or on a day when the dog is not present. Once the client is an agency client, we could then assign the client to a different therapist for ongoing services if they would prefer to work with a therapist who does not have a therapy dog.

In a private practice setting it is equally important to take the necessary steps to ensure that clients who do not desire contact with the therapy dog are not exposed to him. This may be done by screening potential clients over the phone and placing the dog in another room when the client is at the office. The therapy dog would then be present only when the therapist and client both agree that the dog would have a purposeful role. When working with clients who do not want contact with a therapy animal due to fear of allergies, it is important to ensure that there is a designated room that is dander and hair free in which clients with allergies can sit prior to appointments and to meet with the therapist.

Clients are not the only people who need to be provided with an animal-free workplace if desired. On occasion, staff and co-workers will have dog phobias or significant allergies. When designing an AAA/T program it is wise to talk with colleagues and to incorporate these concerns into the plan. We have found that by including them in the planning stage, they frequently become supportive of the program. For example, one of the supervisors at our agency has a significant dog phobia and was very concerned about our idea to implement an AAA/T program. However, once she learned more about the guidelines and limits that would be in place, she become more accepting of the program and gave her consent. Her only stipulation was that she did not want to be surprised by the presence of the animal. So, we agreed that Rocky's work schedule would be posted well in advance so that she would be prepared should she see him in the hallways with me. Initially, Rocky and I avoided her every time we learned she was in the building to increase her comfort level. However, as the months went by she stated that she became more comfortable and that we did not have to avoid her. She even walked beside Rocky on several occasions and talked with me while he was present.

Ensuring That Work Gets Done

Adding the role of handler to the day's work tasks must be done after much consideration and thought. The role of a therapy dog is to enhance the work, not to obstruct it. There are days when the dog's presence is not appropriate and he must be left home. Imperative to maintaining credibility, the dog's presence should always be viewed by others as an asset and not as a nuisance. In addition, it takes extra time to adequately care for the dog; taking walks, advocating for time outs from clients, stopping stressful interactions, etc. Although the dog can be a significant help in building relationships with clients and staff alike and in bridging uncomfortable moments, the presence of a dog adds the additional time commitment of impromptu hallway interactions and discussions that can make a quick trip down the hall a thing of the past. Leaving the office to have a quick discussion with a staff member now requires waking the canine partner, putting on a leash, and taking down the baby gate before venturing out. Every interaction and step becomes highly visible due to the attention that is inherent when working with a therapy dog. One must carefully weigh the potential benefits against the costs prior to committing to adding a therapy dog to a program. Despite the additional time commitment, ways to compensate for the lost time are available. For example I have found that I am now much more purposeful when I leave my office. I never realized how many times I left my office to drop something in the mail or to chat with a co-worker until Rocky joined me. I am now much more likely to pick up the phone or use e-mail rather than go hunt for a co-worker, and I now carefully combine all the small errands that necessitate me leaving my office into one or two purposefully planned trips. Not only does this save the time from multiple trips, but it protects my time from distractions I frequently fell prey to in the past. I have been amazed to see that this small change has more than compensated for the extra time Rocky and I spend visiting with clients and staff alike. This time out of my office and visiting with staff and clients is now very purposeful and planned.

Handler's Potential Dual Role As Therapist

When working with a therapy dog, the handler's number one responsibility must be to the dog. Without this, the dog lacks an advocate and then must rely on himself to make safety judgments and protect himself, elevating the risk to clients and the agency. When working with a resident handler/dog team there are two primary models of interacting with clients: therapist as handler and separate handler and therapist. (When working with visiting dogs, the visiting handler is only qualified to be a handler. Should a therapist be needed, it must come from within the agency, thereby using the separate handler and therapist model.)

In the majority of interactions that occur with a resident handler/dog team, the handler also serves as the therapist or the one who also interacts with the clients/visitors/staff. This is true due to the sheer number of hours that the employee/handler is working with the dog during a given day. It is not practical to have an additional therapist shadow the team throughout the day to interact with clients. This is not usually problematic, for the therapy dog must be well trained to work within the given setting. However, should the dog become overwhelmed during an interaction, the handler's first priority must go to the dog. This is key to ensuring that the dog feels safe and that there is no need for the dog to take a defensive posture (Davis, 2002). As therapists know, under normal circumstances the therapist's first priority is to the client. Therefore, using this handler-as-therapist model has the potential for a conflict of interest should the dog have any needs during an interaction.

During interactions that have an elevated likelihood of being complex or in which the canine member of a resident/handler dog team has an increased chance of needed extra assistance, it is unwise to use this handler-as-therapist model, for the client's needs must then become secondary to the dog's in order to ensure safety, thereby creating an ethical dilemma for the therapist. During these times it is prudent to incorporate a separate therapist whose sole task is to ensure that the client's needs are met. This frees the handler to concentrate on the dog's needs without fear of neglecting the client. Using this separate handler and therapist model is most effective during AAT or during AAA that has an elevated level of unpredictability. For example, Rocky and I frequently walk through the Health Department alone, stopping to interact with clients and staff. However during times in which we are planning to enter waiting rooms or other areas that have children who are not closely supervised and who are playing boisterously, I ask an additional therapist to accompany us. I know that these circumstances increase Rocky's stress, and I need to pay specific attention to him to coach him through these situations and monitor to ensure he is not unduly stressed. The additional staff member's role is to work with the children to interact appropriately and to meet their needs as clients. This staff member can also serve as an assistant by setting limits with the children should I decide that

Rocky needs to leave the situation. Should a staff member not be available to accompany us, we would avoid those situations since the handler-as-therapist model would not be adequate.

When working in private practice and an additional co-worker is not available to utilize the separate handler and therapist model, it is important to use a therapy dog only during times in which the therapist/handler can ethically place the primary priority on the dog's needs without compromising clinical care. This would most likely be low-risk situations in which the therapist/handler is fairly confident that the dog will have minimal needs during a client interaction. In addition, it would be prudent to use an experienced therapy dog that is not easily surprised by normal, yet unpredictable therapy interactions.

The Dog's Needs

Last, but definitely not least, it is imperative that programs plan for and accommodate the therapy dog's physical needs. For visiting dogs, these needs are more limited and include providing access to the outdoors to eliminate before a visit and as needed during the visit, providing clean drinking water, and close monitoring by the handler to avoid undue stress. In addition, all therapy dogs should be closely assessed prior to every visit to ensure they are healthy, in a good mood, and want to visit and interact with people. Knowing your dog is crucial to this assessment, for it is through the dog's behavior that any signs of problems or animal discomfort would arise. For example, I once heard a handler say that if her therapy dog ever didn't get excited when she put on the dog's therapy vest, she would retire the dog. If I used that standard, Rocky would never visit, for Rocky hates having to wear anything (collar, leash, seat belt harness, therapy vest, etc.). Since he was a puppy he has always given me his sad puppy eyes and tried to avoid having to wear anything (similar to a child who hates to wear clothes). However, once he is "dressed," he eagerly hops into the car for the trip, and is clearly happy to be wherever the car stops. This behavior preceded his therapy dog career and even occurs when we let him know we are going to the dog park (his favorite place in the world, and a phrase he understands well). This avoidance of harnesses and other required outdoor equipment soon included his therapy vest. If a stranger witnessed his avoidance of his therapy vest,

Snoot Loop, leash, and seatbelt harness, one might mistakenly think he hates his job. More accurately, he is not able to think past his dislike of the required attire to show his true feelings about the destination. For Rocky it is imperative that I closely monitor his mood prior to introducing the hated equipment and again once he is in the car and when he is at the location to ensure that he demonstrates happiness and an eagerness to interact. Should this not be present, I would immediately need to cancel his day.

Even when a dog's behavior is explainable, as was the case with Rocky and his dislike of required equipment, it is imperative that the handler continue to listen to the dog and to explore if there are ways in which to compromise or make adjustments to minimize the dog's discomfort with an aspect of therapy dog work. For example, although Rocky continued to work despite his expression of dislike toward his required equipment, I began to experiment to see what changes I could make. I stopped putting all of his equipment on him prior to leaving the house and only required that he wore his seatbelt harness prior to riding in the car, leaving the remaining equipment to be put on him in the car prior to taking him into the agency. Although this was significantly less convenient for me, I noticed an immediate, positive change in Rocky's behavior. He was much more tolerant of having to wear the seatbelt harness. In addition, once we arrived at the agency, he seemed to understand the need for the therapy dog vest and leash and appeared almost eager for me to put these pieces of equipment on him so he could get out of the car. Unfortunately, Rocky continued to dislike his Snoot Loop (a head harness designed to gently remind him to walk politely by my side and not to pull when excited) despite these changes. In addition, I noticed that his mood seemed to gradually change at work, and I wondered if it was related to this disliked piece of equipment. Although he had always preferred not to wear his Snoot Loop, he had seemed to accept the necessity of it and to tolerate it for short periods of time. However, I worried that wearing it for an entire shift might be taking its toll. I experimented by taking off the Snoot Loop when he was resting in my office. During those periods of time, his mood seemed to improve. In addition, he seemed more melancholy when I left the harness on him. This posed a significant dilemma, since he completed his therapy dog examination with that particular piece of equipment and was now required to wear it while working. In addition, I was not yet confident that he was mature enough to hold his manners and walk with a loose leash when excited. After a conversation with his trainer about the problem, she suggested an alternative harness called a SENSE-ation that provides a similar benefit yet fastens around the dog's upper chest (see Appendix A for information about both the Snoot Loop and SENSE-ation harnesses). The results were immediate. Rocky's mood was noticeably improved when wearing the new harness. After working with a Delta Society examiner, Rocky was approved to wear the new harness while working. Both of these measures (staggering when the equipment was put on Rocky and changing the harness to one he preferred) made a significant difference for Rocky's quality of life at work, and played an important role in communicating to Rocky that I noticed his discomfort and would advocate on his behalf.

Therapy work is stressful to therapy animals. While under normal, closely monitored conditions, this stress is manageable and is not problematic. Therapy dogs are especially vulnerable to stress since they are not allowed to leave a situation until they are given permission and because the very settings in which they work are frequently stressful in and of themselves (Delta Society, 2003). In order to adequately care for a therapy dog and advocate for his need, the handler must also have a thorough understanding of animal stress and the ways in which the therapy animal communicates this stress. One of the most effective ways that dogs communicate and reduce their stress is through what Turid Rugaas (1997) terms calming signals. These are nonverbal signals such as sniffing the ground, blinking, averting the eyes, turning away, lip licking, yawning, and tongue flicking. Although many of these behaviors in isolation are quite normal and of no concern, when they occur in clusters, in a greater frequency than normal for the dog, or in combination with a high-stress situation, they can be indicative that the dog is no longer enjoying the interaction and is "preparing to control his/her own stress by acting out in a defensive manner" (Delta Society, 2003, p. 21). If the handler is unaware of these common canine communications or ignores these warning signs, the risk of potential injury becomes significantly increased. It is the handler's responsibility to remain alert for animal stress and to advocate for his or her partner and prevent the dog's stress from escalating to that point. In addition, when using a visiting therapy dog team, it is wise for the therapist to be familiar with normal canine calming signals and to alert the handler if these signals are noticed and not addressed, since it is the therapist's ultimate responsibility to ensure client safety.

In addition to regular access to the outdoors, clean drinking water, and close monitoring and advocating by the handler, dogs who are working as a resident handler/dog team have additional needs. Due to the long work day, they need a place of their own to rest and spend unscheduled time during the day. This place should be protected from clients and other intrusions, so that they have a place all their own in which to retreat. In addition, it is important that dogs not be overworked and that the day includes an element of fun. All therapy work is somewhat stressful on dogs, for they are continuously exposed to the unfamiliar, they are expected to remain on their best behavior at all times, and they are not able to sleep undisturbed like they would in their own homes. Because of this, it is wise to plan their schedule in such a way that they only work one consecutive day. This allows them to rest and "just be a dog" on alternate days. This helps to avoid burnout in the animal and health problems due to sleep deprivation. In addition, the handler must be alert to signs that the dog is becoming fatigued during the workday (often shown by lack of eagerness to interact or signs of stress when interacting) and ensure that the dog is given extra down time and protected from client/staff interactions. It is imperative that the dog not be expected to continue to work for convenience when he is emotionally done for the day. Should this regularly occur, it would be wise to rethink his regular schedule to allow for shorter or less frequent days.

In addition, it is helpful to incorporate elements that entice the dog's playful spirit in a fun, and yet controlled manner during the workday. For example, Rocky's trainer suggested that he be encouraged to carry dog toys through the hallways as he and I travel through the building. This exercise hones his attention and obedience skills, for he is transporting an object on command, but it also serves an additional energizing function as well. Rocky always has a more playful bounce in his step when he is carrying a treasured toy, and this simple exercise has a wonderful way of giving him energy and drawing positive attention to him (which he loves) from passersby. He eagerly stops during these trips to show staff members and visitors his favorite toy and to receive a quick pat. (It is important to note that Rocky has been screened to ensure that he is not possessive of these toys and is not at risk of "guarding" them should someone pick up his toy.)

Last, dogs who are working with their handler as a resident handler/dog team need time away during the workday. More than just time to eliminate outdoors, they need exercise and time away from "work." This may be in the form of a walk or it may be in the form of play or cuddle time with the handler. Dogs love just "being" with their handler and being part of the day. (Rocky has been present at my feet for the entire writing of this book.) Ensuring that a dog has this time just being a part of his handler's day and not being expected to "work" is invaluable in preventing burnout.

ENSURING A PROGRAM'S SUCCESS

Once an animal-assisted activities/therapy program has been designed three additional steps are needed to ensure its success. The first is to educate those in power. These people may include the board of directors, regulatory bodies, the CEO, referral sources, other supervisors, officemates, etc. Without purposeful education, the program risks being misperceived as unscientific "fluff," thereby losing credibility. Even worse, the program might be perceived as foolhardy and dangerous. Therefore, prior to introducing a therapy dog into the workplace, it is prudent to educate those who have the potential to negatively impact the program. This education should include the purpose and benefits of using a therapy dog with the agency's clientele, research and case studies that support the use of AAA/T in similar settings, as well as a clear explanation of how all foreseen problems have been anticipated and resolved. It is frequently helpful to attempt to predict others' concerns, for this provides valuable information about what needs to be included in the education. For example, as a county-level health department we were well aware that the primary concerns when introducing a therapy dog into this setting would be allergies, cleanliness, and liability. Because of this we provided an extensive list of articles and research on the subject as well as many examples of how these very concerns had been overcome in local, reputable hospitals and other medical settings. In addition, we provided references from the Centers for Disease Control (CDC) citing their standards for inclusion of a therapy dog in a medical setting. Some of these elements included restricting the dog from clean linen, pharmacy, and food preparation areas. Being able to reference the

CDC as well as local area hospitals and show how we proposed using similar standards significantly increased the credibility of our proposal, leaving little to no room for concern or additional questions.

The second step that is needed to ensure the program's success is to take the time to fully educate line staff and all others who might come into contact with the program. Unfortunately, this step is frequently neglected resulting in subtle erosion of the effectiveness of many programs. It is easy to underestimate the power of casual negative comments made or beliefs held by staff, co-workers, etc. By taking a proactive stance and providing clear, ongoing education for staff and coworkers, many of these problems can be eliminated. For example, Rocky originally wore a Snoot Loop head halter when working. He wore this due to his very young age and due to his tendency to forget when excited that he is to walk beside me and not to pull on the leash. The halter is designed in such a way that it gently reminded him not to pull ahead of me during high-stimulation interactions. Unfortunately, some people who were not familiar with this type of dog collar mistakenly thought it was a muzzle and was used to prevent Rocky from biting. Not only was this perception inaccurate (Rocky could bite just as well wearing the head halter and in fact would not be working as a therapy dog if biting was a concern), it could have significantly damaged the reputation of the AAA/T program if visitors and staff perceived Rocky as at risk of biting. By providing accurate information, rumors can be quickly corrected and co-workers and staff are more likely to readily accept the therapy dog program. In addition, when staff members have accurate information and are accepting of the program, they are much more likely to correct overheard inaccurate information from clients and visitors. Because of the importance of ensuring that staff members and co-workers are fully informed and supportive, we have found it helpful to provide frequent inservices to staff members about the therapy dog program. We use these as forums to ask staff members what they have noticed when Rocky is interacting with clients, what difference Rocky's presence makes, what questions they have, etc. In addition, we use these opportunities to provide general information (frequently the information we provide is corrected information about rumors or questions we have overheard from clients and staff). These educational forums provide valuable opportunities to evaluate our program's effectiveness, see how the program is being perceived, and make needed changes to ensure that the program remains credible and effective.

The third step to ensure that the AAA/T program is successful is to have written policies and procedures in place prior to program implementation. These policies and procedures should include all areas of program design, such as visiting versus resident handler/dog models being employed, credentials for both dog and handler, immunizations and health requirements, areas in which the dog is not allowed, role and obligation of the handler, liability and plan in case of injury, ways in which allergies and phobias will be addressed, the structure for visits, etc. We have included a copy of our policies and procedures as a sample (see Appendix B). Although writing policies and procedures can be a time-consuming and daunting task, they are well worth the effort. They provide a formal blueprint for the program, serve to answer outside questions about intent and protocol, and serve as protection should the program come under scrutiny. Their very existence adds to the credibility and professionalism of the program.

SUMMARY

Adequate time invested into program development and design is crucial to the success of an animal-assisted activities/therapy program. Without this, a great idea and a potential asset to clients might be needlessly lost. Whether the intent is to utilize a therapy dog in an agency or private practice setting, one must carefully plan for ways to adequately address issues such as program credibility, canine behavior, cleanliness, allergies, phobias, liability, program structure, and the dog's basic needs. In addition, co-workers, regulatory bodies, referral sources, and clients who come into contact with the program will benefit from accurate information about AAA/T to ensure the long-term success of the program. With these steps in place, the AAA/T program has a solid foundation, and the therapy animal team can focus on the most important thing: changing clients' lives for the better. The next chapter looks at the powerful role that therapy dogs play in animal-assisted activities in a treatment setting.

Photo by Nancy Braden. Used with permission.

Chapter 5

Using AAA in Solution-Focused Treatment Settings

Unrecognized miracles are all around us just waiting to be named.

Now that all the concerns have been addressed and you have a solid animal-assisted activities program design, you may be wondering just how can a therapy dog really assist in the goals and purpose of a solution-focused therapist or agency. This chapter will explore how a therapy dog team can skillfully impact the treatment environment, thereby paving the way and lightening the load for a therapist to effectively engage and work with clients.

SOLUTION-FOCUSED PRINCIPLES

Solution-focused therapists follow the guiding principles of solution-focused therapy. These principles are readily seen throughout a solution-focused therapist's actions, and many of them can likewise be seen throughout AAA. These principles are summarized by Pichot and Dolan (2003) as follows:

- If something is working, do more of it.
- If it's not broken don't fix it.
- If it is not working, do something different.
- Small steps can lead to large changes.
- The solution is not necessarily directly related to the problem.

- The language requirements for solution development are different than those needed to describe a problem.
- No problem happens all the time. There are always exceptions that can be utilized.
- The future is both created and negotiable. (p. 13)

Let's now explore how a therapy dog team routinely makes use of six of these eight principles to positively impact the environment.

If something is working, do more of it.

Therapy dog handlers routinely scan the environment to identify people who demonstrate an interest in interacting with the therapy dog. This interest may be communicated through a smile, an outstretched hand, or an inviting comment. Once identified, a visit is quickly offered and the handler continues to closely monitor the client for signs that the visit is a positive experience for him or her. In a treatment setting, these signs might be increased verbal interaction, stories of past or current pets, nonverbal signs of enjoyment such as smiling or relaxation, laughing, or seeking increased contact from the dog such as "kisses" or snuggling. Once the handler identifies these positive cues, the handler makes a mental note and continues to offer the client contact with the therapy dog at every visit, seeking to continue an intervention that has been deemed effective with the client. These clients are easily identified, for they frequently will begin to seek out the therapy dog and verbalize their disappointment when the dog is not present upon their arrival. We have even experienced clients who bring their family members to the agency to meet the therapy dog in an effort to share their positive experience with those who matter most to them. Our front desk staff members have joked that they are now taking messages and announcing appointments for a dog. Although they smile as they say this, they clearly recognize the incredibly positive impact that Rocky's presence makes for clients.

If it is not working, do something different.

Most therapists have experienced those frustrating times in which the current treatment plan does not seem to be effective. The client continues to be distant, angry, or blaming despite the best efforts of the therapist. In these cases, SFT would suggest to do something different. The use of an animal in the environment can be that something different. Clients are frequently surprised at the presence of a therapy dog, and this surprise can be just the interruption in the client's thought process that can make a difference. For example, we once had an ethnic minority adolescent client named Sam who was extremely quiet and difficult to read during the group sessions. He would come to the agency early for his sessions, and sit by himself in the waiting room, listening to music through his headphones or sleeping. He didn't smile or interact with staff other than to minimally answer a direct question. His therapist suggested an experiment, "What if Rocky visited Sam? Maybe he would be different." So, the next time Sam came to the agency, I purposefully walked Rocky by where he stood to see his response. He watched the dog, yet made no outward sign of wanting to interact. Since he did not appear fearful at all, I initiated contact, introducing Rocky and asking if he liked dogs. He said yes, and put his hand down to pet Rocky. His therapist, noticing the interaction, quickly joined the conversation asking him if he had any pets. He began to talk about his own dog, and he smiled during the interaction. Sam was more talkative in the session that day following the interaction with Rocky, and the therapist now had more insight into who Sam was and what he enjoyed. Rocky and I continued to interact with Sam every time he came to the agency. I frequently talked to Rocky as we approached the client saying, "Oh look, here's your friend, Sam." As Sam petted Rocky, I often pointed out to him Rocky's wagging tail, saying, "He remembers you." Sam would smile with pride and increase his show of affection to the dog. Rocky had a way of drawing Sam out when we as therapists had been unable. He was just the "something different" that was needed.

Small steps can lead to large changes.

AAA is a small and unobtrusive intervention. Even just the animal's presence as he walks by a waiting room full of clients can have a profound impact on the mood of an agency. An animal's presence frequently invites smiles, interested looks, interruption from complaining and grumbling, and squeals of joy from children. Miller and Berg (1995) state, "The simplest and least invasive approach is frequently the best medicine" (p. 20). Similar to the far-reaching ripples of water caused by the impact of a tiny stone on a still pond, a therapy dog's presence, wag of his tail, tongue licking away a client's tear, or the softness of his fur in a stressful moment can make a client's day, thereby starting a positive chain of events. It lays the foundation for the therapist to then assist the client in identifying and taking responsibility for continuing these events and changing his or her life. For example, one of our clients came to the agency one evening for group. As she sat on the floor interacting with Rocky, she took out her camera and stated that she wanted a picture of her favorite therapist. That therapist was Rocky. While we all laughed at the time, we also knew that there was truth to her words. Rocky had made her time at the agency less stressful and had impacted her life. Although he was just being himself, his presence made a difference to this client.

The solution is not necessarily directly related to the problem.

We are frequently asked, "So what does a dog have to do with therapy?" This question exemplifies this solution-focused principle. The client's solution to substance abuse or depression may not have anything to do with what caused the client to drink or to become depressed. Similarly, the presence of a dog in a treatment setting may have no apparent direct connection to the problems with which the clients present. Frequently clients come to treatment believing they need to analyze the problem in order to find their solution. They are often relieved to learn that the insight that a solution-focused therapist finds most valuable is in what life will be like when the problem is resolved (Berg, 1994). The presence of an animal is often helpful in helping clients to stop thinking about the problem (if only for a moment), thereby clearing mental and emotional space for the client to imagine a life in which the problem is resolved. The presence of an animal can unlock memories, thoughts, and feelings about past and current pets, frequently evoking smiles and fond recollection. A client can also simply enjoy the company and affection of a dog in the moment. These emotional changes in clients (although perhaps only fleeting) can be invaluable for therapists in discovering exceptions and other clues to a solution.

***The language requirements for solution development
are different than those needed to describe a problem.***

Because animals do not speak human language, clients change their way of communicating and interacting to a nonverbal form when interacting with animals. There is a connection between a person and an animal that does not need words. Both easily read the other's body language to know that both are enjoying the interaction. This abandonment of the normal way of communicating and reliance on behavioral indicators for meaning is a wonderful transition to a different way of thinking as the client enters a solution-focused session. Clients frequently come to treatment expecting the problem to be the focus of treatment. Solution-focused therapy places the emphasis on a place in which the problem is solved. This change in focus requires a different way of thinking, a different language, and a willingness to view the world differently.

***No problem happens all the time.
There are always exceptions that can be utilized.***

Clients are frequently momentarily transformed when they are interacting with a therapy dog. It is not uncommon to see clients on the floor, laughing, and smiling as Rocky licks their faces. Clients' faces often light up as Rocky quickens his pace and wags his tail in recognition as they enter the agency. We later learn that they had a bad day or even suffer from clinical depression, none of which we would have guessed from witnessing their interaction with Rocky. These are impromptu exceptions to their problems that occur before our eyes; moments in which their problems do not exist. These are invaluable clues that can be utilized by the therapists to discover additional exceptions that occurred outside of the agency. For solution-focused therapists believe that "solutions to clients' problems are already present in clients' lives. Solutions are present as exceptions to clients' problems, and as personal and social resources that clients may draw upon in solving their problems" (Miller & de Shazer, 1998, p. 371).

As we describe the specifics of how we use animal-assisted activities in our solution-focused agency, we invite you to look for these six governing principles in each client interaction.

GOALS AND PURPOSE

At our agency Rocky visits both general visitors (those who have accompanied a client to our substance abuse treatment program and those who may be at our agency for services outside of our program area such as immunizations or other medical services) as well as those who are seeking substance abuse treatment services. With our general visitors and clients we have the following general goals when using animal-assisted activities: (1) Provide a sense of community, and (2) Challenge the client's concept of what might occur at the agency.

Provide a sense of community.

Rocky provides an incredible service to our general visitors and clients. He is frequently a topic of conversation as he walks by the main waiting room or as visitors notice his many pictures hanging on the walls of the client areas. The very sight of a dog in a county health department is unusual, and worthy of curiosity and conversation. Parents frequently focus their children's attention on Rocky, and the children respond with happy smiles. Visitors frequently offer an outstretched hand to pet him as he walks by, whereas others smile and point in his direction while whispering to those sitting near. The mood in the clinic becomes light and more casual as visitors' focus shifts to the therapy dog. When we have time to stop and visit, visitors quickly engage in casual conversation about their past and current pets, etc. As nurses and other agency staff come to the waiting room to call their clients for appointments, they frequently stop and smile, taking a moment or two to enjoy watching our visitors and clients interacting with the therapy dog. At times visitors and staff sit on the floor to better interact with Rocky on a personal level. This only serves to further the relaxed, informal environment as staff and visitors share impromptu moments. There is a nonverbal disclosure by all who engage in the activity that they enjoy animals, thereby highlighting commonality between staff and clients/visitors.

Challenge the client's concept of what might occur at the agency.

Clients rarely look forward to having to come to a county health department. The services provided there are frequently viewed as intrusive with possible frightening results (i.e., testing for sexually transmitted diseases, immunizations). Even nutritional and behavioral services require the disclosure of very personal information, making the entire process something that most would rather avoid. Those who come to the agency for the first time frequently experience apprehension, knowing the service is needed albeit dreaded. They come to the health department with a negative idea of what the experience will be like. Steve de Shazer (1985) wrote, "What you expect to happen influences what you do" (p. 45). Our visitors and clients' expectations of what the experience will be like frequently results in a seriousness in the waiting room, as they sit quietly, minimally interacting with others. Rocky's presence challenges this idea, lightening the mood. Visitors and clients frequently forget their preconceived ideas as they interact with Rocky and begin to casually chat with those around them. Adults enjoy the reaction of the children, and even admit that they too would like a visit from the therapy dog. As they begin to chat with me as I handle Rocky, as well as other staff, they quickly discover that the health department staff are friendly. Even Rocky appears to "smile" in his relaxed facial expression (Coren, 2000, p. 250), further lightening the mood and increasing the sense of community.

For clients who come to the agency to receive services from the Substance Abuse Counseling Program, we have similar goals. However, these goals are more specific due to the therapeutic nature of the program itself. They can best be described as: (1) Provide a sense of community, and (2) Provide an informal setting for staff to interact with clients.

Provide a sense of community.

In addition to the benefits mentioned earlier for the general population, additional benefits exist for our clients. Those who come to the Substance Abuse Counseling Program face similar dread as that described for the general visitor, for someone (i.e., a social services caseworker, a probation officer, a parent) believes they have a problem with substances and is requiring treatment. Our clients frequently don't agree, and are angry and afraid they will be labeled as a "drug addict" or "alcoholic." Therefore our clients frequently come to our program fearful of judgment by our staff and initially present in a defensive and guarded manner. This makes the creation of a sense of community in our waiting room even more valuable.

Rocky is seen as the program's "greeter," and I regularly take him out to visit with those who are waiting in our waiting room. Some are there for the first time, while others are waiting for treatment sessions. This mix of new with the established clientele is useful as the new clients watch as Rocky greets established clients with happy recognition. They often quickly join him on the floor and enjoy some time before their scheduled appointment, adding to the informality of the room. (As his handler, I almost always sit on the floor to better observe his comfort level and to minimize my role. By me sitting on the floor as the program manager, it further adds to the sense of community and to minimize the power differential between clients and staff.)

Rocky's ability to give a warm greeting that includes a "kiss" and a snuggle serves to give warmth and a personal touch that would be deemed inappropriate by a human therapist. Clients sometimes mention to Rocky that they have had a rough day and that it is nice to see him. His greeting is frequently perceived as being more genuine by clients and therefore more welcome, for he is seen as lacking an agenda. He is seen as able to see past their mistakes and appearances. Our clients rarely trust our human staff members' intentions as quickly as those of our therapy dog. Rocky is able to effortlessly establish rapport while human staff members are initially met with more reserve.

Provide an informal setting for staff to interact with clients.

Therapists frequently stop and join in the casual conversation or do tricks with Rocky while he is in the waiting room. The receptionists stand to get a better view as Rocky "high fives" a client or staff member on command. Clapping is common as clients and staff alike cheer Rocky on. Clients laugh as Rocky occasionally does not obey a therapist and holds out until the therapist finds a treat. Staff and clients joke that it is not just them who sometimes would like to ignore the directives of the therapist. It all adds an element of humanness to the staff that assists in creating the sense of community.

All of this serves to offset the formality of the treatment sessions and the intrusiveness of the personal questions that the therapists are required to ask of the clients. Although our solution-focused treatment model is less intrusive than most, it still maintains a level of power differential inherent in any helping relationship. In an effort to minimize our therapists being viewed as holding the "answers," our therapists do not self-disclose personal information to the clients. This helps to keep the focus squarely on the clients and to avoid the expert role. However, personal information about the therapists is inferred by the clients as the therapists' love of animals and playfulness are observed. This allows the therapists to benefit from the humanness that is frequently a desired quality from self-disclosure while avoiding the pitfalls of distracting from the clients' personal solutions.

Because our clients come to our program on a frequent basis and because we have established formal treatment goals with them to address their clinical needs, we are able to purposefully interact informally with them during AAA in ways that enhance their clinical goals. Our clinical team is small enough (with six therapists and the program manager) to allow all of us to become familiar with the majority of our client cases. We are then able to use informal time to offer compliments, notice differences, and explore exceptions with clients as appropriate in a public setting (such as the waiting room) that target client progress without alerting those around us that we are purposefully intervening.

For example, John was a Caucasian man in his thirties who was referred by Social Services after his children were removed from his custody for methamphetamine use. He had tattoos covering a significant portion of his arms and he frequently came to the agency dirty from work. He and his wife were convinced that his appearance prejudiced his caseworker and treatment providers against him. He presented as very guarded and used sarcasm as a way to avoid personal questions and serious subjects. His attendance in treatment was sporadic which made it difficult to get to know him or to provide the evidence he needed for court that he was remaining substance free. However, he loved Rocky. Every time he came to the agency he sought out Rocky and would kiss him on the nose. He would do this again when he was ready to leave. It was the only time that we saw the gentle, compassionate side of this guarded man. On days that Rocky was not at the agency, he would stop by my office and say, "So, is Rocky doing okay? He's such a good dog. Tell him I said 'hello.'"

At one point in John's treatment, his therapist staffed the case with me. He told me that John was really struggling because his case-worker was going for termination of his parental rights and it looked like there was little he could do at this late point in his case. He said that John was once again questioning if any of the professionals involved in his case really cared about him and could see past his appearance. That evening when I saw John in the waiting room, I snapped on Rocky's leash and we went out to visit. As we approached, I purposefully said to Rocky just loud enough to be overheard, "Hey Rocky! There's your good friend, John!" Rocky responded by quickening his pace and wagging his tail as we approached. As Rocky licked John's face I continued to talk to Rocky saying, "You really like John don't you? He's such a great person." John responded by talking directly to Rocky saying, "I really like you too, buddy." John ruffled Rocky's ears and kissed him on the nose. By seemingly giving Rocky a voice, John was able to hear a genuine, message of caring. It was the only way I could think of to get the message to John that staff at this agency really cared about him. I knew he would believe Rocky.

The informalness of the waiting room often also serves as an opportunity for therapists to notice differences in their clients during AAA interactions and then to casually join the discussion. For example one day as Rocky and I were passing through the waiting room we saw two children and their mother. I introduced Rocky and asked if they would like to see Rocky do some tricks (I didn't know the family, but they were current clients of Marc's). The two school-age children sat quietly on the floor and followed my instructions on how to give commands to Rocky and how to reward him for his good work. Rocky rewarded them with "kisses," and they laughed as they spent some time petting him. I noticed that Marc had come out of his office and was watching the interaction, smiling at the children's reaction to Rocky. As Rocky and I prepared to leave, I overheard Marc say to the mother, "Wow! I am so impressed with how well behaved your children are! You have done a wonderful job with them!" Little did I know that he had been working with this mother on how to manage her children's behavior. Marc noticed right away that the children's behavior while interacting with Rocky was markedly different from previous interactions. He took full advantage of this opportunity to join in our informal interaction, notice the difference, compliment

Mom for the change, and then ask her to think about what she had done differently that had resulted in such good behavior from her children. It was a wonderful impromptu clinical opportunity.

HOW TO INITIATE AND STRUCTURE AN AAA VISIT

Although upon casual observation AAA visits appear natural and effortless, there is significant thought and purposefulness on the part of the handler as to who to visit, how to approach, and how to structure the visit. Without this level of purposefulness the visit may very well be intrusive, thereby damaging the reputation of the AAA program.

Who to Visit

The handler must continuously monitor the environment when working with a therapy dog. The handler is monitoring for positive indicators as well as indicators of concern. Positive indicators are the behavioral and verbal cues from clients and visitors that the dog's presence is welcome and that a personal visit may be desired. These include looks in the dog's direction followed immediately by smiles, pointing, and pleasant conversation. Other indicators are parents initiating their child's or other family member's attention toward the dog, outstretched hands, "doggy" talk directed toward the therapy animal, or movement toward the dog. These signs alert the handler that those in the environment are comfortable with the dog's presence, and depending on the handler's schedule, approaching clients or visitors would be appropriate.

On occasion we will encounter clients and visitors who watch Rocky and me walking through the hallways or interacting with others, and they do not show any interest, but also do not show any concern. By slowly approaching them, observing their response while we approach, stopping a safe distance away, and then introducing Rocky and asking if they would like a visit we can quickly determine if this person might like interaction from Rocky. The majority of times we have found these individuals to be very receptive to a visit and to be grateful we asked. By stopping a safe distance away and only approaching closer with permission we are able to avoid those who would not like contact with the dog.

The ability to quickly notice subtle indicators of concerns is an important skill for a therapy dog handler. Indicators of concern include moving away from the dog, moving a child away from the dog or closer to an adult, prolonged watching the dog without any positive change in affect, freezing in place without a quick and positive recovery (i.e., smile), and cautionary statements made to those nearby (i.e., "careful"). Whenever the handler sees any of these indictors, he or she must quickly determine the best course of action. If the person exhibiting the behavior is in close proximity to the dog a safe course of action is to quickly apologize for the surprise and explain the dog's role and level of credentialing while moving the dog away from the person. For example occasionally Rocky and I encounter a visitor who, preoccupied in thought, suddenly turns a corner and becomes startled by discovering Rocky and I walking in the hallway. The person most commonly stops immediately and stares at Rocky in fear. When this occurs, I quickly stop (to prevent Rocky from walking any closer) and say, "I'm so sorry. I didn't mean to startle you. This is Rocky our therapy dog. He works here." As I am speaking, I am closely monitoring for the person's recovery response. If the person quickly looks at me while I'm talking, gradually smiles, and responds verbally to me, then I most likely would not move Rocky further away. I would simply ask if he or she likes dogs, and if so, offer a quick impromptu visit as a way of introducing Rocky and our AAA program. However, should the person hold his or her gaze at the dog despite my talking, I would quickly back Rocky away from the person to increase the person's personal space. (By the person maintaining eye contact with the dog rather than behaviorally acknowledging me, he or she may be communicating that he or she is feeling unsafe in the dog's presence. Should this occur it is very important that the handler quickly increase the person's level of comfort by moving the dog until the person indicates feeling safe.) Any verbal explanation of a therapy dog's role should only occur once the person is feeling safe and realizes that the dog is under control. Should the information fail to alleviate the indicators of concern, it is imperative that the handler make every effort to keep the therapy dog away from the individual to ensure that he or she feels safe while at the agency. Placing information posters, pictures, and brochures throughout the agency also minimizes any surprise or misinformation about the therapy dog's role. However despite these preventive measures, the handler must remain attentive.

On occasion we have overheard inaccurate information about Rocky and his role as we walk by, and we have found it imperative to be observant of such comments and to immediately correct them. For example, one day when Rocky and I were walking through the clinic waiting room I saw a young child smile with surprise as she saw Rocky walking by. Her mother then stated, "He is a Seeing Eye dog. You cannot touch him." Rocky and I quickly stopped and I said to the well-intentioned mother, "Actually Rocky is a therapy dog and not a service dog. He was especially trained to be safe to have in buildings, and his job is to make people smile. He is the kind of dog that children can touch with permission from their parents. Would your child like a visit from Rocky?" This impromptu education combined with a gentle reinforcement of the mom's authority is an effective way to correct information without any damage to the parent's credibility in front of the child. It is very important that clients and visitors really understand the difference between therapy and service dogs so that they can benefit from the presence of a therapy dog while not inappropriately approaching a service dog they might encounter in the future.

Another commonly overheard comment from our substance abuse treatment clients upon first meeting Rocky is, "So is he a drug sniffing dog?" While employing such a canine might come in handy for detecting recent substance use in our clients, it would greatly hamper the therapeutic quality of our program and would destroy the benefits sought by an AAA program. Our typical response to this question (or to overhearing any hints of this concern) are, "Oh no! Rocky is only here to make people smile and feel more comfortable. He wouldn't recognize drugs if he smelled them!" We then go on to offer a visit while explaining his level of training and the benefits he brings to both clients and staff.

How to Structure a Visit

Once a visitor or client has been identified who appears to be receptive to the therapy dog, it is best to approach slowly, introduce Rocky and his purpose, and then offer a visit (on occasion the person is so excited he or she will approach the dog and handler and this step is not needed). Here are some common statements that I use as Rocky and I approach:

> "Hi. This is Rocky, our therapy dog. He is an official employee here at that Health Department. Would you like a visit?"
> "Hi. You look surprised to see a dog here. He is a working dog. His job is to make people smile. Would you like to meet him?"
> "Hi. Do you like dogs? This is Rocky, our therapy dog."

By giving this quick introduction and asking if the person would like a visit, the handler is able to continue to monitor the person's behavior for nonverbal indicators of permission to approach. It also gives the person time to respond if there is anything of which the handler should be aware (e.g., allergies). One evening as I walked through the clinic waiting room I saw a young school-aged girl leaning back comfortably in a child-sized chair in the hallway watching a child's video playing on the television. Her parents were sitting causally behind her, and I knew all three had been in the waiting room for quite a while. Although none of them appeared to notice as Rocky and I entered the hallway, I thought I would approach and offer a visit to make the wait seem a little shorter. Rocky and I slowed our pace as we drew near, giving the girl and her parents a chance to notice us to avoid startling them. The parents watched as we came near the girl, but did not show any signs of concern, only curiosity. I stopped several feet away and said to the girl so the parents could overhear, "Hi. Do you like dogs? Rocky and I thought you might like a visit." The girl turned, looked, nodded, and quickly slid to the floor. Rocky responded by moving forward to say hello, she began to pet him as I explained Rocky's job to both her and her parents. Her mother's hand quickly reached toward Rocky to pet him, and I gave Rocky a little longer leash so he could visit with all three. As Rocky moved toward the father, he quickly sat back, put his hand up in a stop-sign fashion and said, "Not me. I'm allergic." I quickly pulled Rocky back and allowed him to visit with the girl and her mother. Rocky responded by lying down beside the girl. As I talked with the parents, I made a special point to explain how allergies are controlled for at the agency and then complimented the father for knowing that touching a dog could easily trigger an allergic reaction. As I kept a close eye on Rocky during the conversation, I noticed the girl lean over and hug Rocky around his neck, lying on and enjoying his soft fur.

As this case illustrates, once the visit has begun, the handler's role takes a complex turn, for he or she must closely monitor the animal's behavior for possible signs of stress while carrying on a conversation with, at times, several people. Although the handler often must attend to multiple areas during a visit, it can be useful for the handler to determine the most relevant action occurring during the visit, and place special attention to that while being cognizant that this priority may quickly change. For example during my interaction with the girl and the two parents, I determined that the most important thing to monitor was Rocky's response to the child. Rocky can feel uncomfortable around children who are not respectful of his space or who are loud or boisterous, and I did not know how this child would respond. I deemed the parents to be predictable, while the child might not be. While I talked to the parents, I watched Rocky's behavior very closely to see how he felt around this young visitor. As Rocky lay down and opened his mouth into a relaxed position (Dibra, 1999), I knew he was feeling comfortable. I took a seat on the floor beside Rocky and the girl and settled in to be a part of the interaction. I also gently placed my hand on Rocky's side as he enjoyed the girl petting him, so that I could feel any change in muscle tension as I talked with her parents while watching the AAA interaction.

During an AAA visit, the handler may need to intervene with the client or visit to provide instruction or information about how to appropriately interact with the dog. For example, dogs commonly prefer to briefly sniff the visitor's hand as a greeting rather than for the visitor to suddenly attempt to pet the top of his head. This is something that most people who are familiar with dogs know and readily do when meeting a new dog. Rocky is no exception. Although he tolerates people petting him without the desired greeting, at times he may take a step back or lift his head to lift his nose toward the hand to sniff. On occasion the visitor has stated in response to this, "He doesn't like to be petted." I then quickly correct the misinformation by stating, "He just likes to say 'hello' by sniffing your hand first. It's a kind of doggy etiquette" (as I demonstrate how to approach a dog by extending my hand). Rocky then responds with a quick sniff of the extended hand, and the visit continues with Rocky's full attention.

During the visit the handler may need to make adjustments in the immediate environment: move the dog's tail to prevent it from being stepped on, provide increased structure to the visit, or provide instructions to the visitors. For example, one day as Rocky and I were visiting clients in the SACP waiting room, several children and their mother saw Rocky and came to visit him from the main clinic waiting room. As they approached to visit Rocky, another child banged on the glass that separated the two waiting rooms, startling Rocky and distracting his attention from the children who wanted to visit. Seeing that there were too many distractions in the current environment, I asked the children and mother to follow us to a quieter hallway beside the SACP waiting room away from the glass partition and the loud noises. I then asked the children if they would like to see Rocky do some tricks, to which they happily nodded affirmatively. The combination of moving to a quieter location with fewer distractions coupled with the structure of tricks was just what was needed, and Rocky soon relaxed as he rolled over, caught a bone off his noise, and gave a high-five to the children's delight. Once Rocky was comfortable, I allowed the children to approach and pet him as they said good-bye and thanked him for his performance.

The verbal content of an AAA visit is dependent on the relationship between the handler and the visitor or client. When we are visiting with strangers in the main clinic waiting room, the conversation remains light, asking about pets, chatting about how their day is going, etc. The content of the conversation does not run any deeper than a casual social conversation, for the clients and visitors are there for medical services and did not come to the clinic for any therapeutic reason. However, when we are providing AAA visits to clients of SACP, the content of the conversation can be as deep or personal as the setting and the situation allow. This is appropriate since I (as the handler) am an employee of the agency and because I and any staff who accompany Rocky and me are trained therapists, responsible for the mental health services provided to these clients. As such, the AAA services to these clients are designed to have a therapeutic benefit that compliments their formal treatment services. Therefore, taking advantage of valuable opportunities to give a compliment, notice a change, or explore an exception during an AAA visit only serves to further enhance the clients' treatment experience. (It is important to mention that should an agency utilize a visiting therapy dog model, the conversation should remain casual, with no therapeutic intent.)

Lessons Learned

Aside from the many previously mentioned benefits of using AAA and the lessons we have gained through our application of AAA with our clients, there have been three additional lessons that we believe are important to highlight. The first is the powerful benefit of clients and staff observing one another in a playful and more relaxed stance. Although professional boundaries are necessary, the presence of a therapy dog frequently gives the permission needed to allow a more personal side to be seen while maintaining professionalism. It can be easy to become so focused on the clinical tasks at hand that one over-looks the human spirit in the individual in front of them through all of the paperwork and compliance with regulations. Therapists can fall prey to this with clients. In addition to overlooking who the client is, professionals can also innocently prevent the clients from seeing the human side of them. When a therapy dog is present, it invites both (client and professional) to take a moment to enjoy a snuggle or "kiss" with the animal and interact with the dog in a playful ex-change. These moments, while they feel personal and private due to the degree of genuineness and intimacy, they are done within view of all to see. The public display of humanity has a powerful effect on all. It lowers the public facade that we all display and shows those around us the compassion and appreciation of life that helps to minimize the power differential between clients and staff. What an incredible way to start or end a therapy session.

The second lesson we would like to share is the benefit to staff when they use the therapy dog as a quick break or stress reliever throughout the day. The pace within a treatment center can be hectic as therapists keep pace with a full schedule while managing the crises inherent in a therapist's day. We have found that therapists have been much more likely to take a moment for themselves by stopping and saying "hello" to the therapy dog in passing. Rocky never seems put off by the therapists rushing from appointment to appointment, and he doesn't wait until the pace slows and he's invited before catching their eye or entering their offices to say "hello" whenever their doors are open. In exchange, they find his happy greeting hard to resist, re-sulting in them taking a much needed breather. They have said that these few moments have served a valuable role of clearing the thoughts from their heads, allowing them to enter the next client appointment free from the previous crisis. This allows the therapist to be more fully present for the client who sits in front of him or her and increases the level of clinical care.

Third, we have found Rocky to be a powerful way to assist clients in relaxing from their long and difficult day and to transition to talking about themselves in a group session. As our clients begin to gather in the waiting room for the evening's group session, it is now common for me to bring Rocky out to socialize with the waiting clients. Rocky moves from client to client in greeting, wagging his tail in recognition and giving each a snuggle as I sit on the floor holding his leash. Clients frequently move to the floor as well to better position themselves in order to enjoy moments with him. The clients begin to casually chat with one another, gathering group facilitators, and me, sharing pictures of their children or sharing exciting news from the week. Rocky seems to know who has exciting news, and he quickly elicits laughter as he tries to lick the pictures or steal the attention of the client who is talking. Clients who are new to the group experience a nonthreatening environment in which to get to know both staff and group members, easing their apprehensions about the new situation. This beginning to the evening's treatment group provides a smooth transition for the therapists when the time comes for them to gather the clients and move the conversation into the group room. Clients are now comfortable and receptive to the therapists' efforts to direct the conversation to the clients' personal miracles and future vision for their lives.

SUMMARY

Animal-assisted activities can serve an invaluable role when used to complement the therapeutic services within an agency. Whether this is in a more casual meet and greet for strangers in an agency waiting room or a more purposeful, informal greeting of current treatment clients, therapy dogs have an incredible way of increasing the clients' comfort level, creating a sense of community, and changing the overall environment for the better. The next chapter will look at how solution-focused therapists can create and implement specific treatment interventions that utilize the therapy dog within the therapy session.

Photo by Mark Hochstedler. Used with permission.

Chapter 6

Using a Therapy Dog in Solution-Focused Therapy Treatment Sessions

A life lived in relationship with an animal has the power to make us both fully human and more fully humane.

Suzanne Clothier

Since a therapy dog can have such an incredibly positive impact on an agency and treatment environment, it seems obvious that it would be a good idea to bring the dog into the actual treatment session. However, including a therapy dog in a treatment session simply because the client likes the dog lacks purposefulness and solution focus. This chapter gives clear guidelines for when including a therapy dog in a treatment session is most useful, how to write treatment plans that include a therapy dog as a purposeful intervention, and how to structure a treatment session once the dog is in the room.

PURPOSEFULNESS IN INTERVENTION

Purposefulness is a hallmark of solution-focused therapy. A solution-focused therapist assumes a set therapeutic stance and way of viewing the client, the problem, and what creates change. This stance distinguishes a solution-focused therapist from a problem-focused therapist. A set of solution-focused assumptions and principles are the foundation for a variety of tools or interventions available to the solution-focused therapist depending on the desired outcome. For example, if the therapist needs the client to obtain a clear vision of what life will be like once the problem is resolved, the miracle question is the best tool for this purpose. If the therapist needs to assist the client in exploring his or her current progress toward the desired goal, a scaling question would be the most effective tool, and so on. Although the client in the solution-focused process remains the expert on himself or herself, the therapist must remain the expert on the process and on using the appropriate tools/interventions in his or her tool belt. When introducing a therapy dog into the solution-focused process, this basic concept of purposefulness must remain intact, otherwise the therapist will lose credibility and the session will become less meaningful and effective. The presence of a therapy dog should enhance the process, not change the fundamental concepts within the client-therapist interaction.

The use of a therapy dog during a session can best be understood as one of several tools that a solution-focused therapist has. As such, there should be client-specific, desired outcomes identified by the therapist in order for the "therapy dog tool" to be the most appropriate tool for that purpose. As Abraham Maslow (1969, pp. 15-16) once said, "It is tempting, if the only tool you have is a hammer, to treat everything as if it were a nail." Animal-assisted activities can have a magical quality due to the immediate and personal impact that a therapy dog has on many people. People tend to visibly respond. Therapists can be deeply touched by seeing clients' powerful emotional responses to the therapy dog. However, it is imperative that a therapy dog does not become that "hammer" and that the therapist is able to remain purposeful within the treatment session. So, let's look now at some contexts in which the therapy dog tool is most often optimal.

IDENTIFYING CLIENTS

When the therapists at our agency come to the waiting room to gather their clients for a group session following Rocky's AAA work, it is common for clients to ask, "Can Rocky come to group?" My response is almost always, "How would he be helpful?" I have yet to have a client tell me how he would be helpful to the entire group. However, they have told me some very good ways that Rocky would be helpful to them personally. This brings us to the first clue of when a therapy dog might be useful.

Clients Who Have a Strong Connection with the Therapy Dog

Central to solution-focused therapy, listening to what clients say is important to them is crucial to good treatment. Anytime a client says that something would be helpful, we are all ears. That doesn't mean however, that we simply take them at face value, for we want to make sure that they are thinking in context of their larger miracle. If the client can tell us how including Rocky in a session would be helpful in them doing the clinical work of the session, Rocky is always present in that session. Clients form a strong connection with Rocky, and at times this connection might be valuable in providing just the needed sense of comfort or safety for them to dig in and start their work in a clinical session. A key factor to consider when a client initiates this kind of conversation and requests that the therapy dog be present is how able are they to concentrate on a serious conversation with the dog present. Remember the purpose of including the dog would be to enhance the process, not distract from it. A simple test would be to have the dog present for a conversation and observe the client's response. If the client appears more comfortable and relaxed with the dog present, the therapy dog might be a valuable tool to get this result during a session. If however, the client is overly attuned to the dog's movements and/or loses his or her train of thought, the dog will be a hindrance to the session and should not be included.

It is important in making this determination to compare the client's normal behavior to his or her reaction when with the dog. For example, a child or adolescent might normally behave in a somewhat distracted manner commenting on the surroundings or apparently non-related topics during a conversation with an adult, so in this case the occasional mention of the dog's presence during a conversation would not be a sign of further distraction. In this case, it would be more important to note the overall difference in the client when the animal is present. If the client is able to easily refocus on a therapeutic conversation and the dog has a positive impact on mood or level of comfort, a therapy dog may be beneficial.

When considering including a therapy dog in a family or group session, the therapist must assess whether the dog will be beneficial to every participant of the session. In a group session it is unlikely that each participant would have the same positive reaction. Although the dog may be very relaxing and comforting to some, others may find the dog distracting. In this case the use of a therapy dog would not be appropriate. However, in a family session, the dog may be very appropriate even if only clinically targeting one member (as long as the dog is not a distraction or irritant to other family members). This is frequently the case when the presenting problem involves a child or adolescent who is particularly fond of dogs. In these cases, the child can feel like the cause or center of the family strife, and dread the upcoming session. The dog can serve the role of a "buddy" or ally in the session and make the child more comfortable while the therapist works to identify the family miracle and assist the family in developing a more systemic view of the solution.

Those Who Like Dogs in General

On occasion, clients will volunteer the information that they like animals. It might be in connection to learning that a therapy dog is available, or it might be something that they mention while talking about their history or what is important to them. When assessing the appropriateness of using a therapy dog with clients, it is useful to pay specific attention to comments they make about animals and to explore these further as needed. For example, Susan was an adolescent client in my private practice. Her mother brought her for services because the couple was living apart and they were worried about the impact on their daughter. Susan answered me with monosyllables, and appeared nervous. When I asked about what was important to her, Susan mentioned that she has two dogs. I immediately wondered if Rocky's presence might help her to feel more comfortable in this awkward, professional setting. I briefly mentioned Rocky to her and her mother and told them that he was available to attend future sessions if Susan thought that would be helpful. I noticed that while I was talking about Rocky, Susan was giving me direct eye contact (something that was not happening prior to this conversation) and was smiling. As I walked Susan to the door at the end of the session I said, "Just let me know if you ever want Rocky to attend." She looked at me and said quite seriously, "I think that would be a good idea." After double checking with Susan's mother to ensure that Rocky's attendance would be acceptable to her, Rocky attended all of Susan's subsequent sessions.

Susan's response to the possibility of including a therapy dog is typical of the sorts of clients who might benefit from this intervention. In contrast, when I have brought up the subject with other clients (with whom ultimately I decided not to use a therapy dog), they may seem amused by the subject of including a therapy dog, but their affect and attention level does not change. By only mentioning the possibility once and not revisiting the subject, the client has the option of requesting it or letting the conversation be forgotten. In Susan's case, her affect and attention level dramatically improved when I mentioned including the therapy dog. I offered it a second time at the end of the session because she had shown such a markedly positive response to the idea and because her mother was not present at the end of the session as opposed to when I initially discussed the idea. During the session Susan was much more open with me about what she really thought and what she wanted after her mother left the room. Consistent with this, she quickly told me her opinion when I brought it up without her mother present.

Treatment Goals That Are Known to Be Consistently Enhanced by AAT

Although a therapy dog can be effectively used with many different treatment goals, three specific goals stand out as consistently benefiting from the presence of a therapy animal. Of course in order for this to be appropriate the client has to either have a strong bond with the therapy dog or enjoy dogs in general, thereby wanting the animal to be a part of the process. That being said, the first goal we will discuss is to improve parenting skills.

Improve parenting skills.

Animals provide a wonderful parallel context in which to explore parenting issues. They are dependent on their owners for good care just as children are dependent on their parents. Dogs will avoid things they don't like even when the things are good for them (e.g., grooming) just as children do. Dogs will exhibit out-of-control behavior if it is allowed by the owner, as will children when it is allowed by the parent. Dogs will take full advantage of any weakness in consistency on the part of the owner just as children will of the parent, and so on.

Ironically, dogs learn by the very same behavioral principles that guide child behavior. Now please understand, we are not saying that dogs and children are on the same cognitive or moral level, for they are not. However, despite the more advanced cognitive capacity that humans possess, the basic behavioral principles of learning are similar for obtaining good dog behavior as well as good human behavior, providing the basis for effective behavioral parallels to be created and utilized during therapeutic moments. Why not use these commonalities to help parents explore effective parenting behavior in a more natural and less threatening way?

Some parents are defensive about their parenting since they most often have been doing the best they know how despite child behavioral problems. They love their children, and the very thought that they may not be parenting well or that their children's poor behavior may have a direct connection to their parenting style, is a difficult thing to consider. Even worse is the fear that a professional may deem them unfit to parent. Despite their good intentions, parents are frequently required by professionals such as Social Services to improve their parenting skills for the sake of the children. This can be a difficult topic for a professional to broach.

The use of a therapy dog can allow the therapist to notice times in which the parent is exhibiting good parenting and to naturally compliment it, explore what difference it makes for the children, etc. For example, John's caseworker (from the previous chapter) expressed concern about his parenting skills. He and his wife strongly disagreed with their caseworker, stating that the caseworker was prejudiced against them due to John's many tattoos. Having a direct conversation about parenting (despite the caseworker's desire for this to occur) was very difficult and unproductive. Instead, by taking advantage of John's love of Rocky, the conversation was much more natural and beneficial. The following interaction occurred spontaneously one evening:

JOHN (J): [Smiling as he approached Rocky and very focused on greeting the dog] Hey buddy! How are you doing today? [John affectionately pets Rocky and then kisses him tenderly on the top of his long muzzle. His voice is not too loud. Just as dogs love during personal moments.]

THERAPIST (T): You are so great with him [smiling while watching the interaction]. How did you learn to be so good with dogs?

J: I don't know. I just like them. It just comes naturally.

T: That's quite a gift. A lot of people have no idea what dogs like. I bet you are good with children also.

J: Yeah. I used to kiss my son each time I left and when I came home each day. We are really close.

T: I bet he really liked that. You seem like a very caring father. I can see that by how you interact with Rocky. Dogs can be very good judges of character. I wonder if there are times that your case-worker has been able to see this compassionate side of you . . . how much you love your son.

J: We have supervised visits, but I don't want them to see anything! They are just out to get me! [John continues petting and focusing on Rocky, making no eye contact with me.]

T: I know it has been really tough for you. Suppose she was able to see it. What difference do you think it would make if she could see a moment like this between you and your son?

J: I don't know. Maybe it would make her think I am not as bad as she thinks.

T: Wow! So she would see a part of who you really are. What difference would that make?

J: She might lighten up some and give me a chance.

Using a therapy dog to specifically address parenting issues can be done with an individual client who just enjoys being around the animal such as in John's case, or it can be done with a parent and child together. In the later case, it can be very effective to ask if the dog can join the session to help the parent and therapist to work on the child's behavior. Again it is important to stress that the dog should only be present if both the child and the parent enjoy the dog's company and can focus on the task at hand while the dog is present. Even though the stated goal is to help the child with his or her behavior, the larger one is to identify times in which the parent is currently making parenting decisions that ultimately help the child's behavior. For some clients this focus on the child's behavior in the context of the dog is a much less threatening way to work on parenting skills, yet is equally effective. The following example demonstrates how this is done:

CHILD (C), MATHEW: [The four-year-old boy sits on the floor petting Rocky, clearly enjoying the time with the dog.] Look! He has big teeth! [He points at Rocky's teeth as Rocky's mouth is in a relaxed pose, slightly open with his tongue exposed.]

THERAPIST (T): Yes he does. I brush his teeth every night to keep them very clean and healthy.

MOM (M): Mathew hates to have his teeth brushed. I have given up.

T: Rocky used to hate it too. I use liver flavored toothpaste to make it better for him.

C: Liver! Yuck!

T: [laughing] Yeah that does sound gross. But he loves it. He still hates the brushing part, but it's important to keep him healthy. Since he loves the taste of the paste, he tolerates the brushing.

C: Tommy has bubblegum toothpaste.

T: Really? That sounds better than liver.

C: Yeah. It tastes really good!

M: If I get you some bubblegum toothpaste, will you brush your teeth?

C: Yeah!!

T: Now you can think of Rocky every time you brush your teeth.

C: [nodding as he continues to pet Rocky]

M: [laughing] I guess if the dog can brush his teeth, we can give it another try.

T: I'm impressed that you are hanging in there and doing things that you know are good for Mathew even when he doesn't like them. That can be hard.

During this session the therapist set up a possible direct parallel about good hygiene by volunteering that Rocky gets his teeth brushed on a daily basis. The therapist then took full advantage of a comment from the mother about her son's dislike of brushing his teeth. In response, the therapist provided another possible parallel by volunteering that Rocky also does not like brushing his teeth, but that the flavored paste made the process tolerable. The mother made all the necessary connections for this parenting lesson without any direct teaching from the therapist. The therapist then summarized the teaching moment with a compliment about Mom's parenting skill. If the therapist had taken a more problem-focused approach, this session could have easily resulted in a perceived reprimand to the parent about not brushing Mathew's teeth and education about the possible ill effects. The mother already knew that it was best to brush Mathew's teeth, but was not sure how to proceed given his dislike of the process. Taking a more directly educational approach would have most likely resulted in the mother becoming defensive. By capitalizing on Mathew's innocent comment about Rocky's teeth and creating possible parallels between dog and child hygiene, the mother and child suggested their own solution.

Sometimes the therapist may use interactions with the therapy animal to purposefully set the stage for future therapeutic conversations. Such is the case in this example with a client named Karen. Karen was a young, ethnic minority mother whose daughter was removed from her care by Social Services due to abuse and neglect and due to Karen's substance dependency. Karen loved Rocky, and although she avoided most interaction with staff, she sought out interaction with him. Karen did not see any need for treatment services other than to get her caseworker "off of my back." She did not see any problem with her continued alcohol use while in treatment for substance dependency since alcohol is "legal" and her daughter was not in her care anyway. In addition, discussing parenting with Karen was challenging at best, and a direct approach was not effective. During an interaction with Karen one evening, Karen asked if she could give Rocky a treat (something she loved to do). I granted this request, and handed her a treat from my pocket while reminding her that Rocky must earn the treat by performing a trick at her request. Upon seeing that Karen had a treat, Rocky quickly sat down, doing his best to charm the treat from Karen's hand. Before I could intervene, Karen had given in, and handed Rocky the treat for sitting, although Karen had not given the command to sit. Karen then hurried off to her treatment group.

Later that evening, following Karen's treatment group, Karen stopped by my office to say good-bye to Rocky. One of the therapists was in my office interacting with Rocky. Karen stood by the doorway watching the interaction. As the therapist asked Rocky to give her a "high five," Rocky turned his head away to look at Karen, and did not comply with the therapist's command. The therapist looked as if she was ready to give up with her request for a trick. Remembering Karen's lack of follow through earlier with Rocky, I decided to make this a teaching moment:

HANDLER (H): [Said to the therapist loud enough for Karen to overhear] Don't let him get away with not following your command. Here, get his attention. Remember? Tap your eye and say, "watch," and then try again. He needs to take you seriously. Rocky will try to get away with whatever you let him. You need to follow through with him and not give up once you ask him to do something.

THERAPIST (T): Okay [as she patiently tries again]. Rocky, watch! [She taps the corner of her eye to get Rocky to focus, and then gives the hand signal to high-five. Rocky looks around the room to see if he really has to comply since the therapist does not have a treat and is not his handler. As the therapist gently persists, Rocky then slowly lifts his paw and high-fives the therapist. Karen, the therapist, and I cheer.]

KAREN (K): He didn't bow to me when I asked earlier [said rather disappointedly].

H: You just need to be patient and not let him get away with not listening to you. He's just like a child. He has to know that you are serious. Let's try again. Rocky, come! [Rocky quickly comes over to Karen and me at my request.] Remember the command to bow? Now tap your eye to tell him to focus on you. And give the command.

K: [Karen obediently taps the corner of her eye as Rocky focuses in.] Rocky, bow! [Rocky glances at me as if to ask, "Do I have to listen to her?" I quietly give the body command for "bow" to reinforce the client's efforts.]

H: Say it again, Karen [as I help to get Rocky to take the client seriously. Rocky then takes an obedient bow to the delight of Karen.] See, you just have to hang in there, and insist that he listen to you, just like a child.

K: That's so cool!

Knowing that Karen has difficulty with this very same issue (following through with requests to demonstrate she is serious) with her child was key to designing this spontaneous teaching intervention.

By using Rocky as an example of the importance of patiently insisting that he follows requests, and teaching Karen that he will do whatever he is allowed to do (i.e., ignore requests) the stage is now set for transferring this learning more directly during future treatment sessions. In addition, Karen can also apply this learning herself as a result of the parallels that were created during this interaction. The therapist in my office was unaware of the teaching I was doing with Karen, as she did not know the parenting issue and had not witnessed the previous interaction that I had with Karen earlier that day. This is a nice example of how subtle interventions can be, allowing those around the therapist and client to naturally play a part without necessarily being privy to the purpose behind the interaction.

Finally, the therapist can use the handler and therapy dog's relationship to model and create possible parallels for a healthy "parent-child" relationship. Therapy dogs, like children, can become distracted. Rocky, for example, frequently breaks from his disciplined, loose-leash walking when we are walking down the hallways when he sees a familiar client or staff member. He wags his tail, and makes it clear to me that we should stop or change direction and spend a few minutes visiting with this friendly person. I appreciate this sociable quality in him, and I value his opinion about who he would like to visit. This quality is also really appreciated by clients and staff, for it is apparent to them that visiting them is Rocky's idea at times and this is just the greeting that makes their day. (I don't demand robotlike obedience from Rocky and our setting does not require this level of discipline.) How the handler responds to the therapy dog's interest and "requests" can serve an important role in teaching parents how to respectfully handle their children's normal interests, desires, opinions, and distractions.

In the real world, it is all too common to see a person who is walking a dog on the street yank on the leash and drag the dog away from whatever has caught his eye during the walk. This kind of interaction is very similar to some of our clients' responses to their children when the child becomes distracted. The parents impatiently insist that their child keep moving by pulling on the child's arm as they move along, or alternately, they resign themselves to having no control over the child, and just yell for the child to return to their side. Neither approach demonstrates the respect for the child, nor the important and necessary ability to control the child's behavior in a win-win fashion.

Clients and visitors are frequently surprised to see how I respond to Rocky's interest and distractions. The following is a common scenario while walking down the hallway at the agency:

> Rocky interestedly looks to the left as we pass the walking room and then suddenly shows recognition of a client by slightly lowering his head, wagging his tail, and making a left turn to approach the recognized person; his whole body showing excitement and his doggy "smile" resulting in a return smile from his intended visitor. Upon seeing his reaction and his efforts to approach the client I stop and say, "Hey, there's your friend! We need to put this down first and then we will go visit."

Now remember, when saying this I am fully aware that Rocky has no idea what my words mean. My words are meant to give Rocky a voice to those around me and to explain why, despite Rocky's warm welcome, we will not be stopping to visit right then. It also provides a form of positive reinforcement to Rocky for his friendliness and communicates to him that while I will be redirecting his interest momentarily, I fully appreciate his love of people and that his interest is not in any way a problem or an undesirable behavior. I then gently and respectfully get Rocky's attention to insist that he come with me to finish our errand. I may use my hand to gently tap him, very gently give a tug on his leash, or redirect him verbally knowing that, like a child, he very well may be so excited about seeing this client that he has forgotten to listen to me (Clothier, 2002). This patient insistence that Rocky be "with me" (Clothier, 2002, p. 73) despite the distraction is a powerful way to role model how a parent can effectively work with normal child distractions. My gentle taps, quiet verbal commands, and even a soft hand redirecting Rocky are similar to how I would treat a fellow human being who had forgotten in all the excitement that I was still beside him or her. There is an insistence that I be remembered, yet a genuine appreciation for Rocky's interest (even a curiosity and validation on my part of what caught his eye and what interests him). This respect, curiosity, and genuine appreciation, combined with an insistence that Rocky cooperate with me despite his interest and desires provide a powerful role model for parents who are struggling with their young children's behaviors and personalities. Although the therapists and the handler may not make any direct verbal connection between the therapy dog/handler relationship and the client's parenting goal in the moment, the therapeutic parallel has been set in place for future use.

Improve attention or concentration.

Some people do best when they have something to fiddle with when nervous or when discussing difficult things. For others the very act of fiddling may result in increased comfort, attention, and relaxation. This might be part of who the person is, a symptom of the presenting problem, or situational to coming to treatment or to a new setting. While traditional therapy might include analyzing the behavior to determining the cause, solution-focused therapists find the cause much less relevant, choosing to focus instead on the desired solution. Solution-focused therapists believe that regardless of the cause, if it would be helpful for the client to fiddle, it is best to provide the opportunity to fiddle and simply accept this as part of who the client is, thereby providing the necessary therapeutic opportunity to focus on the desired solution.

People's natural reaction to a therapy dog is to touch—to pet the soft fur, to flop the tail or ears, to touch the wet nose or tongue, or to explore the rougher textured pads on the feet. There are many textures on a dog, and the very presence of a therapy dog gives permission to indulge in touch and to casually fiddle during a conversation. It is common to observe clients in the waiting room run their fingers through Rocky's long fur as they continue a conversation with a staff member or fellow client. Others sit on the floor and touch his tail or feet absentmindedly as they discuss clinical issues with their therapist. There is a casual and relaxed feel in this type of interaction. Clients are not alone in their need to fiddle. We find that staff members are just as prone to fiddle during staff meetings and supervision when Rocky is present. I have even found myself slipping off a shoe during a meeting and gently petting Rocky's side with my socked foot as he sleeps at my feet. There is a calming effect in this type of touch.

Therefore, it is wise to be observant of how clients respond to the presence of the therapy dog and to notice when clients absentmindedly fiddle with the dog. When this occurs, notice the effect on the client. Should this effect be one that would be desirable during a therapy session (i.e., increased concentration or comfort level) consider including the dog in the session to achieve this effect. The very presence of the therapy dog in the session can also be a wonderful way to explore this desired trait in more detail during the session as well. The following describes how this might occur:

THERAPIST (T): I notice that you seem so comfortable and relaxed as you pet Rocky.

CLIENT (C): Yeah. He's a great dog.

T: It reminds me of the peace that you mentioned in your miracle day. Is it at all similar to what you described?

C: Yeah, I guess it is. I hadn't thought of it in that way.

T: So a little part of your miracle is occurring right here?

C: Yeah! [said with increased vocal energy as she starts to make the connection]

T: So, what other parts of your miracle have already occurred, even for just a moment or two?

C: Well, I've had times that that peace has happened at home as well.

T: Really? Tell me about them.

Rocky's presence with the client resulted in a calming effect that was similar to one of the desired traits that the client described when answering the miracle question. By observing this positive change in the client while she interacted with the therapy dog in the session, the therapist was able to recognize an exception that was occurring in the moment and to assist the client in exploring this exception to the problem. This exception could then be expanded to ones that occur outside of the session in the client's natural environment.

Improve ability to manage depressive symptoms.

Clients who struggle with depressive symptoms frequently present with a serious tone, with minimal affect or vocal animation. Sadness and tears can become the norm. Depending on the severity of the symptoms, the client may give a professional minimal eye contact, have slower movements, or even believe that they are unlovable or worthless. Animals can have an incredible impact on some clients who are struggling with these symptoms. In this day and age, it is inappropriate for a therapist to freely offer physical affection to clients. Even appropriate touch such as an empathic touch on the shoulder is often withheld due to fear of how it might be perceived. A therapy dog knows no such limits. Therapy dogs genuinely show recognition and interest in people as they wag their tails and give a happy "doggy smile" as they approach. A dog can freely approach a client (once permission is received of course) and joyfully lick the client without abandonment, frequently resulting in a smile if not full-blown laughter. Some of our clients have not experienced such a happy greeting by anyone in years. The very fact that the greeting was given by a dog (rather than the therapist) frequently adds to the therapeutic element, for the dog is not perceived as having an agenda or being able to fake such enthusiasm. The following is an example of how we have used a therapy dog with a depressed client:

THERAPIST (T): Wow! Rocky sure is happy to see you today!

CLIENT (C): Yeah. [A faint smile emerges as she continues to pet Rocky as the session begins.]

T: So, what's different since last time we met?

C: Nothing, really. I really didn't do anything. I don't have any friends anymore.

T: So what did you do to keep things from getting worse?

C: I just stayed home. It's lonely. None of my family or friends want to be with me anymore. I guess I'm no fun anymore.

T: Rocky seemed pretty interested in being with you today. He's not one to hide his true emotions.

C: Yeah. [She smiles as she pets Rocky.]

T: So, I'm just curious, what do you think that Rocky knows about you that other people don't know? Maybe even something that you forgot about yourself?

C: Humm . . . I guess that I really do like him.

T: And what does he see in you that lets him know that about you?

C: That I don't push him away when he comes up to me; that I pet him and interact with him.

T: And what difference does that make that you don't push him away and that you interact with him?

C: He stays and wants to interact more.

T: How does this fit into your miracle that you described a while ago?

C: Well, I want people to stay and interact with me?

T: So, what parts of your miracle are occurring now in your relationship with Rocky?

C: I'm not pushing him away.

T: And what are you doing instead.

C: Letting him know that I want him around.

T: So if we put all this on a scale with 10 equaling that you are living your miracle and 1 equaling that it is so bad that even a dog wouldn't give you the time of day, where would you say you are?

C: [laughing] Well, it's not that bad! I guess I would say a three.

T: Wow! A three! So what lets you know you are a three and not a two?

C: Well, there's Rocky. And, I've actually been talking to my neighbor when I'm out watering the flowers.

T: Really! Tell me more about that.

Rocky's natural exuberance toward the client made it very difficult despite her depression for her not to smile at times during the session. By noticing this exception to her depressive symptoms the therapist was able to use this when traditional questions initially yielded little reward. The therapist was able to use Rocky and invite the client to give Rocky a voice. It was through this voice that the client could explore what she was currently doing that encouraged the very relationships that were part of her desired miracle. By playfully including a dog in the definition of a one on the ten-point scale, the client was able to continue a more lighthearted response and she was required to give herself credit for the efforts that she exhibited with Rocky during that session. Once the client was able to acknowledge some progress, the client more readily acknowledged her progress in other areas outside of the therapy session, with her neighbor.

Acknowledging and using behaviors that the client offers during a session (such as positive interactions with a therapy dog) is especially useful with clients who provide minimal answers to questions either due to depressive symptoms or fear of the therapist's response (i.e., externally motivated clients). We find it a very effective way to both highlight exceptions to the presenting problems as well as to demonstrate to the client that our role is to focus on what the client wants and to notice positive behaviors. This frequently serves as a jumping-off point to exploring other positive behavior that has been occurring in the client's life that was previously not mentioned or noticed by the client.

Other Considerations When Identifying Clients for AAT

Some of the important factors to consider when screening clients for the appropriateness of AAT can seem rather elementary, however we would be remiss not to mention them here. The first is making sure that the client desires the interaction and that the client does not have any condition such as animal-related allergies that would make it a negative experience. Although we discussed allergies at length in Chapter 4, due to the increased length of time that the client may spend with the animal during an AAT session, it is very important that the client does not have allergies that would be unduly exacerbated by the therapy dog's presence. Some clients who have mild allergies welcome casual contact with dogs, knowing that their allergic symptoms will be very mild, and they view the contact as well worth the inconvenience of allergy symptoms. However, having a client come into a treatment room in which the dog spends a significant amount of time will increase the client's exposure to allergens and may cause an increased allergic reaction. In addition to all of the precautions that are mentioned in Chapter 4 to control for allergens, the client should be made aware of this possible increased risk when engaging in AAT if he or she suffers from allergies. If the client is a child, the parent should be apprised of the increased amount of exposure to allergens and should give consent prior to an AAT session. In addition, there should be an alternative room available that is free from allergens in which the therapist can provide treatment services for those clients whose allergies would be exacerbated by allergens left behind despite regular janitorial care.

Second, parental permission is essential for the involvement of any child in AAT. This is important not only to screen for possible medical conditions and phobias, but also to ensure that the parent truly understands the methodology behind the use of the animal so that the parent continues the work outside the session. The use of a therapy dog, while fun, is not for entertainment. Parents can mistakenly view the presence of a dog to be solely for the purpose of making the child happy (similar to giving out candy after a doctor's appointment). If a parent's perception of the therapy dog is left unchecked the therapeutic impact of the AAT session can be lost. Parents should be encouraged to continue to work with their children to notice positive behavior in everyday life, and to utilize parallels and lessons learned while in the dog's presence. For example, let's revisit the case we mentioned earlier about Mathew brushing his teeth. The mother may be encouraged to continue to playfully remind Mathew about Rocky's liver-flavored toothpaste and how much it helps him to tolerate brushing his teeth. In addition, this lesson will also help the mother remember the importance of doing her part in getting child-friendly paste and toothbrush and in persevering during difficult times with her son.

Third, the therapy dog must truly enjoy being a part of the AAT session and a part of the intervention or role necessary for the particular client. Dogs do not show the same amount of interest in all clients, and it can do damage to a sensitive client to include a therapy dog that does not show any interest in the client or who would rather be somewhere else. On occasion, the lack of the therapy dog's interest can be used in a therapeutic way (to point out cause and effect of the client's behavior), however the dog's feelings and welfare must be paramount during every intervention. This type of intervention is often best done without ever involving the dog by simply observing a client and then using the content in a session. For example:

CLIENT (C): I want my little brother to leave me alone when I want him to. I don't like being bugged.

THERAPIST (T): I noticed that Rocky seemed to know to leave you alone as you walked by today. He's usually so friendly, but he steered clear of you today. What do you think he saw in you to know that he shouldn't bug you and that he should leave you alone today?

C: That I was walking fast and didn't look at him.

T: Okay. I can see how that would send him that message. What else do you think he saw?

C: That I was really focused.

T: How would he know that?

C: Because I was serious.

T: So, in your miracle, what is your little brother seeing in you to know when not to bug you?

C: I guess the same things. I might have to remind him though. He forgets sometimes.

In this example having Rocky in the session would not be appropriate or necessary. The therapist is using an observed interaction (or lack thereof) with Rocky to explore behavioral aspects of the adolescent client that might occur during an exception to his problem with his little brother. Having Rocky present in the session would not only be unwelcome by the client (as evidenced by his ignoring the dog), but might be unwelcome by Rocky (as evidenced by Rocky's lack of interest in the client). This example also serves as a good reminder that a significant amount of clinical work can be triggered by the presence of a therapy dog, while not requiring the dog to actually be present for the session at all.

Fourth, when working with a therapy dog in an AAT session it is imperative that the therapy dog be comfortable with the client and the surroundings, both for safety and therapeutic reasons. Should the dog be uncomfortable, the dog might feel a need to take protective action. In addition, the client may sense the dog's uneasiness and might personalize the dog's behavior in an untherapeutic manner. Dogs vary in the amount of unpredictability with which they are comfortable. The handler must be aware of the dog's comfort level and make efforts to maximize the comfort for the dog. One way of doing this is to have the clients work with the dog in a room in which the dog is familiar and feels comfortable. By bringing the clients to the dog (versus requiring the dog to move locations), the dog's stress level is decreased (Davis, 2002).

As part of ensuring the therapy dog's welfare, the therapist must ensure that the client's behaviors are appropriate for the inclusion of a dog and do not pose a threat to the animal. Clients who have difficulty controlling impulsive behaviors or who are unpredictable in their actions may need to work with the therapist prior to introducing a therapy dog to the session until the client is able to respond predictably to the therapist's directives. Because protection of the therapy dog is critical to both an effective and ethical AAA/T program, we strongly recommend that clients are never allowed to be alone with a therapy dog. Clients frequently come to us with horrific pasts, and often have behaviors that can be harmful to others. Many have histories of sexual and/or physical abuse. Others have histories of perpetrating these forms of abuse on others. Although these histories alone are not something that preclude the clients' work with a therapy dog, the therapist/handler must be alert to the need to closely monitor the clients' behavior with the animal and be prepared to intervene immediately to advocate on the dog's behalf as needed. It is the professionals' responsibility to keep the therapy dog safe at all times and to never put him in harm's way. Therapy dogs cannot communicate to us their concerns or their discomfort if we are not present to notice or listen.

GOALS AND PURPOSE

Having clear and defined goals and desired outcomes prior to utilizing a therapy dog with an individual client are the hallmark of AAT. Without it, any work with a therapy dog falls into the category of animal-assisted activities instead. These goals and outcomes should be written into the client's case file and progress notes are needed to track the services provided as well as the outcome of the intervention. Although this may seem rather daunting, the creation of an AAT treatment plan is no more complex than those utilizing any other intervention. There are two ways that AAT treatment plans can be written: specific in the treatment plans or more broad as a tool to change the therapeutic environment of the session.

AAT As Specifically Written into the Treatment Plans

When thinking about writing a treatment plan for a medical intervention (such as developing the muscles in an arm), the intervention seems rather straightforward and easy to write. Incorporating an animal into a medical treatment plan simply involves identifying the traditional physical treatment, and then utilizing animal-related activities that will simulate those same movements. For example, the following might be the goal and steps for such a treatment plan:

Goal: The client will develop fine motor skills in her right arm.
Steps:

1. The client will fill the therapy dog's water dish, using her right arm to turn on the water faucet and to assist her left arm in holding the dish and setting it on the floor, one time each session.

2. The client will throw the ball for the therapy dog with her right arm for a minimum of five repetitions each session.
3. The client will brush the therapy dog with her right arm using long strokes from the dog's neck to tail for ten minutes each session.

In this example, it is clear how the filling of the water dish, throwing of the ball, and brushing of the dog would result in the client utilizing the muscles in her right arm, thereby furthering the development of fine motor skills. These exercises are similar to the movements that would be traditionally prescribed, however they are animal-related in this AAT session. It is also very evident how by completing these tasks, the client would make significant strides toward independent living skills outside the treatment session. There is an obvious cause and effect relationship between the two. However, it is more challenging when writing a mental health treatment plan. It is further complicated when the therapist is using a solution-focused approach since in such an approach the therapist believes that it is the client who is the expert on himself or herself, and that the therapist is only an expert on the process. Such a therapist would rarely prescribe such a clear intervention as described earlier. Solution-focused treatment plans are much more process oriented, prescribing various interventions (such as the client answering the miracle question or a scaling question) while allowing the client complete freedom within the intervention to explore and discover the necessary steps needed to resolve the problem. The therapist then holds the client accountable to achieving the goal through the use of questions throughout the session, thereby assisting the client to discover the steps necessary to reach the desired outcome. Despite such limitations and challenges, it is possible to write a solution-focused treatment plan that includes AAT interventions and still holds true to the basic tenets of solution-focused therapy. We have found that the key is to put the therapy dog intervention under the therapist's steps rather than the client's steps (similar to how we would list a group-setting modality). This allows the client to complete traditional solution-focused interventions, while allowing the therapist to involve the therapy dog as a tool or modality to elicit exceptions to the problems, compliments, etc.

For example, let's look at an ethnic minority client by the name of Samantha. She was referred to our agency by Social Services due to concerns that her children were not receiving adequate care stemming from their parents' substance dependence. There was no missing Samantha and her children when they were at the agency. Staff members described it as a whirlwind as the children ran out of control, touching, yelling, running, etc., down the hallways, while Samantha made feeble efforts to control them, to no avail. Staff members would heave a collective sigh of relief when the ordeal was over and the family headed into the parking lot to go home.

In the beginning of this case, I kept Rocky behind closed doors during the family arrival because of Rocky's dislike of loud, out-of-control children. However, one day, there was a knock on my door while Marc and I were in supervision. Upon opening the door we found one of the therapists asking if Rocky could come out and meet some children for her. I quickly snapped on Rocky's leash, and we headed out into the hallway. There we found three wide-eyed young boys (between the ages of three and five years old) standing there with toys beside their smiling mother, all quietly staring at Rocky with wonder. Rocky eagerly wagged his tail in anticipation. Considering that the hard plastic toys could be a potential hazard to Rocky once they began to clumsily pet him, I suggested that they ask their mother to hold the toys for them as they enjoyed a visit with Rocky. They quickly pushed the toys into their mother's open arms and then sat on the floor in a row (including the mother) as per my request, each boy the model of obedient eagerness. They then laughed as Rocky snuggled with them, licked their faces (with mom's permission of course), and performed tricks. I then asked them each to pick a trick to ask Rocky to perform, allowing them to "give Rocky a treat for being such a good boy." I explained that Rocky only gets a treat after he has listened carefully and obeyed. After approximately fifteen minutes, the family said their good-byes as Rocky bowed to them to their delight. Marc and I returned to my office to finish our supervision. The therapist then came into my office and thanked us for coming out with Rocky. She then said that was Samantha and her children, and she had told the children they could meet a wonderful dog and have a visit if they walked slowly and quietly in the hallways. I was shocked! I didn't even recognize Samantha, and would never have guessed those well-behaved children where the same kids who previously created havoc at our agency.

As a result of that therapist's idea to change the children's behavior at our agency by promising a visit from Rocky, we learned many things about what works for this mother and her children. During that visit, I noticed that Samantha responded well to my suggestions to her children (e.g., "How about you have your mom hold your toys so you can pet Rocky." "Let's sit on the floor so we can watch Rocky better.") She quickly assisted her children in following my suggestions (even modeling good behavior by sitting on the floor with them) and appeared to understand her role in helping her children to comply with these vague directives. She worked as a team with her children so they could enjoy the interaction. These were all valuable behaviors we had not previously seen from the family. We also learned that her children responded well to a positive incentive for desired behavior. This was an important lesson that Samantha noticed as well. These were valuable observations that could later be used in our work with Samantha. This impromptu AAA visit was the foundation of a treatment plan that was subsequently created for future AAT sessions.

From this AAA visit, we created a treatment plan to assist Samantha in developing the skills necessary to effectively manage her children's behavior in a purposeful manner (see Figure 6.1). The client steps in this treatment plan are the sort of traditional solution-focused therapy interventions that you would find in most of our client treatment plans. They include tasks such as answering the miracle question, making a list of current skills, and noticing times when she is using environmental cues (such as my suggestions to her children during our AAA visit) to manage her children's behavior. All of these tasks are designed to assist Samantha in envisioning how life will be once she is able to effectively manage her children's behavior and in identifying and continuing behaviors that she finds effective.

Upon a cursory look at this treatment plan, it might appear that AAT interventions are not being employed. The Therapist's Steps however are the key to understanding the modality and tools that the therapist will be using as the client completes the solution-focused work. The therapist's role is to not only ask solution-focused questions such as the miracle question throughout all sessions, but to also facilitate AAT family sessions and to provide solution-focused feedback to Samantha about her parenting. The therapist must carefully listen to Samantha's miracle and how she wants to parent her children,

INDIVIDUAL TREATMENT PLAN

CLIENT NAME: CLIENT #:

THERAPIST NAME: DATE:

****

GOAL: The client will develop the skills necessary to effectively manage her children's behavior in a purposeful manner.

SHORT-TERM OBJECTIVE: The client will identify specific skills she needs to effectively manage her children's behavior in a purposeful manner.

DUE DATE: 6/1/04

CLIENT'S STEPS:
1. The client will describe how her life will be different when she is able to manage her children's behavior in a purposeful manner x 1. (MQ)
2. The client will make a list of the skills she is currently using to purposefully manage her children's behavior x 1.
3. The client will make a list of skills she could begin using to more effectively manage her children's behavior in a purposeful manner x 1.
4. The client will notice times that she uses environmental cues to purposefully manage her children's behavior 2 x per week.

SHORT-TERM OBJECTIVE: The client will practice using the skills necessary to manage her children's behavior in a purposeful manner.

DUE DATE: 6/1/04

CLIENT'S STEPS:
1. The client will continue to do the things she is currently doing that assist her in managing her children's behavior in a purposeful manner 1 x per week for five weeks.
2. The client will practice at least one new thing each week from her list of things she could begin doing and share her progress with the therapist 1 x per week for five weeks.
3. The client will notice what difference it makes when she is cognizant of environmental cues to assist her in managing her children's behavior 2 x per week for five weeks.

THERAPIST STEPS:
1. The therapist will facilitate AAT family session 1 x per week for five weeks.
2. The therapist will provide feedback about the client's parenting 1 x per week for five weeks.

_____   _____   _____   _____
CLIENT SIGNATURE   DATE   THERAPIST SIGNATURE   DATE

****

_____   _____
DATE CLIENT COMPLETED GOAL   THERAPIST SIGNATURE

FIGURE 6.1. Sample Treatment Plan

and then provide compliments, acknowledge differences, notice exceptions to the problem, etc., that occur during the family session.

The therapist may learn the specifics about Samantha's miracle during the family session or individually during other interactions with her. The family sessions provide an opportunity for the family to interact together with the therapist present and for Samantha to practice new skills, etc. The therapy dog's presence simply provides further opportunities for the therapist to notice, compliment, and ask additional questions about what is working as she parents. In addition, the therapist and handler can model limits, give suggestions to the children about how to interact with the therapy dog, etc., all providing opportunities for Samantha to practice using environmental cues similar to what might occur naturally in the environment to purposefully manage her children's behavior.

Although the content of the family sessions could occur without a therapy dog present, the therapy dog lightens the mood and adds a happy energy for all, which allows the session to feel more like a special treat, rather than therapy. Rocky's presence and behaviors can also be used by the parent or therapist as a reward for good child behavior. For example, should the children become unruly, Rocky would need to leave the session, for he is not comfortable with such behavior. This is an excellent cause and effect lesson for the children. They can then take pride in how safe they made the environment during the session for their new friend, so he could stay and play with them. This also assists in building empathy and nurturing skills for children.

Following a family session the therapist would chart the progress of the AAT session. For example, the following note might be written following a session with Samantha and her children:

> The client and her three children attended an AAT session (separate handler/therapist model used). The client was attentive to the handler's suggestions throughout, and the children quickly responded to the client's guidance in assisting them in interacting safely with the therapy dog. The client was attentive to her children's affect, and was able to effectively remind her son about the rules and redirect him when he began to escalate without incident. The client rated her ability to effectively parent as a 6 on a ten-point scale (10 = goal is complete and 1= no control over her children's behavior at all). We discussed ways that the client can give the children a reward to look forward to

and to reward the children's good behavior at home. The client suggested planting a garden with the children to assist them in learning and working together.

Sometimes clients present with only vague problems, citing that they simply need to attend treatment in order to meet their goals. Such was the case for Julie. Julie was a young Caucasian mother whose daughter had been removed from her care by Social Services due to her substance dependency and resulting child abuse/neglect. In Julie's mind, her caseworker was unreasonable and no changes were necessary in order to get her daughter returned. Julie loved Rocky, and frequently sat on the floor to better interact with him. While with Rocky, she comfortably chatted about her daughter, visits at Social Services with her daughter, employment struggles, etc. She expressed disappointment on Rocky's days off, and was clearly more relaxed and happy when interacting with him. Her mood quickly changed when it was time to attend treatment groups or to meet with her therapist. Talking about personal subjects was challenging, and Julie complained of feeling "quizzed" in these settings. Julie was asked to leave group session on several occasions due to her difficulty following the group leader's directives and her "short-fuse temper." After much discussion about how we could help her, she and her therapist agreed that helping her to better cope with authority figures and to be perceived accurately by others would be a place to start.

Since Julie appeared so markedly different when interacting informally with Rocky, this seemed an important component to include in her treatment plan. However, since Julie did not believe she had a problem nor needed treatment, suggesting Rocky as a therapy tool would most likely be ineffective. (We did not want to change her view of Rocky as the only therapist at our agency who did not have an agenda. By including him in a structured treatment session, we might have changed her view of him, and therefore the benefit of the visits.) Therefore, we simply included the AAA visits into the treatment plan under the Therapist's Steps (see Figure 6.2). By including the therapist in the AAA visits that were already occurring, the therapist could then purposefully notice exceptions to the problem (e.g., times in which Julie was responding well to staff directives, times she was being perceived how she would like to be perceived, times she was happy and smiling despite a difficult day), provide compliments, etc. The content of these visits could then be used during the more formal

INDIVIDUAL TREATMENT PLAN

CLIENT NAME: CLIENT #:

THERAPIST NAME: DATE:
****

GOAL: The client will develop the skills necessary to be perceived how she would like by others.

SHORT TERM OBJECTIVE: The client will identify specific skills she needs to be perceived how she would like by others.

DUE DATE: 6/15/04

CLIENT'S STEPS:
1. The client will describe how her life will be different when she is able to be perceived how she would like to be by others x 1. (MQ)
2. The client will notice when she is perceived how she would like to be by others x 1.
3. The client will make a list of things that she is doing when she is perceived how she would like to be by others x 1.
4. The client is make a list of things that she could do to increase the likelihood of being perceived how she would like to be by others 1 x per week.

SHORT TERM OBJECTIVE: The client will practice using the skills necessary to be perceived how she would like to be by others.

DUE DATE: 6/15/04

CLIENT'S STEPS:
1. The client will continue to do the things she is currently doing that assist her in being perceived how she would like to be by others 1 x per week for five weeks.
2. The client will practice at least one new thing each week from her list of things she could begin doing and share her progress with the therapist 1 x per week for five weeks.
3. The client will scale how accurately she is perceived by important others (1= not at all and 10=very accurate) 2 xs per week for five weeks.

THERAPIST'S STEPS:
1. The therapist will provide AAA visits 2 x per week for five weeks.
2. The therapist will provide group sessions 2 x per week for five weeks.
3. The therapist will assess clients progress as needed and once at the end of five weeks.

_____ _____   _____ _____
CLIENT SIGNATURE   DATE   THERAPIST SIGNATURE   DATE

****

_____   _____
DATE CLIENT COMPLETED GOAL   THERAPIST SIGNATURE

FIGURE 6.2. Sample Treatment Plan

sessions in addition to purposeful compliments and differences that could appropriately be made in the waiting room or hallway settings. These interactions were then charted in the client's file. While to the casual observer, the staff interactions with Julie might appear unplanned and spontaneous, in reality, they were a structured part of her treatment plan, with the therapist's comments having the purpose of highlighting client progress. This made the AAA visits very purposeful and therapeutic for this client, therefore falling into the category of AAT. The following is a sample note that might have been included in Julie's file following one of these visits:

> The client completed an AAA visit prior to her group session. She sat on the floor and playfully interacted with this therapist, the handler, and the therapy dog. She spoke about a visit with her daughter at Social Services today. She stated that she brought her daughter some carrot sticks and juice for a snack. She stated that she believes the case aide at Social Services noticed her efforts to bring a nutritious snack for her daughter. She stated that despite her anger at "being watched" during the visit, she was proud of how she handled herself. When asked how she was able to do so well during the visit, she stated that she "just focused on how much I love my daughter. She's all that matters." She stated that she has been actively looking for a job in order to provide for herself and her daughter.

AAT with General Goals

Despite the specificity of the treatment goal, for some clients the desired outcome for using a therapy dog is more general and does not lend itself well to inclusion in the treatment plan. In such cases the decision to use a therapy dog should be clearly noted in the client's file under an assessment and treatment recommendation section, although the use of AAA/T would not necessarily have to be noted in the treatment plan. (If the therapist decided to include it in a treatment plan, it would best be listed in a manner similar to the case example in Figure 6.2.) This type of decision is akin to a therapist choosing to use an individual versus group treatment modality, in which the desired outcome could occur in either modality, but a specific modality is chosen due to the perceived additional benefit of one over the other. In these cases the abbreviation AAA/T noted in the client file is an accurate way to describe the intervention, for it indicates that it is really a combination of AAA and AAT. An intervention labeled AAA/T contains the purposefulness and client-specific design of an AAT intervention, however the intervention itself may take more of an AAA structure even though it is provided during a treatment session. Let me give an example to explain.

Let's return now to a previously mentioned client, Susan, the adolescent client who I saw through my private practice. I offered to include Rocky in our sessions due to her apparent discomfort in the therapy session and due to her marked change in affect when I mentioned the possibility of involving a therapy dog. In addition, her mother was concerned that Susan might be suffering from depression and wanted my assessment. Given Susan's behaviors in my office I was initially unsure if her one- or two-word answers were due to a depressed mood, nervousness, or attitude. My hypothesis was that Rocky's presence would allow me to see the "real" Susan. If it was nervousness, then she might feel more comfortable around the therapy dog and begin to warm up quicker than she would without him. If it was depression, then I would expect to see an initial improvement in affect, but I would expect to see her mood return to a depressed state if the depression was endogenous and psychotropic medications were needed. If indeed it was depression and her depressed mood was more situational in nature (as I initially suspected), I would expect her mood to initially improve once she met Rocky followed by an increased comfort level talking to me about what was going on, thereby allowing me to ask solution-focused questions to help her resolve her difficulty. Finally, if it was attitude, I would expect a subtle positive change in her behavior when interacting with Rocky when she "forgot" I was looking followed by a return to the attitude when she "remembered" I was there. This could easily be overcome by focusing more on Rocky's presence and taking less of a "therapy" tone in the session.

My initial purpose in involving Rocky in Susan's sessions was that of a diagnostic tool. Animals have a wonderful way of helping human beings be more genuine and in the moment. That is precisely the outcome that I needed with Susan. In order to help her, I needed her to let me know who she really was. She was unable to tell me with words, so using a therapy dog seemed an effective way to reach this goal.

The outcome of including Rocky in this case was amazing. Rocky was able to draw Susan out of her shell during the very first session. Susan smiled with happiness as soon as Rocky and I greeted her and her mother at the door the following week. "You brought him!" she exclaimed as she patted him on the head and followed us back to the office. Although she remained rather tentative (she remained on the couch in my office while I sat on the floor with Rocky), she laughed and smiled as Rocky did his best to snuggle and engage her. Soon she was asking him to perform tricks and then squealing with mock disgust as only an adolescent can as Rocky drooled on her leg while enjoying a treat she had given him. Rocky's presence also gave me an excuse to sit on the floor and take a more informal stance in the session. Kicking off shoes and sitting on the floor all seem to make sense when a dog is in the room (even with adults), while it can be perceived as rather odd and even unprofessional without one. I soon learned that my initial assessment was correct. Susan was suffering from situational depression, which lent itself readily to solution-focused techniques. Rocky's presence also provided the perfect excuse to take a short break from conversation when the subject was too hard. Occasionally Susan would stop mid conversation and say, "Can I have Rocky high-five?" We would pause for a few moments of laughter and playful interaction, and then I would segue back to solution talk once again. Rocky would comfortably take his place on the floor at Susan's feet and beside me, and she would pet his soft fur with her toes as we talked. All of these interactions were charted in Susan's file, noting them as AAA/T.

OTHER ISSUES COMMON TO AAT

Before finishing our discussion about using therapy dogs in actual client sessions, a few additional matters should be briefly discussed: how to proceed with a scheduled AAT when a therapy dog cannot attend, the importance of termination with the animal, and self-disclosure.

When a Therapy Dog Cannot Be Present

On occasion the question has arisen, "What if the dog is ill and can't attend a scheduled AAT session?" Because the therapy dog is a tool used by the therapist, the session can continue without the therapy dog. Although the client will most likely be disappointed, the work of the therapy session is not dependent on the presence of the dog. The foundation of animal-assisted solution-focused therapy is still solid solution-focused therapy. The therapy dog simply enhances the work and makes the therapist's job much easier. Take the case of Samantha and her children for example—while the children would be disappointed if Rocky was not present for a session, the therapist can still observe the family's interaction as they play with toys, draw pictures, etc., thereby continuing on with the solution-focused treatment plan in the dog's absence. The primary difference will be the lack of energy or emotional spark that the presence of an animal has on people. When a therapy dog is ill or not able to attend due to medical concerns it is also important to notice and acknowledge the caring and concern that clients express on the animal's behalf. These are very caring gestures that are worthy of compliments, and can be utilized therapeutically. Clients become attached to therapy dogs in much the same way as they form attachments with other staff members. Just as efforts would be made to terminate with human staff members, care should be taken to not overlook these bonds and to assist clients in saying good-bye to the therapy dog as treatment ends.

Self-Disclosure

As a rule, our staff members do not use self-disclosure with clients. We believe that it could be distracting for our clients to know very much about our history and current personal lives, because while two people may share similar problems, frequently their solutions are different. When self-disclosure is used, it can be tempting for clients to view the therapist as the expert and forget to remain focused on discovering the best solution for themselves. We find it best to help our clients to remain solidly focused on their own miracle and in exploring what their own solutions will be. Clients seem to really appreciate our position on this once we take the time to explain it, and rarely ask questions about our personal lives.

We have found that adding Rocky to our staff has had a slight impact on this subject, however, for his very presence is a form of self-disclosure. As his handler, I am frequently asked where Rocky goes at night as clients and visitors are curious to learn about the life of a therapy dog. Being around a working dog is a new experience for many, and they are curious about who owns the dog, how he acts on his leisure time, how he ended up in this line of work, his level of training, etc. The answers to all of these questions are very important in order to maintain the credibility of using such an intervention in a professional setting. However, the answers to all of these questions contain information about my personal life.

Initially, as I began to answer these questions, I was leery as to how personal these questions might become. I understood the importance of answering every question that was directly about Rocky's profession and qualifications (similar to questions I would deem appropriate about my qualifications and training), however, the answers to these questions were close to information about my family and personal values which I feared, if made public, would become a distraction to our clients. I soon discovered that clients and visitors had an uncanny way of stopping the questions just short of personal information about me or my family. These disclosures about Rocky's life remained on the same professional level as we strove to keep other conversations between staff and clients. However, they had a more casual feel that often led to more therapeutic conversations about parenting or being consistent. For example, as people asked about Rocky's eating habits, I frequently mentioned that he does not eat table scraps and the importance of this to prevent begging in a therapy dog. This kind of conversation frequently leads to conversations about how difficult it is to say "no" to children or pets. This provides me the opportunity to empathize in a therapeutic manner by saying, "Yes, it can be very hard, however, I have found it very worthwhile in the end. How have you said 'no' to your child when it really counts?" Amazingly enough, this kind of conversation does not lead to clients then asking me if I have children, etc. The focus just stays squarely on the client and his or her desired solutions.

SUMMARY

Including a therapy dog in a treatment session can have an incredible impact for the client and can make the therapist's work much easier. However, the hallmark of good solution-focused therapy is purposefulness and working from a place in which the problem is resolved. Including a therapy dog in this process does not change these basic tenets, it enhances them. The therapist must have a clear purpose for including the therapy dog in the treatment session, a desired therapeutic outcome, and documentation that describes this process and outcome. The next chapter will look at specific considerations when working with special client populations.

Photo by Nancy Braden. Used with permission.

Chapter 7

Applying AAA/T to Special Populations

> Listening means an awareness, an openness to learning something new about another person . . . listening with the intent to learn is an approach to a different type of conversation.
>
> Elizabeth Debold

As a social worker by profession, I (TP) learned from the start of my career the importance of valuing and respecting a person's culture, gender, developmental stage, sexual orientation, religion, and every other part of a human being that makes up the uniqueness of his or her essence. However, I will never forget that moment in graduate school when I first realized how easy it is, when focused so intently on learning every possible classification of demographic differences, to succumb to the all-too-human trait of generalizing accepted information about a group of people and no longer recognizing or truly valuing the uniqueness of the human being in front of me, undermining the very efforts of understanding and respecting differences. On this occasion we were asked to write a case study about a client from our internship and to include details about how treatment should be modified according to the client's ethnicity, gender, etc. When I thought about this client, I realized how different she was from the stereotypical information I was learning in school. As I talked to my clients, I realized how unique each one was, and how inaccurate my assumptions would have been had I used the general information about their identified culture as a foundation for understanding them. Although some of what I was learning was accurate for a few of my clients, it began to make more sense to assume nothing and simply ask my clients directly.

The more I learned about the general characteristics of Hispanics, African Americans, Catholics, transgendered individuals, adolescents, females, or any other group of people, the more I forgot to find out about the person in front of me, i.e., who he or she is, what he or she values, or how he or she views the world. Despite (or perhaps because of) my training, I had to take a step back, put the academic learning into perspective, and reclaim my natural curiosity and desire to truly listen to the wonderfully unique human being right in front of me. The information this person shared was by far more useful than any book learning about cultural sensitivity and differences could ever be.

Taking the time to explore various client populations and how they might be uniquely impacted by or benefit from animal-assisted activities and therapy (AAA/T) is important in order for the reader to fully appreciate the power of AAA/T. However, such a chapter also runs the risk that I discovered in graduate school: that of overshadowing the importance of being curious and really listening and valuing the uniqueness of the person sitting across from us, as our brains review the theoretical information and drown out the client's words and our own curiosity. Despite the possible risk, we have decided to include such a chapter, believing the benefits outweigh the possible risks. We do so with a cautionary observation from Suzanne Clothier (2002): "A dancer who concentrates on technicalities may forget to hear the music" (p. 44). As you read this chapter and apply this information to your work with clients, never forget to let your clients' music fill your heart.

WORKING WITH CHILDREN

As Insoo Kim Berg and Therese Steiner's (2003) book, *Children's Solution Work,* so eloquently explains, solution-focused therapy is a natural compliment to how children think and view the world. Children are experimental—they accept their reality for what it is without the need for analyzing the cause, and they move quickly to solution building. Similarly, AAA/T fits naturally into a child's world. Children are taught from an early age to love animals and to associate them with positive and playful experiences. Animal characters are present in children's lives frequently from the very beginning. Animal characters are on the baby's toys, clothes, furniture, sheets, and wallpaper just to name a few objects. In addition, animals are commonly the theme in nurseries as well as in pediatric and maternity hospital wards. As if that isn't enough exposure to the animal world, adults naturally animate stuffed animals during interactions with babies and young children and give the animals human characteristics (e.g., making the stuffed bear appear to talk and dance to the child's delight). Children soon learn to associate animals with comfort, play, and home (Sussman, 1985). As the child grows, cartoons and books are full of talking, dancing, and thinking animal characters. These animal characters take the role in story books to teach the child about potty training, obeying mom and dad, looking both ways before crossing the street, and other necessities of life.

Whether it is H.A. and Margret Rey's stories about Curious George, Stan and Jan Berenstain's lessons told in the pages of the Berenstain Bears, or even the classic Dr. Seuss tales, most of us have fond memories of some animated animal from childhood books. Life's lessons are naturally taught through parallels from animals' lives, and children readily understand and apply the embedded lessons. Creating therapeutic parallels using a living therapy animal is a natural way to work with children and to utilize this already established and highly effective method of learning.

Matching the Therapy Dog to Children's Work

Working with children comes inherent with its unique challenges for dogs. Children can be loud, boisterous, unpredictable, and lack motor skills. They are similar to adults from the dog's perspective, but they move and sound so different! They are known for running, screaming, making odd noises, and many other qualities that can be unnerving at best for dogs. Because of this, it is imperative that a therapy dog who is expected to work around children for a significant period of time be specifically matched for his ability to not only tolerate these things, but to enjoy the experience. It can be a challenge to find such a dog. When working closely with a therapy dog organization such as the Delta Society or Therapy Dogs, Inc., using a visiting dog model, professionals from these organizations can help to identify a therapy dog team that is highly skilled and comfortable working with this population. However, if you are using a resident handler/dog model, it can be more challenging due to the significant amount of time the dog spends at the agency, the wide variety of possible situations the therapy dog team may encounter, and the lack of close guidance from a governing therapy dog organization. In this setting, a resident handler/dog team must be well matched for the population with which it is working the majority of the time.

In addition, the dog must be able to be well controlled when encountering individuals from other populations as well. The handler must also have a specific plan to address or avoid situations with which the dog may not be comfortable and be able to control the environment to minimize stress on the animal should a difficult situation occur. Working closely with a professional dog trainer who is well versed with the specific needs for both the animal and the agency's clientele when doing therapy dog work and who can design training lessons specific to the agency's and animal's needs is very helpful and can prevent potential problems. (This is a wise precaution to take for continuing education for the therapy dog team regardless of any specifically identified stressor.) Finally, knowing the therapy dog well and respecting the dog's preferences, have an important role as well. This allows the handler to predict possible problems and to act in a proactive manner.

Dogs who have difficulty around children frequently have a specific age range or specific child behaviors that they find stressful. Dogs rarely are all-or-nothing in their preferences. For example, Rocky usually prefers to not be in close proximity to most children between the ages of two through six due to their difficulty controlling their movements, high excitability, etc. He is especially uncomfortable with a group of such children who are boisterous. Specifically, he dislikes it when children run toward him, squeal, or exhibit other similar unpredictable movements, regardless of the child's age. However, he enjoys children in this age range who are relatively quiet, who are responding to adult directives, and who move slower. Because of this, I began private lessons working with a professional therapy dog trainer who designed and taught me ways to increase Rocky's comfort level in these situations. However, I continue to carefully watch for children while Rocky and I are working and assess if their movements will be problematic to Rocky and if they will cause stress beyond his training level. If I determine that Rocky will be uncomfortable, I take another path through the agency whenever possible. When not possible, I decline any visits with children if I don't have a second therapist with me to help manage the children's behavior with regard to Rocky. When Rocky is requested to work with a specific child, I first assess if the situation is appropriate for Rocky and then I educate the child and parents about how to respond to Rocky in a way that maintains his comfort. This then becomes part of the designed intervention, adding the element of empathy for Rocky's feelings as well as cause and effect for the child. (Rocky will need to leave if the child will not comply with the behaviors Rocky needs.) For example, when working with Rocky the child needs to use an "indoor voice," allow Rocky to approach rather than run toward him, and engage in quieter activities such as coloring or drawing, talking, playing with puppets, etc. These limitations work fine in our setting since the majority of Rocky's work is with adults and children over the age of six, however Rocky would not be an appropriate dog in a school setting or child treatment center.

Common Interventions

Once the appropriate therapy dog has been found, there are many ways to integrate a therapy dog into working with children. The ways are only limited by one's imagination. As Berg and Steiner (2003) repeatedly stress, the key to working with children is to really hear them and to use mediums that are consistent with who the child is and how they best communicate. According to Berg and Steiner (2003), "The underlying principle is to listen to them to learn how unique each child is and how each one makes sense of the work in a unique way" (p. 14). Similarly, the most appropriate therapy dog intervention will take into account the activity level of the child, if the child likes to read, draw, is more tactile, etc. All of this will be integrated into an intervention that keeps the desired goal in mind. Frequently the intervention itself is "dog inspired" but does not actually require the dog's presence, leaving the dog free to be present or not at the handler's discretion during the actual intervention. Here are a few ideas and examples.

Stories and Books

As mentioned previously, a common child-teaching technique is to use animals to tell stories that contain lessons. Childhood books are filled with animal characters and most books have a lesson that becomes clear in the end. For example, Stan and Jan Berenstain's Berenstain Bears series has stories about moving, helping others who are in need, arguing with siblings, blaming others, etc. All of these stories strive to help the reader to learn an important lesson while enjoying the antics of the Bear family. When a therapy dog is present, children are frequently curious to learn about the dog, who he is, what he likes, what the child might have in common with the dog, etc. This natural curiosity allows the therapist to pick and choose stories about the dog's life that contain similar teachable moments that are therapeutically appropriate to the child's treatment goal. For example, the following story might be helpful when working with a child who does not like having to listen to his mother's limits, even though the limits are to keep the child safe.

THERAPIST (T): When Rocky was a puppy, he was very curious. He would put his nose into everything! See how long that nose is? Can you imagine what all that nose was in? He was very cute, but I worried about him. I worried that he might put his nose in the oven when I took out the dinner, or that he might put his nose in the electrical socket or chew on a cord. I also worried that he might run into the street to chase a squirrel if I didn't keep him on a leash.

CHILD (C): Ohhhh! [very worried] He could get hurt!

T: Yes! He could. I was very worried. He was just a little puppy, and he didn't understand that I just loved him and didn't want him to get hurt. He would get mad at me for telling him "no" all the time. He didn't understand why I said "no." He just wanted to see what everything was. He was very curious.

C: But you had to keep him safe.

T: Yes, even though it made him mad.

C: Did he bite you?

T: No, he knows that it is not okay to bite or hurt me no matter how mad he feels, but I'm sure he might have been so mad at me he thought about it.

C: What did he do when he was mad?

T: He knows that it is okay to be mad, and he does things to make himself feel better that doesn't hurt anyone. He has bones to chew on, and he would go play with his toys and growl at them until he felt better. When he came back he felt much better. He knew that I was okay that he was mad, but he couldn't hurt me when he was mad.

C: Is he still mad at you?

T: No, he learned that I only wanted to keep him safe. He trusts me and that when I say "no" I have a good reason because I love him. He also learned how to stay safe. He is very wise. He knows not to sniff the dinner when I pull it out of the oven, and he knows to not chew on electrical cords and other things that would hurt him. He is a very smart dog.

This story provides a possible parallel to the presenting problem and to the mother's stated solution for the therapist to then explore with the child how the child's mother keeps him safe, how the child remembers that his mother does it because she loves him, etc. It also provides a valuable teaching opportunity about the difference between feelings and actions. This work combined with working with the mother to teach her how to use these kinds of child-friendly teaching tools, provide a language which the child understands, validates feelings, sets limits, and strengthens the relationship between mother and son. Rocky was present during this story, increasing the power of the story, as the child looked over at Rocky at various times, deepening the child's concern through the reality of a real dog who could be hurt. Rocky's presence also demonstrated Rocky's positive relationship with me now (Rocky showed no sign of ever being "mad" at me), providing a visual that anger is an emotion that passes. However, his presence would not be required for such an intervention.

According to Sussman (1985), children often view pets as an extension of themselves and treat pets as they would want to be treated. Using this concept to allow children the opportunity to create their own stories about animals is a powerful way to understand a child's heart. When a dog is present and children are encouraged to write their own story or draw a picture, it is very common that the dog will appear in their story or drawings. It is a safe way to express what is in the child's heart and forefront in the child's mind. The therapist can then ask questions about the child's drawing or story to better understand and then therapeutically guide the conversation. For example, the following conversation is common using this intervention:

THERAPIST (T): Wow! What a great picture! Tell me about what you drew.

CLIENT (C): There's me, Dad, my brother, and Rocky.

T: That is quite a nice picture. What are you guys doing?

C: I'm watching TV. Dad and Robert are fighting. Rocky is scared.

T: That's right, Rocky doesn't like it when there's a lot of yelling. It looks like you are helping Rocky feel better in the picture. What are you doing?

C: I'm covering his ears.

T: That is so nice of you! I'm sure he really appreciates you thinking of him and keeping him safe.

C: What else do you think might help Rocky feel better when he is scared?

A lot of valuable information was disclosed by the child in this picture. Although Rocky is not a part of her family, she included him in the family picture without direction since he is part of her session today. It is very common for children to include animals in their stories and pictures and to have the animal express their feelings, thoughts, or desires. By asking questions about this, children frequently give clues as to what they wish someone would do for them or about what makes their lives just a little better.

A key difference that makes the session solution focused is that the therapist's questions focus on understanding the child's perspective of the solution and what works, rather than about the problem. In addition to working with the child about coping strategies, feelings, and behaviors, the therapist can then work with the parents to help them make necessary changes in the environment to address the child's discomfort and fear.

Another useful way to use stories and books is demonstrated through the more formalized R.E.A.D. (Reading Education Assistance Dogs) program. This is a volunteer program through Intermountain Therapy Animals (see Appendix A for additional information about this resource) and utilizes registered therapy dogs and their handlers to improve literacy. The dog (and handler) serves as listener and facilitator as the child reads animal-related stories. Beyond the educational intent of the program, additional possible benefits would be to increase the child's self-esteem, provide positive attention to a child accustomed to negative attention, role model to the parent how to positively attend to the child, increase empathic skills ("find a book the dog might enjoy" or "make the dog feel comfortable"), and improve the child's social skills while interacting with both the dog and the handler. Although this is traditionally done using a visiting dog model, it could be done using a resident handler/dog team using the R.E.A.D. format and materials as well (see Figure 7.1).

Dog Photo Album

It is common for therapy animal handlers to carry a small photo album with them containing carefully selected pictures of the dog at various stages of his or her life. This can be particularly helpful in a therapy setting. For example Rocky's photo album contains pictures of him from puppyhood to the present. Included are his very first puppy picture, photos of him behind his baby gate, playing with his favorite toys, wearing a protective "lamp shade" after a visit to his doctor, playing in the snow, camping in the woods, learning to climb

FIGURE 7.1. Child "Reading" to Rocky Through the R.E.A.D. Program (Photo by Susan Trimmer. Used with permission.)

stairs, working with his teacher at school, working with clients at work, and so on. Each photo has the potential to be the beginnings of an effective parallel for a child. For example, the following conversation occurred while a child was looking through Rocky's photo album:

CLIENT (C): What is he doing here?

THERAPIST (T): That's Rocky at school with his teacher, Patti. He had to concentrate really hard to understand what she was asking him to do. Rocky didn't understand English when we got him, so he had to go to school to understand what we were saying to him. See how hard he is working?

C: Um hmmm. School is hard.

T: Yes, it can be very hard. What helps you get through the tough times at school?

Children tend to be the most curious about photographs that contain parallels to their own struggles and issues. This provides a natural forum for children to see the dog in similar settings to their own (e.g., with family, playing, sad after a doctor's visit, at school). This allows the children to relate to the dog and put themselves in the dog's "paws." Including pictures which allow the children to project their own feelings onto the dog can be especially helpful, for example:

C: He looks sad in this one.

T: Yes, sometimes he's sad.

C: What makes him sad?

T: When he has to stop playing, when he has to take a bath, when he has to go to bed and he doesn't want to. All kinds of things.

C: I don't like to be sad.

T: Yeah, being sad isn't fun. What helps when you are sad?

C: Drawing pictures.

T: What do you draw that helps you when you are sad?

Finally, photo album interventions can be used to teach basic hygiene or safety skills. This may be done by including pictures of the therapy dog wearing a seat-belt harness for the car, wearing various outdoor equipment such as a leash or harness, or pictures of the handler brushing the dog's teeth or other grooming. Children are fascinated by the life of a dog, and these types of pictures provide excellent parallels to hygiene or other safety activities in the child's life as well.

Direct Interaction with the Dog

Children who are more action oriented frequently benefit from doing things with the therapy dog. Conversations between the child and therapist during the activity are a natural result and can be about the therapy dog activity or simply derive from therapeutic parallels. In addition, more action-oriented children frequently benefit from instruction about how to safely meet a new dog and how to treat a dog with respect, for they are at higher risk of rushing toward or invading a strange dog's territory in the community without thinking about the possible consequence. Learning these lessons with a highly trained therapy dog and his handler as the teachers is a good way to learn about not only dog safety but empathy and thinking before acting as well. These are valuable lessons to include in a therapy session.

Once a child knows the basics of how to interact safely around a therapy dog and how to consider the dog's feelings, interactive activities can begin. Two examples of possible activities are taking the dog for a walk around the facility and asking the dog to do simple obedience tricks. Let's look at these two interventions in more detail.

Walking a therapy dog contains valuable lessons and potential therapeutic parallels for a child. Now it is important to note that under no circumstances would we ever recommend that anyone other than the handler actually handle the dog. This would create undo stress for the therapy dog and would create potential safety risks. However, there are ways in which a child can safely walk the dog while the handler still retains full control of the animal.

For example, by using a standard six-foot leash (or one that contains a second handle close to the dog), the handler can hold the leash close to the dog, while giving the end of the leash to a child to hold. The dog can then walk between the handler and child, as the dog responds to the handler's lead. The child then happily holds the end of the leash during the walk, and the dog is provided necessary guidance from the handler while the handler's hand close to the animal protects the dog from sudden jerks on the leash by the child. The therapist/handler can use this opportunity to talk about how to walk a dog, how to respect an animal's feelings, or about any number of things. Many therapeutic parallels can come from such an interaction. For example:

CHILD (C): Look! I'm walking Rocky!

THERAPIST (T): Yes! Look how well he is walking with you. He looks very happy. Look at how his tail is wagging as he walks. That's how I know he is happy. How would I know if you are happy?

C: Well, I'd be smiling. See? [shows a big smile] I'm happy too.

T: I see! What makes you happy?

C: Walking Rocky.

T: That makes me happy too. What makes you happy on other days? Days that you can't walk Rocky?

Walking together through the agency allows the child some private, personal time with a caring adult, and also provides him or her with the pride of seemingly handling an animal (this can be especially empowering when the dog is large). Children are frequently exposed in the community to dogs who lack good manners, and seeing a well-controlled dog is oftentimes a rare experience for many. This only adds to the pride a child may feel about being able to "control" such an animal.

It is not uncommon that some children confide their belief during this exercise that "control" comes from force. This may take the form of the child running ahead to try to drag the dog or give the dog loud or harsh commands. This is a wonderful opportunity for the handler not only to protect the animal but to teach the child that control comes from respect and partnership. The handler can show the child how the dog responds to just a quiet whisper or even a hand movement. This provides a powerful parallel for the therapist to use with the child during future sessions.

During walks with the therapy dog and handler, the child may gain additional positive attention from others who witness the child with the animal during the walk. It is common to hear the child say to others during the walk, "See, I'm walking him!" This can lead to positive conversations with the child about other tasks in which the child excels or takes pride in his or her accomplishment. For children who are timid or fearful, the fun of successfully walking a large animal can provide just the needed motivation to face their fears and to take a risk. Children frequently say "yes" in nervous excitement to the opportunity to interact with a therapy dog, the excitement and love of animals overcoming the natural apprehension and fears of interacting with a large animal. The therapists can then provide compliments to the child for being so brave, and then explore other times that the child has been brave. It is a wonderful opportunity for the therapist to explore how a child knows when taking a risk is a good idea, etc.

A second activity that children frequently enjoy is asking the therapy dog to do simple obedience tricks. Having the dog trained in both verbal and hand signals can be very helpful for this, for this allows the handler to give subtle hand signals to the dog if the dog fails to understand the child's poor enunciations. Commands such as "sit," "down," "shake," and "roll over" are all good commands for a child to give to a dog. Commands that require more physical contact with the dog, such as "high five," catching a treat off the dog's nose, or "jump" (through a hoop or over an obstacle) are often best done by the handler as the child observes. Asking a therapy dog to follow commands can be an empowering experience for a child. A therapy dog may be the first creature who has listened and responded to the child with such enthusiasm and genuine compassion. This can result in the child feeling heard and important. Teaching the child to respond to the animal with praise and appreciation are equally important lessons, for it is often the social relationship and interaction between the child and therapy animal that hold the most profound learning. This type of interaction teaches children to respectfully make requests and then to express gratitude when the request is granted. It further holds lessons about the importance of speaking in a way that the listener can understand (the child needs to use commands that the dog understands in order to get the desired response). The handlers can provide treats for the child to give to the dog in addition to verbal praise if the dog is sufficiently trained to take treats gently. Children frequently enjoy being able to feed a dog and witnesses the dog's enjoyment in receiving a tasty morsel. Therapeutic parallels about nutrition, weight, earning rewards, etc., are easily created from adding the elements of treats to the session. The following exchange demonstrates a possible parallel:

CHILD (C): Wow! Look at how he doesn't eat the bone! [watching Rocky balance a dog bone on the end of his nose at my command]

HANDLER/THERAPIST (T): Rocky, take it! [Rocky effortlessly flips his head and grabs the bone and begins to enjoy his well-earned treat to the child's delight.]

C: Why didn't he grab it sooner?

T: Because I asked him to leave it on his nose. He knows that he should trust me if I tell him not to touch something.

C: That must be very hard for him. He loves bones.

T: Yes, I'm sure it is. That's why he looks at me during that trick to know when he can take it. How do you keep from doing stuff that you really want to do, but you know that you shouldn't?

C: Well, my friends offer me pot all the time, but I know that I shouldn't do it.

T: What reminds you that smoking pot isn't something that you really want to do right now?

Visit/Session Reminders

Children enjoy mementos of their time with a therapy dog. These serve as a keepsake of their time together as well as a reminder of the lessons learned during the session. The types of useful mementos are limited only by the imagination of the therapist, and the most appropriate kind of memento is best tailored to the individual agency setting. Some ideas of mementos are instant photos of the child with the animal, a bookmark or business card that contains the dog's picture, or cards that contain personal facts about the dog (such as the dog's birthday, favorite activities, breed, etc).

We have designed "business cards" for Rocky that contain his photograph as well as a few fun facts about him that we give to children (see Figure 7.2). The children, as well as the adults, enjoy these cards and find them an enjoyable way to end a visit. The excitement from receiving the card and the child's eagerness in looking at it, help to offset the disappointment of ending time with the therapy dog. Because we use the cards during casual visits as well as more formal therapy activities, we have included facts on the cards that add to the credibility of the animal program (such as Rocky's credentials) as well as facts that increase familiarity and make visitors and clients smile (such as Rocky's favorite games). These cards also serve as a way for visitors and clients to share their experience meeting our therapy dog with others after they leave the agency. We have had

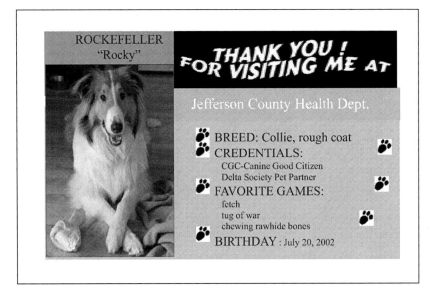

FIGURE 7.2. Rocky's Business Card (Photo by Mark Hochstedler. Used with permission.)

many clients return and tell us that they gave the card to a family member or a friend and request another one. These cards play an important role in encouraging clients to talk about their experience at our agency and the lessons learned here outside the agency and into their day-to-day lives.

Photo Identification Badge

Many agencies require that all employees obtain and wear a photo identification (ID) badge during working hours. When agencies utilize therapy dog teams, it is often helpful for the therapy dog to also obtain a photo ID badge. Although this may seem rather frivolous at first thought, the therapeutic parallels and the conversations that result from visitors, clients, and even other employees seeing the dog's ID badge are invaluable. The photo ID badge adds credibility to the therapy dog team, demonstrating that the agency fully endorses the animal program and the dog as an "employee." This sends a powerful message to clients and visitors, and frequently results in questions about the dog's training and job role. The following conversation is common when clients observe Rocky's ID badge (see Figure 7.3) for the first time:

CLIENT (C): Look! He even has his own ID badge.

THERAPIST (T): Of course! All employees are required to wear their ID badge at all times.

C: That's really cool. So what does he do around here, anyway?

T: Well, his job is to help people be more comfortable. Research shows that people tend to be more relaxed, their blood pressure and heart rate may go down, et cetera, when a dog is around. A lot of people really don't want to come here initially, and we find that Rocky makes it a little easier for them.

C: I can see that. I really didn't want to come today either.

T: I'm glad you came anyway. What let you know that coming here today was a good idea even though you didn't want to come?

FIGURE 7.3. Rocky's Employee ID Badge

Having therapy animals wear ID badges further reinforces to visitors and staff that dogs with these official badges are allowed into the agency because of their credentials and qualifications. Requiring ID badges minimizes visitors from mistakenly thinking that they are allowed to bring their own dog into the facility just because they see that a dog is allowed into the building. When we first developed our therapy dog program, we initially experienced an occasional fellow staff member who brought his or her uncredentialed dog to work to interact with clients once he or she saw that the administration was supportive of utilizing the therapeutic benefits of animals. Although these employees' intentions were clearly in the right place, the risk to clients and to the agency's credibility by their actions was high. While it is important that agency management sets clear limits and ensures that this type of maverick intervention is swiftly corrected, there may be a short period of time in which the dog is in the facility before action can be taken. By requiring that any dog who is allowed into the facility obtain and wear an ID badge, the agency has some protection from situations such as this, since unauthorized animals are quickly identified as nonsanctioned by the agency through the lack of an official badge.

WORKING WITH ADOLESCENTS

Adolescents can be a challenging population for many professionals. Many professionals find themselves taking a polarized stance on the subject, stating that they either love working with adolescents or they hate it. By their very nature, adolescents frequently delight in challenging adults' norms and ideas of how the world should be. Yvonne Dolan tells the story of her experience working with this population and playfully contributes her premature gray hair to her struggle to find a way to connect in a meaningful way to these kids despite their prickly exterior and shock-value stories (Pichot & Dolan, 2003).

Although it is easy to forget in the moment, adolescents' developmental task is to find their own way, to challenge the norm so they can determine who they are, what they believe, how they fit into the world, and what world views they will espouse as their own (Werner-Wilson, 2000). Adolescence is the time to challenge one's thinking and to hone the ability to think critically. It is a time to do this from the safety of the family, while there are loved ones on which to rely.

The Role of Values

Families pass on their values to their children. There are many life lessons parents must teach their children, and each family has strong beliefs about how these values are best taught. For example, my (TP) family strongly believed that every important life lesson could be learned through nature. They further believed that a simple life was best, thereby gravitating toward the wonders of nature, reading, and time without the distractions of the newest things that money could buy. They not only told me this, but they demonstrated this belief in how the family spent its time and resources. This resulted in a strong connection, respect for, and love of animals, plants, and people. Some of my favorite memories of family outings were to the zoo, the aquarium, the park, the botanic gardens, and camping. Although my family took us to ball games and other common family attractions, these places were not presented to me as rich in learning and did not hold the same value in our family. Weekends were not spent watching ball games on television (while we did watch the occasional Super Bowl or World Series), playing video games, or shuttling from sporting event to sporting event, but with picnics, gardening, and other nature-related activities. Walks with our dog and other family members were highly treasured, and lessons abound in the flowers, plants, and other living treasures along the pathways. Other families take very different paths to teaching necessary values to their children. For example, I have friends whose families strongly believed that every important life lesson could be learned from sports, and they tell a similar experience, substituting sports for every nature-related activity in my life story. They don't see the beauty and energy I find in nature and simplicity, and I don't find the excitement or meaning they find from a football game or from purchasing the newest gadget. Neither way of learning life's lessons is better than the other; just different. However, each stems from a different value system, and each instills a very different way of looking at nature, including dogs. How a child is raised and the degree to which the importance of animals and nature is taught in the family plays a tremendous role in how a person eventually views animals.

As I went through adolescence and challenged my parents' way of viewing the world I rejected many things as I discovered my true self, however I kept this value of nature and of a simple life. I would gladly trade fancy vacations and things for a quiet afternoon with my family and dog. Somewhere along the way, a deep love of dogs had taken hold. Not only did I fully appreciate the lessons that dogs held, but I felt a sense of happiness in their very presence. I found myself incapable of holding back a smile when a dog was present or a chuckle at canine antics. I truly admired the honesty and genuineness that dogs so freely offer to all around them. Their world of no "white lies" and not having to read between the lines was refreshing. I was in the fullest sense of the words, a "dog person."

Classifications of People Who Are Naturally Drawn Toward Animals

When working with people using therapy animals, it is important to recognize two distinct groups of people who enjoy and benefit from a therapy dog's presence. They are (1) people who have been taught or who have discovered that incredible lessons can be learned from nature (including animals), and (2) people who have an instinctual love of animals.

People Who Understand the Lessons Dogs Hold

As children, we are naturally drawn toward animals. Some parents encourage and nurture this attraction and others do not according to the family's value system. People who truly understand the value and the lessons that a dog holds by his very presence are easy to spot in a crowd. They rarely question the presence of a therapy animal in a professional setting, and if they do, they quickly nod with understanding when the benefits are explained to them. It is common to hear a client or visitor from this group say as they finish a visit with a therapy dog, "This is a really good idea. I wish more places included therapy dogs." They may or may not get on the floor with the therapy animal and fully engage with the dog. They can be more reserved in their interactions, but are clearly approving of the clinical purpose and role of the animal. They commonly tell others of the presence of a therapy dog and may bring family members (frequently children) to learn about and experience the therapy dog.

Adolescents can present as more reserved, especially when they are with their friends or peers. Adolescents are "other focused"; they are acutely aware of how they might appear to those around them. This concern about how they are perceived can take precedence to who the adolescents really are or what they truly want. Therapy is an opportune time to assist adolescents in exploring what they really value, and their opinions about animals can be a great place to begin. Adolescents will often welcome contact from a therapy dog, however they may not initiate it. We commonly first identify these adolescents sitting with their parents in the waiting room. As the parent shows overt signs of welcoming a visit from the therapy dog, the adolescent may sit more quietly, preferring to maintain his or her image. The adolescent may appear disinterested, but when asked if he or she likes dogs, the image quickly softens and the dog is welcomed. These adolescents may initially view the dog as being "for the kids" and view themselves as being "too cool" for the dog. However, these same kids are frequently seen sneaking a quick pet as they pass the therapy dog in the hallway. Although the adolescent may not initiate conversation or show interest while with peers, the therapist can use the adolescent's interest in dogs during private sessions as a way to learn more about the client and about what he or she truly values. This can be a valuable way to help the adolescent explore who he or she really is and the role the adolescent wants animals to play long-term.

People Who Have an Instinctual Love of Animals

Some people simply fall in love with animals and are drawn to them. These people may or may not come from an environment that actively taught them about the lessons animals can teach or the core values that animals share with the human race. While many come from families who purposefully taught their children about the values of animals, others seemingly discovered this on their own. By following their hearts and taking advantage of opportunities to associate with animals, some people have discovered the lessons that animals hold despite the lack of external education and reinforcement about the benefits of animals. Although all children seem to have this "instinctive gravitation toward animals" (Clothier, 2002, p. 2), some children outgrow it. However, for others the gravitation is so strong that despite the lack of reinforcement from their environment they find themselves unexplainably drawn toward animals.

These clients are impossible not to notice in a professional setting. They smile, point, and otherwise actively engage with the therapy dog. They frequently engage with the dog before acknowledging the handler, and their day is obviously made by simply seeing a dog. It is common for people from this group to sit on the floor, initiate "doggy kisses," and take other measures to put themselves in the best possible position to fully enjoy a moment with the therapy dog. They are the most genuine in these moments, for they are showing the therapist and all those around them something they love and a part of who they are.

Although adolescents in this group are notoriously more reserved, they cannot help but show interest. Some haven't had the opportunity to learn about animals or associate with dogs, but the interest and natural love is there. There is a natural spark that the therapy dog's very presence ignites. We have learned that when an adolescent expresses interest (whether verbal or nonverbal) in the therapy dog, this should be quickly and positively acknowledged and reinforced, for they are taking a risk of being viewed as "uncool" by stepping outside the typical adolescent facade and are showing the therapist a glimpse of themselves. This is a sign of thinking critically and discerning who they really are; the role of adolescence.

Common Interventions with Adolescents

A therapy dog is frequently used with adolescents in a similar fashion to how the dog is used with adults. There is no use of animal-related story books or walking the dog around the agency. Those are for children (as adolescents will quickly tell you). In order to communicate that I recognize they are no longer "children," I frequently find myself saying to my adolescent clients, "I sometimes have the kids brush Rocky or do tricks with him during a session, but the adults and people your age typically just like to have him hang out as we talk." This lets the adolescent know that adults use Rocky as well, but in a "more adultlike" fashion. This helps to justify their desire to include the therapy dog while ensuring that they are not using a child's intervention. Ironically, they (like the adults) frequently ask to feed Rocky treats and engage in tricks with the therapy dog, thereby blurring the line between child and adult interventions.

During the session, the role of the therapy dog can be quite varied. The dog may sleep unobtrusively through the session while the client gently pets him or fiddles with his fur (providing comfort during difficult conversation). Alternatively the dog can serve as a foundation for therapeutic parallels or the topic of initial questions about what really matters in the client's life. The following interaction demonstrates this:

THERAPIST (T): You are really good with animals. Look how comfortable Rocky is sleeping right next to you.

CLIENT (C): [Smiling as she gently pets Rocky.] Yeah, I like dogs.

T: How did you get to be so good with them?

C: My dad used to have one. I really liked hanging out with him. His name was Sam. My dad had to get rid of him though.

T: Oh. That's too bad. How did Sam make your life better when he was there?

C: He kept me company. It was great having someone to hang out with. He followed me everywhere. It was really fun [smiling again, clearly enjoying the memory].

T: How did having Sam make the times you weren't with your dad better?

C: I was happy. I knew even during the hard times that Sam would be there.

T: Tell me about the happy times now.

The therapy dog can even take a more active role in the session as the therapist utilizes the dog's reaction to the client, thereby providing a way for the client to learn about cause and effect. The following excerpt demonstrates how this is done:

CLIENT (C): Come here! [The client begins to be irritated that Rocky does not want to sit with him during the session.] Why won't he get over here? He is here as part of my session!

THERAPIST (T): Yes, he is here for your session, but he does have his own thoughts and opinions. I don't make him do what he doesn't want to do, just like I don't do that to you. Let's just go on with our session, and pay attention to when he does decide to come over.

C: Okay [clearly not amused by my idea].

[During this session we ignored the dog and went on with a typical session. At one point Rocky decided to go to the client, sniffing in interest, and expressing the desire to interact with him.]

T: Wow! Rocky decided that now was a good time to come sit with you. What do you think he saw that let him know now was a good time?

C: [Smiling and petting Rocky] I'm not so angry. He probably knew I wouldn't be any fun to be around before.

T: Hmmm. What did you do to help you not be so angry so you would be more fun?

Regardless of the role, the presence of a therapy dog helps adolescents to view the therapist and, by extension, other adults as being more approachable. This can be extremely valuable when working with adolescents who have had negative experiences with adults and who may view adults in a more authoritarian way. The presence of a therapy dog encourages smiles and playfulness. Taking the time to demonstrate tricks and allowing the dog to be himself (by carrying a dog toy through the hallways or playfully interacting with staff and clients) can work wonders in lightening the mood and starting a session off in a more productive fashion. Both the therapist and adolescent are seen by the other in a more genuine and human light.

WORKING WITH ADULTS

One of the most challenging aspects of working with adults can be how seriously they tend to take themselves and everything around them. Although therapy addresses deeply important and often painful matters and is therefore deserving of one's full attention, the absence of laughter and the positive spectrum of human emotion is frequently untherapeutic. Adult clients sometimes come to therapy with the assumption that they must explore their darkest secrets and confess their most horrific mistakes, thinking that somehow the answers to their problems will only be revealed as a result of engaging in these painful acts. Both solution-focused therapy and AAA/T challenge this thinking, postulating that change often comes from the most unexpected places, a time when things were just a little better or even from something as simple as a smile triggered from a dog's happy greeting. This can be a difficult paradigm shift for many adults to make. Herein lies the challenge (and paradoxically the beauty) of pairing SFT with AAA/T when working with adults.

Adults who have a love for animals or who appreciate the lessons that animals have to teach, often are already aware of the potential cumulative power of small, seemingly unrelated changes as an agent of change—they just may not have made the connection to how this knowledge might be related to solving their current problem. Our adult clients are quick to tell us (when reminded by the presence of a therapy dog) how much better their pets make their day. For some it is the quiet purring of their beloved elderly cat after a stressful day, while for others it is the warm greeting of their golden retriever when feeling unloved, or the companionship of a cocker spaniel on an afternoon walk when feeling abandoned by humankind. All of these are exceptions to problems that would otherwise go forgotten and possible solutions that would be unrecognized. These clients have experienced the change in mood and thinking that animals have made in their lives, and they know the lasting and profound impact that these animal-initiated changes have made. Having a therapy dog in the treatment environment allows the therapist to observe the client and to uncover solutions that the client might never otherwise bring into the therapy room (and a therapist might therefore forget to ask). While the clients might no longer have an animal of their own, the presence of a therapy dog serves as a gentle reminder that solutions are frequently not found by traveling the most painful path. This can be a wonderful therapeutic parallel for the therapist to use to help the adult client to begin the paradigm shift to searching for solutions rather than solving problems.

Taking advantage of parenting parallels is a wonderful way when working with adult clients. Clients who love animals enthusiastically volunteer to spend time with both handler and therapy dog regardless of their motivation for seeking treatment services. The majority of clients at our agency are mandated for services, making certain necessary topics difficult at best to broach. The following is a conversation that occurred spontaneously in the hallway with one of our pregnant clients:

CLIENT (C): Can Rocky visit for a minute?

HANDLER/THERAPIST (T): Sure! How are you doing today?

C: Good.

T: Have you met Rocky before?

C: No. I've seen his picture, but I haven't had a chance to meet him. He's really nice! Is he good with kids too?

T: Yes, he really likes kids.

C: How did you get him to be good with kids? They can be so mean to animals.

T: Yes, that can be tough. Kids and dogs both have to be taught how to treat each other. They don't know how without someone taking the time to teach them.

[This was said very purposefully to create a possible therapeutic parallel if needed since the client was pregnant and children and parenting are obvious possible issues. This lays the foundation for the client to take the conversation wherever the client desires while I am able to highlight the importance of teaching by a parent.]

C: My little boy (he's four) is really mean to our cat. He's a stinker.

T: I am very careful to protect Rocky from kids who don't know how to treat him nice. I find that kids really want to interact with him, so if I say they can only interact with him if they act a certain way (and I take the time to teach them) they try very hard. I make sure that I am always right there to protect Rocky and stop the child from interacting if he can't follow my direction.

[My response to the client's disclosure was very purposeful and conservative. I carefully only answered the question that she specifically asked me, thereby allowing the client to continue to lead the conversation and not feel threatened by any move on my part to change the conversation and discuss her own child.]

C: Yeah, I think my son would do okay if I took the time to teach him.

T: Great! What lets you know he would do well?

C: I don't think he really wants to hurt the cat, he just doesn't know how rough he can be. I think I need to teach him how to be gentle now since, when I have the baby, I need him to be nice to the baby too.

T: What a wonderful time to teach him!

WORKING WITH SUBSTANCE-ABUSING CLIENTS

While the integration of a therapy dog is clearly not limited by the scope of the client's presenting problem, we have had significant experience working with substance-abusing clients with our therapy dog since this is our primary clientele at our program. (It is important to note that the term "substance abusing" bears no correlation to any clinical diagnosis, and is used as a general term to describe behavior and not to define psychopathology. In actuality, the majority of our clients have abused substances to the degree to which that they qualify for a diagnosis of "dependence.") The majority of things that we have learned seem to transcend the presenting problem, and we have found no reason to this point to make any connection between the lessons learned and the client's substance abuse. However, there does seem to be a specific benefit of the use of AAA/T with this population that warranted special mention.

As clients succumb to a life of drugs and alcohol, they frequently lose sight of who they are and what really matters to them. Many of the simple things in life that were once cherished become overshadowed and neglected by a need for fast cash and a lifestyle of suspicion, violence, dishonesty, quick highs, and painful lows. This lifestyle is frequently incompatible with appreciating a child's smile or dog's wagging tail, and the crying of a child or the whining of a pet are seen as annoyances if seen at all. Thus, many of our clients become involved with Child Protective Services due to the child neglect and abuse that is inherent in this lifestyle. It is when our clients' lives are at their worse that we first meet. Their worries are dramatic, and large steps are court ordered. Our clients have lost the ability to notice and appreciate the simple, small occurrences that truly matter and soften the human spirit. Dishonesty has often become a way of life, and hiding who they are is commonplace.

AAA/T and SFT are a perfect match for clients in these very predicaments, for these approaches embrace noticing and value the tiniest of steps. While our clients often have temporarily lost the privilege of raising their own children, they can begin to remember to notice and appreciate the signs of affection that a therapy dog can offer. They can remember the joy of being recognized for just being them as they witness Rocky's unabashed enthusiasm as they entered the agency. All of this serves as a kind of melting of the heart as the clients rediscover who they really are and what truly matters in this world. Honesty and genuineness can be reexperienced, as a dog can be and understands nothing less. It is a reintroduction to the simple life once left behind.

CULTURAL CONSIDERATIONS

No discussion on special populations would be complete without taking a look at cultural considerations, yet ironically little is written about this subject and AAT. The love of animals appears to be rather universal, transcending most cultural barriers. At the time of this writing our country is at war. Images of war and destruction are a daily occurrence and fill the news. While the war is not being fought on American soil, there are images in print and on television that seem to show the humanness of the people in countries continents away; it is the occasional image of a person standing devastated, holding his or her pet. Although little else about the picture of a person standing amidst a war-torn landscape reminds most Americans about our current lifestyle and culture, the love and dedication to a pet in a time of sorrow strikes a chord. Likewise, headlines such as the one in Denver, Colorado, on July 12, 2004, which stated, "Iraqi Kitten Reunites with Fort Carson Soldier" (Associated Press, 2004), remind us that pets are in many countries and animals play a therapeutic role in countries and cultures as far away as Iraq. Stories from China tell us that despite laws that make pet ownership difficult, people in that country remain so dedicated to their beloved pets that they risk legal sanctions by breaking the law and keeping a pet despite their inability to pay the required exorbitant pet licensing fees (Eckholm, 2001). This and many other stories from countries all over the world tell the stories of a human-animal bond no different from what we find within the confines of American culture.

At our own agency, we serve Russian, Hispanic, African-American, and Native American clients, as well as clients from many other cultures. Many do not speak English. However, through the use of interpreters and primitive hand gestures, we have learned that the love of animals is common to all. Smiles, happy chatter and pointing, and encouraging children to look and learn from an animal are found in all cultures and are easy to recognize despite language barriers. The lesson that we take from this is that the love of animals is universal. However, it is important to also remember that some people from other cultures do not like animals, and some Muslim sects for example, even consider touching an animal something that is forbidden (Intermountain Therapy Animals, 2003-2004). Therefore, it is imperative that we don't assume and that each and every person is asked before including a therapy dog in the interaction.

SUMMARY

Animal-assisted solution-focused therapy is a powerful approach to working with people of all ages, presenting problems, and cultures. Although each subpopulation brings unique challenges and considerations, many specific interventions have already been developed and are readily adapted to the setting at hand. Additional interventions and ways of working with clients are limited only by one's imagination. While in this chapter we have taken a look at special considerations and have provided general guidelines, we hope that the reader will use these as a foundation only and will take the time to learn the uniqueness of each client and listen to who the client truly is, for this is at the heart of effective work with any special population.

Photo by Mark Hochstedler. Used with permission.

Chapter 8

Using Animal-Assisted Activities with Employees and Agencies

Dogs find our soft spots, keeping us in touch with a more honest vision of ourselves that doesn't buy its own facade.

The Monks of New Skete

Although we have spent the majority of pages discussing the positive impact that a therapy dog has on the clients of an agency, we would be remiss to not spend an entire chapter discussing the incredible impact that the presence of a therapy dog has on the handler and the professionals in both the agency and the community. This chapter explores this subject and explores how one can purposefully use the benefits of AAA to transform an agency setting.

IMPACT ON THE HANDLER

As a rule, I (TP) am rather shy. I enjoy solitude and prefer time with immediate family and a few close friends. Over the years I have found a way to disguise that fact rather well while in the workplace, for I am passionate about my work and am able to quickly lose myself in helping clients and staff. I enjoy talking about solution-focused therapy and teaching these concepts to professionals, even giving presentations to large groups and effectively facilitating group discussions. However, when the work day is over, I shy away from personal conversations with strangers. I'm a private person, and really don't like disclosing personal information. Ever since I was a small child, I have been misperceived as aloof and standoffish, while in reality . . . I am just shy. When working with my clinical team and with clients, I often forget how shy I truly am around strangers. Ten years of working with the SACP clinical team has bred familiarity and gradually worn down that shyness, exposing my sense of humor and a more personal side in the workplace. However, I have never been one to take significant steps in building personal relationships with other employees outside of my direct program. Although I have always ensured that working relationships were in place, I rarely initiated more than a polite, "Hello. How are you this morning?" in passing.

When the plan to bring Rocky into the workplace was approved, I had no idea how much bringing a therapy dog to work would impact me personally as the handler. I assumed the impact would be primarily for the clients and perhaps to my immediate staff. Rocky was already in my life as my pet, so it never crossed my mind that his presence at work as my partner would transform me and therefore my professional relationships as well. There is something about a genuine relationship with a dog that touches the soul. Because it is built upon a foundation in which words are not important, subtle movements and expressions hold tremendous meaning of what is in the heart. Some authors define this relationship as a path to spirituality saying, "Companionship with a dog touches the broader issue of our relationship with all of creation and with the creator" (Monks of New Skete, 2003, p. 60).

As Rocky joined me in the workplace, I found that the separation between who I was personally and the parts of me that I disclosed around strangers was harder to maintain. Rocky knew who I really was, and he depended on that same personal communication with him regardless of the setting. This meant that the silly, softer, playful side of me, the goofy voice that I typically used to give Rocky messages of praise and encouragement, and the signs of spontaneous affection that Rocky had become so accustomed to in private, now crept into the workplace. This not only relaxed Rocky, but his reaction to the "real me" and his spontaneous return of the affection relaxed me as well. Our relationship and companionship became a part of the work environment. Sitting on the floor with Rocky both in my office and in public places, kissing him on his nose, and affectionately ruffling his ears are now commonplace. Although my immediate employees had seen signs of this other side of me before, this was completely new to co-workers and other agency employees.

IMPACT ON AGENCY STAFF

Prior to Rocky joining our staff, our agency was similar to many agencies in that staff members frequently kept to their own departments and social cliques were common. Assumptions were frequently made about people about whom nothing personally was known. It was not uncommon for an employee to enter the agency, and the front desk staff not to smile in recognition or say "hello" to the individual. In return, the entering employee would remain focused on his or her destination without venturing to break the impersonal pattern. When Rocky entered the agency to begin his new job as therapy dog, the impact on the agency staff was almost immediate. Although agency supervisors and directors were well informed of the plan to add the AAA/T program, frontline staff members were full of questions as to the purpose of a dog in the Health Department. Other staff members did not seem to care about the clinical role or about the safety measures that had been taken prior to Rocky's arrival. They were simply excited to have a dog around. Employees quickly sought him out to visit and get to know him better. They smiled, laughed, initiated conversation, and shared personal animal experiences, all things that in the previous nine years they had never done around me. I saw a different side of these employees, a side that made me feel comfortable interacting with them on a more personal level and made me want to get to know them better. In response I was more genuine and relaxed around them as well. Rocky was like a social magnet for staff and was a topic of conversation; his very presence was an ice breaker. Rocky had a way (as most dogs do) of comfortably drawing humans out of themselves.

As Rocky and I walked through the hallways that first week staff members spontaneously smiled as we approached (something that rarely occurred previously). Sometimes they stopped and said "hello" to Rocky, asked questions about this new "employee," or talked about their own pets. Other times they simply smiled and patted his head in passing. There was a sense of warmth and a sign of acknowledgment of co-workers from other departments. I made an effort to learn their names and began to enjoy this contact as well. A sense of community was beginning as the perceived barriers between departments began to crumble.

As the weeks passed Rocky and I developed a sense of who really enjoyed visiting with him and who rarely if ever took the time to stop and visit as we passed. It seemed a natural progression to set aside time during each of Rocky's workdays to purposefully walk through the entire Health Department to take a few moments to make sure these staff members who really enjoyed time with him had a chance to visit. It clearly made their day, and truth be said, I really enjoyed seeing their reactions to Rocky and the sense of community that was being established. Without the reserved time, my busy schedule would have made this impossible. Staff members began to expect us to make our rounds, even calling my office to ask about Rocky if we did not show up. Employees started to bring dog treats for their visitor, and began to look forward to Rocky performing a trick or two in their offices to earn a reward. This served as a valuable break to their hectic day as they and other employees and visitors around them paused, snuggled with Rocky, and laughed at his antics. As the Monks of New Skete (2003) write, dogs "soothe the chaos of our own lives by the peace that is their fruit" (p. 25). Rocky certainly had a soothing effect on staff. His visits began to provide a much needed interruption and something to which to look forward as the challenges and headaches of normal health department life remained unchanged. These visits continue to be a highlight of our normal week.

Without Rocky, these twice-weekly visits would most likely be met with suspicion, for what would a supervisor be doing spending forty-five minutes to an hour going from employee to employee within other programs and divisions to chat? Without the therapy dog, the time would likely be perceived as wasteful and odd. However, with Rocky by my side the entire process makes perfect sense to all; a perfect break in an otherwise stressful day. Even supervisors and directors quickly saw the benefit of these visits on the staff members and were supportive.

Rocky's very presence by my side serves as a nonverbal self-disclosure that I love dogs. Everyone knows that Rocky is my personal pet, opening this area of my life up for questions and casual conversation. It allows a part of myself that would not otherwise be known to be seen by both staff and clients. Those who respond to Rocky and welcome visits from him are likewise publicly disclosing their love of animals. A natural response to this shared knowledge about each other is more disclosure about the shared commonality. Employees smile and laugh as Rocky comes in from the snow wearing snow boots, and questions about how I keep him so clean are the norm. Stories and updates about employee's pets are now part of the regular visits. Tips on training, animal mishaps, and pet upkeep are commonplace. As small groups gather to enjoy Rocky's company or to watch his tricks, all listen to updates about the family pets, children, and vacation plans. The conversations are always positive and laughter is the norm.

As is part of life, some of these pets have since died and others have experienced illness. Rocky's visits serve as a natural way to share these personal stressors and grief in an appropriate fashion with co-workers. For example, one day as Rocky eagerly pushed open one nurse's office door to greet her, we found her crying, with her eyes swollen with tears. She motioned us in, and Rocky rushed up to lick her face in his standard greeting, followed by a quick bow to request a treat. She could not help but to laugh at Rocky through her tears as she hugged him. She went on to tell me that her beloved pet may have cancer and that she had just finished scheduling medical procedures to get the lump she discovered that very morning diagnosed. During subsequent visits, Rocky and I made sure we checked in with this nurse about her pet. Rocky gave the physical affection that she so clearly needed and as only a canine can do. Rocky was also there to share her joy when she later learned the lump was benign and that her pet would remain a part of her family. During Rocky's first year at the Health Department three employees' pets had to be put to sleep due to illness, while another was hit by a car and lost a leg. We heard the stories of them all and shared the tears of sorrow. I even received an occasional e-mail from staff members informing me of an employee's loss and possible need for comfort from Rocky. After each loss of a pet, I gently inquired if Rocky's presence would be helpful or more of a painful reminder of what they had just lost. Each quickly answered, "Oh no! I was looking forward to hugging Rocky today. Please keep coming."

In addition to losses and illness in employee pets, employees throughout the department who have become part of our routine visits at times have personal crises and are absent from work. Rocky's regular visits add a level of closeness making it a natural next step to express concern for the employee. For example, when Rocky first started work as a therapy dog an employee named Laura was immediately drawn to him due to her love of animals. We visited Laura every chance we could. She walked with a crutch, and although Rocky was initially cautious of the crutch, Laura patiently showed Rocky it was okay by placing treats on the crutch. She took great pride in her role in helping Rocky become comfortable with crutches so he could pass his national therapy dog test. Rocky loved Laura, and would get excited every time he heard her crutch squeak in the hallway. Laura went on medical leave and was gone for a significant period of time. Rocky faithfully checked her cubicle for weeks during our visits looking for Laura. Upon her return, Rocky quickly resumed his visits and made it clear that Laura was remembered and welcomed back to work. She seemed to look forward to seeing Rocky her first day back as well.

These positive relationships and interactions continue even on days that Rocky is not at work. Although the conversations are frequently centered on Rocky, the interaction allows the relationship to continue in Rocky's absence. For example, the following interaction is very common as I walk down the hallway:

EMPLOYEE (E): Where is our buddy, Rocky, today?

TP: He's at home relaxing and catching up on his sleep. He'll be here tomorrow.

E: Oh. Well, he deserves it. I'll have to see him tomorrow then.

TP: Yeah, he works hard. I'll make sure and bring him by. Are you having a good day?

E: Yeah, it's been pretty busy, but it's going okay.

TP: Great! We'll see you tomorrow.

Such interactions were rarely if ever initiated by line staff of different programs prior to Rocky's presence. Now they provide opportunities to enhance the comfort level of the environment, to bridge programs, and to better meet client needs.

In addition to the wonderful personal connections and stress relief that are inherent in our visits with staff, a surprising amount of work takes place on these bi-weekly visits. These regular informal meetings with employees throughout the Health Department are a wonderful way to check in about work-related matters, explore possible areas of collaboration, and learn about each others' work projects. They serve to jar each others' memories about ideas and small details that might otherwise remain overlooked. For example, one day one of the nurses caught me during an AAA staff visit and asked, "Hey did you get my message yesterday?" I hadn't, and if she had not have seen me and checked it out, she might have assumed that I had purposefully overlooked her request to staff a case. Our impromptu AAA visit resulted in us taking the time right then to staff the client's case and offer additional collaborative services between our two departments.

During the staff visits throughout the Health Department, Rocky and I occasionally encounter outside visitors who would like a visit. We always do our best to take a few moments and introduce them to Rocky and his role at the agency. Visitors and clients always come first. This occasional interruption in our routine has a wonderful benefit in that employees throughout the agency have an opportunity to watch Rocky and I interacting with clients (something they rarely get to see given the separateness of SACP and our clientele). For example one day as Rocky and I walked past the main entrance to the agency we saw three young children waiting for their immunization with their parents. I watched as the children's faces lit up with excitement as they noticed Rocky. The parents smiled and pointed in Rocky's direction. Rocky and I quickly changed directions and slowly approached the family, offering a visit. Rocky laid down in the entryway and settled in for being petted by the young children. A conversation with one of the children ensued:

HANDLER (H): Rocky's soft, isn't he? Do you like dogs?

CHILD (C): [nodding and beginning to gently pet Rocky's side] Does he bite?

H: Oh no [saying loud enough to ensure the parent overheard]. Rocky went to school for many months to make sure he is very safe. He's a very good dog.

C: A dog bit me. Right here [pointing to a scar on her face, while still petting Rocky with her other hand].

H: Oh, I'm so sorry. That must have been very scary. Are you okay now?

C: Yes. Would Rocky bite if someone hurt him?

H: It's my job to make sure no one ever hurts him. He is very safe.
Who keeps you safe?

C: My mom. I'm safe now [smiling, still petting Rocky].

The parent motioned for the child as her name was called for an immunization. The child hugged Rocky and ran off to join her parents. As I stood up with Rocky to resume our staff visits, I turned and saw four or five staff members smiling, watching the child run off. "I just love watching Rocky with children. My dog would never be so patient," one said. Rocky wagged his tail and quickened his pace as he walked toward the staff members to visit.

In order to share Rocky with clients from other departments I frequently bring Rocky and walk through the immunization clinic as families wait with their children, offering a visit or asking if the child would like Rocky to show off his tricks. During those few minutes, staff members smile and pause, enjoying watching Rocky interact with children. Other staff members stand in the doorway and observe the playful scene, and share in the clapping to cheer Rocky on. These moments add credibility to both the AAA/T program as well as to the SACP program as a whole, for agency staff members are able to witness a level of caring and compassion by SACP staff to which they are rarely privileged. In addition to creating a sense of community for clients, this adds further mutual appreciation for the work done by staff throughout the agency.

Impact on Direct Staff

Rocky has had a tremendous impact on the therapists and staff in SACP. He has become their co-worker. Rocky's excitement and joy to see the SACP staff each morning is clearly apparent. No other staff member exhibits the same level of pure joy to arrive at work. He wags his tail and does his best to pull in their direction to greet each and every one. As we begin our morning by filling up his water dish and checking my mail box, Rocky insists on stopping at every office. It has now become part of our routine that I drop the leash at each doorway allowing him to happily enter and greet each employee. The routine continues down the hallway to each office. He even remembers when an employee was not available for his morning greeting, and he insists on stopping and saying, "hello" when he sees them later that day. Rocky's way of insisting that proper "good mornings" are said sets a positive norm on our team. One can't help but smile and pass on the more casual way to begin the day.

When therapists stop by my office throughout the day for impromptu supervision or to ask a question, Rocky frequently grabs his bone or a toy and offers it to the therapist to play. Although he usually takes the hint when the therapist is too busy to play, this gesture is a wonderful reminder not to take the work too seriously. (It's hard not to smile when a slobbery stuffed duck is suddenly dropped in your lap, and a happy canine looks hopefully into your eyes.) It also allows the therapist the opportunity to pet his soft fur or to partake in a quick snuggle to relieve the day's stress. On occasion, a therapist has come into my office for the sole purpose of needing a few minutes with Rocky. At times a quick hug or a few lighthearted tricks are just the things that are needed to clear one's head. As staff members pass my office, Rocky frequently is standing at the baby gate with his head casually resting on top. This perch allows him the best view of the waiting room and hallway, and, as he has learned, frequently attracts staff attention and affection.

Rocky takes part in all staff supervision and meetings on his work days, and his canine groans while he sleeps or stretches add levity to the sometimes serious conversations. On quiet paperwork days when a break is clearly needed, staff members occasionally take a few minutes to sit on the floor in the hallway with each other to play with Rocky. During these times Rocky happily goes from person to person, clearly enjoying the personal time. Laughter is always a part of these interactions, only serving to further increase staff morale. It is a rare scene in most agencies to find a program manager, clinical and clerical staff, and a dog happily sitting on the floor laughing and joking. However it is rather commonplace at SACP, and I cannot help but credit this type of environment as having a powerful role in the high quality of client care that exists. While taking these moments may initially seem counterintuitive to high productivity, in reality they provide the additional energy that is needed to decrease staff burnout and allow them to work as hard as they do.

In addition to this positive change in the work environment on our team, there has been a more personal impact as well. When working closely with a therapy dog, it is natural to fall in love with the process and want to become more involved. That happened to me (MC) following the introduction of the AAA/T program at our agency. As I began the process of working with Teri and Rocky, I began to see firsthand the impressive therapeutic benefits of working with a therapy dog. I noticed how Rocky changed the work environment with staff, and the impact he made with clients. I became enthusiastic and decided that I too wanted my own therapy dog. I talked to a number of people in professional organizations who explained some of the pros and cons of working with my own dog and training the dog for therapy work. Finally, I made a decision to adopt a dog.

After a few weeks of going from shelter to shelter looking for the ultimate therapy dog, I thought I found him. Joey was a yellow lab mix with a sweet personality. He was abandoned at a local shelter by an owner who had obviously taken time to care for him. I watched him closely as he interacted with other families and children visiting animals at the shelter, and was encouraged by his calm, curious personality in the midst of chaos. I had my parents bring their two dogs to the shelter to see how the dogs would interact, as my plan was to have my parents watch Joey during my long days at work. A few hours later, Joey was on his way home with me.

Never having owned a dog as an adult, but having several dogs at home while growing up, I asked myself how much more demanding could owning a dog be than the two cats that were already part of my family? I soon found out how much more demanding it is. The challenge of being single, having a very active social life, living in an apartment in a large metropolitan city, and owning a dog soon became apparent. My commitment to Joey took precedence over the time I used to spend with friends and family. I began training classes almost immediately and was encouraged by how fast Joey picked up verbal and visual commands. We went to class every week and then spent hours practicing what we were being taught. Joey became the center of my life, and my leisure time soon became focused upon Joey. As months passed, I discovered the unexpected surprises of having a dog and two cats in a one-bedroom apartment. From the multiple "accidents" on the floor that greeted me on Thanksgiving morning, to Joey's attempts to dig through the floor of the apartment, to the ultimate irony of Joey making a snack of a newly purchased dog training book, I began to become worn down with the new responsibilities. I came to realize that as much as I had been inspired by my interactions working with Teri and Rocky, owning a dog and training him to be a therapy dog at this point in my life was not the best idea.

As hard as it was for me, I knew I had to find a new home for Joey, and I eventually found a wonderful new home for him in the foothills of the Rocky Mountains. He now has a yard and two other dogs to play with, as well as an owner who is at home most of the day. I have come to realize that Teri, Rocky, and I can work as a team, and I don't need my own dog to enjoy the benefits of working with a therapy dog. We now do our best to spread this message on to others whose first response is that they want to get their own dog as a result of meeting Rocky. Utilizing a volunteer therapy dog team with clients is a great way to begin AAA/T work. Dogs are an incredible responsibility and the adoption of one should not be taken lightly.

Ways to Spread the Positive Impact

Our agency is rather large and has multiple locations throughout the county. Over time, staff members from these other locations have met Rocky as they have come to our location or during times when Rocky and I have traveled to another location for a meeting. Rocky is always popular and most often draws a crowd. On occasion, staff members have mentioned that they wished that Rocky could visit their worksite on a regular basis, stating that his very presence would be a positive impact on their work setting.

Although it is not possible to visit all of the other sites on a regular basis due to my work obligations, I did wonder what difference it would make on staff morale if I were to bring him one or two times per month to one other location. Rocky had had such a positive impact on morale at our location, maybe Rocky's presence might make a similar impact on a second location of the Health Department. So, an experiment began. I began taking Rocky to a second location, bringing an SACP therapist along whenever possible to help assess the benefit of spreading the positive impact of AAA. We chose a location that would greatly benefit SACP should we be able to improve relationships between our staff and the employees at this location.

On our first visit, the impact was overwhelming. The front desk staff member saw Rocky coming, and quickly greeted us at the door. As we entered the building, she was playfully on the floor with her arms outstretched in welcome. Rocky quickly responded by licking her face and wagging his tail in greeting. Within minutes, two other staff members joined us in the foyer and took part in interacting with Rocky. My immediate supervisor watched the staff reaction from a distance, curious to observe Rocky's impact on this new location. Rocky, the SACP staff member, and I began our visiting from office to office. Staff members readily came out of their offices, interacted with Rocky, asked questions about him, and took time to visit. The environment was instantly transformed. Employees whom I had never met in my ten years at the Health Department quickly came forward to interact with Rocky, sitting on the floor, petting him, and commenting about his clean coat or good behavior. Even a staff member who had been previously aloof came forward and watched quietly. Suddenly he asked, "Can he sit?" I quickly responded, "Of course! He can even high-five!" The employee smiled (one of the first smiles I had ever seen from him) as Rocky obediently gave me a "high five" on command. What a wonderful way to impact an environment. This was just the first of many visits, all with very similar responses to Rocky's presence.

Our clinical team frequently offers to teach solution-focused principles and concepts to members of other agency departments in an effort to positively impact the agency as a whole. During a yearly all-staff meeting, our team members led the entire staff of approximately 140 employees in answering the miracle question as a team building exercise. Each of the staff from our program led a group of twenty employees from all departments in brainstorming what would let them know that a miracle had happened the previous night, and the health department was now the greatest place to work despite the remaining funding and regulatory limitations. It was an incredible experience. Although some sat quietly, wondering what all this miracle talk was about, others quickly joined in the conversation and threw out ideas of what they would notice: "People would say 'good morning,'" "There would be smiles and a sense of community," "Coffee would be made." Responses ranged from serious to more playful, such as "Therapy dogs in every location" and "There would be chocolate." The next morning as our staff returned to work, we were struck by the employees' response to our team-building exercise. The front desk staff smiled and said good morning with a twinkle of remembering in their eyes. They then playfully stated, "We didn't find any chocolate this morning!" After engaging in wonderful conversations with members from many departments about all the differences that had occurred that very morning, one of our therapists suggested buying chocolate candies for our staff members to give out to employees in all Health Department locations throughout the county as a reminder of the possibility of the agency's miracle occurring. And so it began. As part of this plan, a therapist and I took Rocky to visit and pass out chocolate throughout two of the five locations. As we stopped by and visited with staff, many recognized that chocolate and a therapy dog were two of the things mentioned in their miracle day. It was a playful way to continue the solution-focused message to all staff that miracles do happen, and it's all a matter of on which one chooses to focus.

IMPACT ON COMMUNITY RELATIONSHIPS

The transition from problem-focused to solution-focused therapy has been challenging for our agency. Although it has greatly impacted our clients and staff in a positive way, it has been difficult for us at times to maintain strong, working relationships with our regulatory bodies. While we did our best to demonstrate to these regulatory agencies how SACP met and frequently exceeded state regulations, it was difficult for some auditors to really understand this when we approached client cases in such radically different ways.

For example, traditional substance abuse treatment utilizes curriculums and topics during group sessions to address needs that clients often have. In using a solution-focused approach, we do not use these predetermined agendas, and instead listen to each client to determine the individual changes that are necessary. Although the desired goal is the same, the approach and professional language to attain the goal are quite different. This lack of seeing eye-to-eye resulted in political tensions and hard feelings. Our focus was now on what clients really wanted and on exploring with them what their lives would be like once their problems were resolved. We assisted our clients in finding and utilizing their own resources and in holding them accountable for their own actions. We encouraged them to think systemically, and allowed them to make their own choices while requiring that they explain how these choices helped them to get closer to their long-term goals and to benefit all of those involved in their lives. These were such different approaches compared to the traditional methods of generously giving out resources, and having predetermined ways to address issues of gender, culture, and treatment needs. At times our staff members were viewed as being naïve and even as being neglectful of clinical issues when we trusted a client's judgment that her past history of sexual abuse, for example, had truly been resolved without treatment, or that she could receive good clinical care in a mixed-gender setting rather than in the traditional women's only groups. "Clients won't tell you the truth" they said. Despite the accusations and difficult times, we held strongly to our solution-focused approach, and worked harder to demonstrate how we were indeed being respectful of client needs and were in full compliance with all regulations.

When we decided to add AAA/T to our services at SACP, we informed our state regulatory agencies immediately. As I cautiously described the potential benefits to our clients and staff to one of our auditors, I was pleasantly surprised at her response. She said, "Dogs make a big difference. I think it is a good idea." I was shocked. Although this was not one of the auditors who had previously challenged us on our philosophical stance, I was braced for the worse. At her next visit to our agency, I quickly made a photocopy of our AAA/T policy and procedure as well as a lengthy bibliography. I was eager to prove the credibility and amount of research and thought that had gone into this program. She took the material and then asked if she could have a picture of Rocky. Surprised, I immediately printed a copy of the poster that hangs throughout our agency that explains Rocky's role and contains his picture in his working vest. In addition, I asked if she would like to accompany me to the public relations office to review some recent photos taken of Rocky with an employee's child for advertisement of our program. As the auditor and I walked through the halls to the other side of the building where the public relations office is, staff members asked (as usual), "Where's Rocky today?" After answering their questions, I turned to the auditor and explained the difference that Rocky has made on agency morale. She responded, "I can see that. I would like to meet him someday." She smiled and laughed as we thumbed through the snapshots, clearly enjoying the pictures of Rocky and the child. After picking three or four that she wanted to take, she asked permission to hang the pictures on her office door. She stated that she thought it would be a wonderful way to attract attention to SACP and get her colleagues to ask questions about the dog's purpose.

Our agency participates in quarterly meetings with other substance abuse treatment providers with one of our regulatory agencies, and agencies are frequently asked to give updates about new services available to clients. During one of these meetings, I began to describe our new AAA/T program, giving examples of how Rocky breaks barriers to treatment and assists us in parenting interventions. This auditor was present at the meeting. As I looked over to her, I saw her smiling and nodding in approval as other treatment providers shared the enthusiasm of this innovative way to reach this challenging client population. The benefits of AAA/T seemed to transcend differences in treatment philosophy and somehow created an area of commonality. The therapeutic use of a dog made sense to these other providers even when our solution-focused way of viewing clients remained controversial. They appeared to overlook philosophical differences, and simply hear the power that the therapy dog had on people.

As the months passed, this auditor made occasional comments about how interested her colleagues were in our use of Rocky, and how the pictures of Rocky were having the precise impact that she had hoped. Rocky was making a difference, even on people whom he had never met. Our most recent audit by this regulatory agency was a very pleasant experience. The auditor held us accountable and questioned our methods in various treatment areas, yet she was open to our answers and seemed to understand that our clients are truly receiving good client care despite of our different philosophical stance. As I walked with her through the agency hallways to show her framed photographs hanging on the walls that demonstrated Rocky working with children, she stopped and said, "Adding Rocky to your staff was the best political decision you ever made." Shocked, I asked her to explain. She stated that although she knew this was not our intention, the image of Rocky working with children had touched the hearts of the animal lovers at the regulatory agency, allowing them to overlook and forgive, previous political tensions and philosophical differences with our agency! In many ways, Rocky had allowed us to have a second chance to make a first impression. Those images had resulted in an emotional attachment to our program, resulting in a curiosity and openness about the work we do. Rocky, assisted by our auditor, had managed to repair years of political damage done during our transition to solution-focused therapy, damage that I, with my years of education and expertise, had been unable to repair. It took a therapy dog to put things back on track.

Since Rocky has joined our team there have been many other times that he has seemed to steal the attention and positively impact SACP. My job requires that I attend a significant number of meetings. When scheduling meetings outside of our agency, I typically offer days on which Rocky is not working. (Although Rocky is welcome in our agency, I would need special permission to bring Rocky to another agency since he is not a service dog and is not protected by service dog provisions.) When scheduling one such meeting of administrators from several local agencies, we could not seem to find a common date, so I offered the option of additional days with the condition that Rocky could attend with me. No one at the meeting had ever met Rocky, and I was unsure of their position about animals. To my surprise everyone quickly agreed it would be no problem and the meeting was readily scheduled. Permission was arranged for Rocky to attend a meeting at the same building in which county courts reside.

As we arrived for our meeting that day, we stopped at the front desk to confirm that Rocky's presence was approved due to the high level of visibility of the county courthouse. The staff enthusiastically confirmed that they were expecting him, and they smiled and commented on how beautiful Rocky was. After taking a few moments for them to visit with Rocky, we left to attend our meeting. Once in the meeting, the other attendees quickly came over to Rocky to visit prior to the meeting starting. Even the chairperson of the meeting laughed and began to interact with Rocky. Meeting attendees who had previously never taken the time to initiate any conversation with me were now sitting beside me and asking direct questions about Rocky's role and the impact on clients. There was an unprecedented interest in our program and services! As the meeting began, Rocky obediently fell asleep under the meeting table. Those around us gave an occasional smile when they glanced in his direction and witnessed how unobtrusive he was to the professional setting. During the meeting on two separate occasions following group discussion on a topic, the meeting chairperson directed his attention to me and asked, "Teri, what do you think we should do." Initially shocked, since he had never called on me directly before, nor sought my opinion in a public forum, I then gave my opinion.

I left the meeting that day marveling at the difference Rocky's presence seemed to have made in the level of interest in SACP and in my opinion. As we left the courthouse that day, one of the officers from the sheriff's office saw us. As he approached he said, "There's that famous dog." He affectionately ruffled Rocky's ears and then noticed Rocky's employee badge hanging from his work vest. He laughed and said, "Look at that! If Rocky can wear his employee badge in a government building with no problem, the other employees should have no excuse for forgetting theirs." Rocky seems to invite a playful spirit in all who meet him.

SUMMARY

The impact of a therapy dog is far reaching. Not only does a therapy dog change the therapeutic environment for clients, but it has the potential to change the working environment for program and agency staff. Therapy dogs have the ability to touch the heart of those who cross their paths in a way that humans can only imagine. Their very presence implicitly evokes curiosity, compassion, forgiveness, and a desire to reach out to others. Although the purpose for bringing a therapy dog into a treatment setting is for the clinical benefit of clients, the secondary gain of increased employee morale and positive community relationships should not be overlooked.

Photo by Teri Pichot.

Epilogue

Know what's weird? Day by day, nothing seems to change, but
pretty soon . . . everything's different.

"Calvin" from *Calvin and Hobbes*

As I (TP) sit reading over the pages of this manuscript, finalizing
the text before we send the final draft to the publisher, I realize that
a chapter has occurred over these past few months that we would be
remiss not to write. It has been well over a year now since the idea of
this book was developed, and it has been an exciting process putting
the story into print. This past year, both in writing this book and in
continuing our work with Rocky, has further convinced me that working with a therapy dog can work miracles that a human alone can
never do. I can't imagine not having the option of partnering with a
therapy dog.

I had been contemplating adopting another dog, not only for a family pet and a buddy for Rocky, but as a potential second therapy dog.
One never knows when a therapy dog will be suddenly unable to
work (much like a human), and the idea of having two working dogs
opened countless opportunities: volunteer work in hospitals, additional locations and days within the Health Department itself, etc. Although our family was finally enjoying the quiet routine that comes
when a family pet matures and the damaged drywall, furniture, and
other collateral damage of Rocky's puppyhood had been repaired, my
husband and I decided that it was time to add a second dog to our family. (More honestly, I decided and my husband supportively went
along with my dreams.) Jasper, a tri-color, rough coat collie from a local collie rescue, was the perfect puppy. He was four months old, and
in need of a good home. Our lives have not been the same since that
day in early October 2004 when he joined our family. How easy it is
to forget the disruption and chaos that accompanies a cute, loveable
puppy—from housebreaking, sleepless nights, countless obedience

classes and homework sessions, to fresh holes in the repaired drywall from rambunctious pups running playfully through the house in cramped quarters.

The addition of Jasper to our family allowed us to see how much we had learned about canine culture through training Rocky, and Jasper learned incredibly fast. Sitting and waiting for permission prior to bounding enthusiastically out the door, and laying down quietly when the human members of the family eat were just a couple of the lessons that Jasper naturally learned by watching and emulating Rocky and through our gentle and persistent prompting. We live by the general rule that we don't allow a puppy to do what we would not want to see an eighty-pound dog (or a well-trained therapy dog) doing.

Although the overall training was routine, we had much to learn about how to build a solid relationship with a puppy (which is key to a good therapy dog) when a second dog is present. As Rocky's therapy dog consultant repeatedly reminded us, dogs will always bond to other dogs over humans given the chance. Although it is common to leave multiple dogs home together to keep each other company, we were encouraged to keep our dogs separate when we were not home. She coached us on the most effective way to balance our dogs' needs for canine companionship with our goal of raising dogs that are fully bonded to people and who are well-trained and effective therapy dogs. We began the time-consuming daily tasks of ensuring that each dog has alone time (to prevent separation anxiety), time to play with each other (to enjoy all the normal dog interactions they need for mental health), time as a family (important "pack" time for a sense of belonging), and private time with each "parent" (to enhance human bonding and a solid relationship between each dog and human). The dogs needed to learn to look to us for direction and to respond to direction despite the excitement and fun of another dog's presence (a tall order for a puppy, and not so easy for Rocky either). All of this required purposefulness during all interactions with both dogs and hours of direct training each day. Although quite daunting at times, the resulting bond we soon began to feel with Jasper and the level of partnership are worth the effort. Jasper still has a long way to go should he end up as a credentialed therapy dog. Regardless of the outcome, he is an incredible dog and family pet.

The day we met Jasper at the Collie Rescue was one of extreme emotion. On that day we adopted a wonderful new family member, but we also received incredibly sad news about our beloved Rocky. We learned that despite our best efforts screening for a reputable breeder, Rocky's breeder was now known to be responsible for horrendous breeding practices that resulted in many of her collies needing assistance from the Collie Rescue. Heart-wrenching stories of medical deformities and genetic mishaps were now attributed to this breeder. While our wonderful Rocky seemed healthy and free from such tragedy at that moment, my heart knew he was most likely headed for a difficult path. Previously unexplained medical problems that Rocky had experienced now seemed like an ominous sign that his genetics were also tainted. This information, while incredibly painful, somehow helped to make sense of an unexpected seizure that Rocky suffered the following month, and eye abnormalities he developed during the winter months.

Regular visits to his veterinarian and multiple specialists have become the norm as they monitor his health and treat symptoms. In addition, Rocky's therapy dog consultant plays an invaluable role monitoring his behavior, providing behavioral interventions to address concerns, and monitoring for appropriateness to continue working as a therapy dog. We have been fortunate in that Rocky's symptoms have not been problematic for him nor caused him any known pain. However this may not always be the case, and this is a reality with which I have had to come to terms.

It has been an important reminder for me as a handler and a therapist. I have invested so much into Rocky's training and into the reputation of our therapy dog program. Throughout this process he has become my close friend. The thought of losing him as a professional partner (my little work buddy) with my clients and staff seems unfathomable. I find myself wanting to hold on to our close working relationship despite these new developments. In an odd way, the handler relationship is a necessary form of nepotism. It is this close familial relationship that is needed to ensure safety, yet it is also this close relationship that clouds objectivity. This necessitates that we as handlers create a strong network of animal experts and depend on them for guidance when medical and behavioral changes occur. Although I don't believe I would ever ask Rocky to work when it is not in his best interest, I am now painfully aware how difficult it will be to say good-bye to this wonderful work relationship when the time must come. Therefore trusting his animal consultant and specialists will be the key. For today, I cherish each day we have together as we walk through the office hallways, and am so grateful for each wag of his tail that tells me he's glad he came to work today.

Although Jasper will never replace Rocky, it is a poignant reminder of the fragility of life. One never knows what tragedies will come our way or how many days we have on this planet. We are wise to enjoy each moment to the fullest, while planning for the unexpected. Jasper is a constant reminder that my professional dreams live on through my new friendship with him and future pets. Life goes on. While in AAA/T the therapy dog is viewed clinically as a tool that a therapist can use with clients, we all know a dog is so much more. A tool can be quickly replaced when lost or damaged. A friend and partner cannot. The emotional toll of AAA/T is new ground for me, yet it brings a welcome gift. It reminds me that the most important part of living is being willing to take the risk of losing.

Appendix A

AAA/T Resources and Information

While we have included our favorite resources, this list is by no means intended to be comprehensive of all information available. Contact your local humane society or obedience training professional or organization to find more information.

General Information

American Humane Association
63 Inverness Drive East
Englewood, CO 80112
303-792-9900
www.americanhumane.org

The mission of American Humane, as a network of individuals and organizations, is to prevent cruelty, abuse, neglect, and exploitation of children and animals and to ensure that their interests and well-being are fully, effectively, and humanely guaranteed by an aware and caring society.

American Kennel Club (AKC) Headquarters
260 Madison Ave
New York, NY 10016
(212) 696-8200
www.akc.org

This organization provides information on AKC-affiliated clubs and classes, as well as information on obtaining the Canine Good Citizen credential and patch to add to a therapy dog vest.

www.dog-play.com/therapy.html

This Internet site provides a list of resources about animal-assisted activities and therapy. It lists additional state programs and contact information.

Intermountain Therapy Animals (ITA)
P.O. Box 17201
Salt Lake City, UT 84117
(801) 272-3439
www.therapyanimals.org

This Delta Society affiliate provides information about how to become credentialed to participate in the Reading Education Assistance Dog (R.E.A.D.) program as well as other information. The mission of the R.E.A.D. program is to improve the literacy skills of children through the assistance of registered Pet Partner therapy teams as literacy mentors.

Latham Foundation
1826 Clement Avenue
Alameda, CA 95401
(510) 521-0920
www.latham.org

This organization provides pamphlets, books, and videos on various aspects of the human-animal bond. If you are looking for research support on how visiting animals benefit patients, seniors, and others, this is a place to start. The *Latham Letter* is published regularly to address studies and emerging issues.

North American Riding for the Handicapped Association (NARHA)
P.O. Box 33150
Denver, CO 80233
www.narha.org

This organization is the equine credentialing body, and is an excellent resource for hippotherapy information.

Pawsitive Connection
1207 East Elm Street
Fayetteville, AR 72703
www.geocities.com/pawsitiveconnection

This Web site describes the screening process (Delta Society guidelines) for their program, discusses communicable disease concerns (zoonoses), outlines methods of enhancing therapeutic treatments, and answers frequently asked questions.

Pets and People, Companions in Therapy and Service
P.O. Box 604
Citronelle, AL 36522

(251) 455-7866
www.petsandpeople.org

This Web site provides information about education and certification of therapy animals.

Therapy Pets Animal Assisted Therapy
P.O. Box 10265
Fargo, ND 58106-0265
(701) 588-4592
www.therapypets.com

Here you will find links to therapy dog volunteer organizations and therapeutic riding and hippotherapy programs.

National and International Therapy Dog Registries

Delta Society
875-124th Ave NE, Suite 101
Bellevue, WA 98005-2531
(425) 226-7357
(425) 235-1076 (fax)
info@deltasociety.org
www.deltasociety.org

This organization provides information on the requirements for membership as well as volunteering. Delta provides instructors and training materials to teach the skills needed to visit safely with an animal in hospitals, nursing homes, classrooms, and other facilities. Regular publications keep participants up to date on emerging issues, research, and a wide variety of information on the human-animal relationship. With successful completion of the registration requirements you receive liability insurance, referrals to facilities, newsletters, and continuing education opportunities as well as networking support.

Therapy Dogs, Inc.
P.O. Box 20227
Cheyenne, WY 82003
(877) 843-7364
(307) 638-2079 (fax)
www.therapydogs.com

The goal of Therapy Dogs Inc. is to help dog owners use their dogs for therapy work in various places such as nursing homes, hospitals and schools, as well as work with the mentally and physically handicapped.

Therapy Dogs International, Inc.
88 Bartley Road
Flanders, NJ 07836
(973) 252-9800
(973) 252-7171 (fax)
tdi@gti.net
www.tdi-dog.org

Therapy Dogs International, Inc. (TDI) is a volunteer group organized to provide qualified handlers and their therapy dogs for visitations to institutions, facilities, and any other place where therapy dogs are needed.

Equipment and Supplies

Drs. Foster and Smith
P.O. Box 100
Rhinelander, WI 54501-0100
1-800-381-7179
www.drsfostersmith.com

This company sells a wide variety of animal supplies and information including the mukluks (snow boots) that Rocky wears during snowy weather.

Itzadog
191 University Blvd. #316
Denver, CO 80206
(303) 322-4114
www.itzadog.com

This company created the Quiet Spot, which is a unique pet tag protector that is useful for working dogs since it keeps the dog's ID tags from making noise. Jasper's Quiet Spot can be seen on his Epilogue picture.

Ruffrider
2980 Sugarloaf Road
Boulder, CO 80302
(720) 249-2986
www.ruffrider.com

This site offers a popular and well-made travel harness that is used by many therapy dogs. This is helpful to ensure the therapy dog's safety while riding in an automobile.

Sitstay
5831 N. 58th Street

Lincoln, NE 68507
(800) SITSTAY (748-7829)
www.sitstay.com

This Web site offers many useful items. This is where we purchased the therapy dog patches that Rocky wears on his vest when working at the agency.

Snoot Loops
102 Canton Court
Brooklyn, New York 11229
(800) 339-9505
(718) 891-4200
(718) 891-0741 (fax)
www.snootloop.com
animbehav@aol.com

This company sells the head halter that we initially used for training Rocky and Jasper. It is an excellent halter for initial training or for ongoing use for younger, more energetic dogs.

Softouch Concepts
29460 Union City Blvd.
Union City, CA 94587
(866) 305-6145
www.softouchconcepts.com

This company offers the SENSE-ation and SENSE-ible harnesses. The SENSE-ible harness is the one we use with Rocky as it appears he finds it most comfortable.

Wolf Packs
P.O. Box 3195
Ashland, OR 97520
(541) 482-7669
www.wolfpacks.com

This is where we purchased the plain, green work vest that we used during Rocky's training. (We added the "in training" patches we purchased from Sitstay.com.) This allowed Rocky to become familiar with wearing a vest. We then later added his therapy dog patches when he became credentialed. They offer other pet equipment as well.

National Dog Trainer Organizations

The Association of Pet Dog Trainers (APDT)
150 Executive Center Drive Box 35
Greenville, SC 29615
1-800-PET-DOGS
1-800-738-3647
information@apdt.com
www.apdt.com

The Association of Pet Dog Trainers is a professional organization of individual trainers who are committed to becoming better trainers through education. They refer, but do not endorse, members listed in their membership directory to clients who call or visit our Web page on a daily basis looking for a trainer in their area.

International Association of Canine Professionals
P.O. Box 5601156
Monverde, FL 34756-0156
(407) 469-2008
(407) 469-7127
iacp@mindspring.com
www.dogpro.org

National Association of Dog Obedience Instructors (NADOI)
Attn: Corresponding Secretary
PMB #369
729 Grapevine Hwy, Suite 369
Hurst, TX 76054-2085
www.nadoi.org

State Organizations

Alabama

Hand in Paw
2616 7th Ave. South
Birmingham, AL 35233
(205) 322-5144
www.handinpaw.org

Pets and People: Companions in Therapy and Service
P.O. Box 604

Citronelle, AL 36522
www.petsandpeople.org

Arizona

Companion Animal Association of Arizona
P.O. Box 5006
Scottsdale, AZ 85251-5006
www.caaainc.org

Gabriel's Angels, Inc.
220 South Mulberry St.
Suite 24, PMB 102
Mesa, AZ 85202
www.petshelpingkids.com

Therapeutic Riding of Tucson (TROT)
P.O. Box 30584
Tucson, AZ 85751
www.horseweb.com/client/trot/index.htm

Tucson Area Pet Partners
10567 N. Camino Rosas Nuevas
Tucson, AZ 85737

Arkansas

Pawsitive Connection
1207 East Elm Street
Fayetteville, AR 72703
www.geocities.com/pawsitiveconnection

California

CC/SPCA Pet Facilitated Therapy
103 S. Hughes
Fresno, CA 93706-1207
www.ccspca.com

"Create a Smile" Animal-Assisted Therapy Team
237 Hill Street
Santa Monica, CA 90405

Foundation for Pet-Provided Therapy
P.O. Box 4115
Oceanside, CA 92052
www.loveonaleash.org

Friendship Foundation
P.O. Box 6525
Albany, CA 94706
www.friendship-foundation.org

Furry Friends Pet-Assisted Therapy Services
P.O. Box 5099
San Jose, CA 95150
www.furryfriends.org

Lend a Heart-Lend a Hand Animal-Assisted Therapy, Inc.
P.O. Box 60617
Sacramento, CA 95860
www.lendaheart.org

San Francisco SPCA Animal-Assisted Therapy Program
2500 16th Street
San Francisco, CA 94103-4213
www.sfspca.org

SPCA Los Angeles Animal-Assisted Therapy Program
5026 West Jefferson Boulevard
Los Angeles, CA 90016
www.spcala.com/pages/aatherapy.htm

Therapy Pets
P.O. Box 32288
Oakland, CA 94604-3588
www.therapypets.org

Colorado

Cadence Center for Therapeutic Riding
P.O. Box 9009
Durango, CO 81302
www.cadenceriding.com

The Children's Hospital Prescription Pet Program
www.thechildrenshospital.org/public/helpkids/volunteer/pet.cfm

The Children's Hospital in Denver offers a dog-assisted therapy and visitation program.

Colorado Boys Ranch
P.O. Box 681
La Junta, CO 81050
www.coloradoboysranch.org

Denver Pet Partners
P.O. Box 270113
Littleton, CO 81207
www.denverpetpartners.org

Human-Animal Bond in Colorado (HABIC)
Colorado State University
School of Social Work
127 Education Building
Fort Collins, Colorado 80523-1586
(970) 491-2776
(970) 491-7280 (fax)
www.habic.cahs.colostate.edu

HABIC (Human-Animal bond in Colorado) is a program that celebrates the bond between humans and their companion animals, and puts that bond to action in service programs that provide an environment of animal-assisted activities and animal-assisted therapy. They provide training and placement for those interested in becoming credentialed through them.

Humane Society of Boulder Valley
2323 55th Street
Boulder, CO 80301
(303) 442-4030
www.boulderhumane.org/help/volunteer.htm

The Humane Society of Boulder Valley, Boulder, Colorado offers volunteer opportunities in animal-assisted therapy.

Larimer Animal People Partnership
www.colapp.org

This Delta Society affiliate provides social visits in the Fort Collins area.

Table Mountain Animal Center
Pet Therapy Program
4105 Youngfield Service Road
Golden, CO 80401
www.tablemountainanimals.org

Connecticut

Tails of Joy Therapy Dog Program Connecticut
9 Iron Gate Lane
Cromwell, CT 06416
www.tailsofjoy.org/index.htm

Florida

Freedom Ride, Inc.
1905 Lee Road
Orlando, FL 32810
www.freedomride.com

Gulf Coast Chapter Delta Society Pet Partners
10501 FG-CU Boulevard South
Ft. Meyers, FL 33965-6565
www.fgcu.edu/cfpa/pettherapy/index.html

Sarasota Manatee Association for Riding Therapy (SMART)
P.O. Box 9566
Bradenton, FL 34206-9566
www.smartriders.org

Georgia

Happy Tails Pet Therapy
P.O. Box 767961
Roswell, GA 30076
www.happytailspets.org

Iowa

Miracles in Motion
P.O. Box 14
Cedar Rapids, IA 52406-0014
www.miraclesinmotion.net

Illinois

Chenny Troupe, Inc.
1700 W. Irving Park Rd.
Chicago, IL 60613
www.chennytroupe.org

The Lincolnshire Animal Hospital Pet Visitors Group
Lincolnshire Animal Hospital
420 Half Day Rd.
Lincolnshire, IL 60069
(847) 634-9250

Pegasus Special Riders
P.O. Box 293
Oregon, IL 61061
(815) 732-3189
www.pegasusspecialriders.org

Kentucky

Exceptional Equitation
Spruce Point Farm
2107 Massie School Rd.
La Grange, KY 40031

Wags Pet Therapy of Kentucky, Inc.
P.O. Box 91436
Louisville, KY 40291-1436
www.kywags.org

Louisiana

Visiting Pet Program
5831 South Johnson Street
New Orleans, LA 70125
www.visitingpetprogram.org

Maine

Equest Therapeutic Riding Center
P.O. Box 935

Kennebunk, ME 04043
www.equestmaine.org

Flying Changes Center for Therapeutic Riding
Route 201
Topsham, ME 04086
www.flyingchanges.org

Maryland

Back to Fitness Therapeutic Riding
Morgan Run Stables
801 Bloom Road
Westminster, MD 21157
www.bcpl.net/~gharris/btf.html

Great Strides Therapeutic Riding
26771 Howard Chapel Drive
Damascus, MD 20872
www.greatstrides.org

Massachusetts

Dog B.O.N.E.S.
480 Commercial St.
Provincetown, MA 02657
www.therapydog.info

White Oak Farm
411 North Street
Jefferson, MA 01522

Michigan

Children and Horses United in Movement (CHUM)
P.O. Box 14
Mason, MI 48854
www.chumtherapy.org

Offering Alternative Therapy with Smiles (OATS)
3090 Weidemann Drive
Clarkston, MI 48348
www.oatshrh.org

Minnesota

Bark Avenue on Parade
P.O. Box 24071
Minneapolis, MN 55424
www.barkavenue.org

Helping Paws of Minnesota, Inc. Service Dogs
P.O. Box 634
Hopkins, MN 55343
www.helpingpaws.org/AAAProgram.htm

Mounted Eagles Therapeutic Riding Program
7305 Dressage Rd.
Brainerd, MN 56401
www.mountedeagles.org

Pals on Paws
14051 55th Street, NE
St. Michael, MN 55376
www.geocities.com/Heartland/Meadows/1442/Pals.htm

Missouri

Magic Moments Riding Therapy
394 County Lane 125
Diamond, MO 64840
www.geocities.com/heartland/ridge/9220

Pet Therapy of the Ozarks, Inc.
P.O. Box 9462
Springfield, MO 65801
www.geocities.com/petttherapyoftheozarks

Support Dogs, Inc.
11645 Lilburn Rd.
St. Louis, MO 63146
http://supportdogs.org

Nebraska

Heartland Equine Therapeutic Riding Academy
P.O. Box 260

Valley, NE 68064
www.hetra.org

Paws for Friendship, Inc.
P.O. Box 12243
Omaha, NE 68142
http://pawsforfriendshipinc.org

New Hampshire

Dog Logic Therapy Dog Team Training Program
3020 Brown Avenue #10
Manchester, NH 03103
www.doglogic.com/therapymain.htm

New Mexico

Cloud Dancers of the Southwest
Equestrian Therapy and Recreation for the Disabled
P.O. Box 14058
Albuquerque, NM 87191-4058
(505) 363-1277
http://home.att.net/~c-dsw

Southwest Canine Corps of Volunteers
Albuquerque, NM
sccv@comcast.net
http://home.comcast.net/~sccv/

New York

Astride, Inc.
P.O. Box 5241
Syracuse, NY 13220

Long Island Riding for the Handicapped
P.O. Box 352
Glen Head, NY 115743
www.lirha.com

Pal-O-Mine Equestrian
829 Old Nichols Road

Islandia, NY 11749
www.pal-o-mine.org

Winslow Therapeutic Center
328 Route 17A
Warwick, NY 10990
www.winslow.org

Ohio

Doggie Brigade
Akron Children's Hospital
One Perkins Square
Akron, OH 44308
www.akronchildrens.org

Equine Assisted Therapy
7908 Myers Road
Centerburg, OH 43011
www.equineassistedtherapy.org

Miami Valley Pet Therapy Association
P.O. Box 675
Troy, OH 45373
www.mvpta.org

Oklahoma

Paws for Friendship
10724 S.E. 29
Oklahoma City, OK 73130

Oregon

Adaptive Riding Institute
P.O. Box 280
Scotts Mills, OR 97330
www.open.org/~horses88

Equitopia
28970 Hwy 34
Corvallis, OR 97330
www.equitopia.org

Project Pooch
Oregon Youth Authority MacLaren School
2630 North Pacific Highway
Woodburn, OR 97071
www.pooch.org

RideAble
P.O. Box 71092
Eugene, OR 97401
www.rideable.org

Pennsylvania

Animal Friends Pet Therapy Program
2643 Penn Avenue
Pittsburgh, PA 15222
www.animal-friends.org/site/petassist.jsp

The Capital Area Therapeutic Riding Association (CATRA)
P.O. Box 339
Grantville, PA 17028
www.catra.net

South Carolina

Charleston Counseling & Support Services
P.O. Box 30082
Charleston, SC 29417
www.geocities.com/animalassissistedtherapy

SCDogs Therapy Group
501-8 Old Greenville Hwy
Clemson, SC 29631
www.scdogs.org

Tennessee

Shangri-La Therapeutic Academy of Riding (STAR)
11800 Highway 11E
Lenoir City, TN 37772
www.rideatstar.org

Texas

All Star Equestrian Center
P.O. Box 392
Mansfield, TX 76063
www.allstarfoundation.org

Ride On Center for Kids (ROCK)
P.O. Box 2422
Georgetown, TX 78627
www.rockride.org

Riding Unlimited
9168 T.N. Skiles Road
Ponder, TX 76259
www.ridingunlimited.org

Self-Improvement through Riding Education (SIRE)
Route 2, Box 56
Hockley, TX 77447
(281) 356-7588

Utah

Intermountain Therapy Animals
P.O. Box 17201
Salt Lake City, UT 84117
(801) 272-3439
www.therapyanimals.org

Utah Animal-Assisted Therapy Association
P.O. Box 18771
Salt Lake City, UT 84118-8771
www.uaata.org

Vermont

Therapy Dogs of Vermont (TDV)
P.O. Box 1271
Williston, VT 05495
www.therapydogs.org

Virginia

Animal-Assisted Crisis Response Association
c/o Lois C. Hardy
5314 Sunrise Shore
Chincoteague, VA 23336
www.aacra.org/index.html

Paws for Health
c/o Richmond SPCA
1600 Chamberlayne Avenue
Richmond, VA 23222
(804) 643-6758
www.pawsforhealth.info

The Shiloh Project
12210 Fairfax Town Center
Fairfax, VA 22033
www.shilohproject.org

Washington

Reading with Rover
P.O. Box 2569
Woodinville, WA 98072
www.readingwithrover.com

Sirius Healing Animal-Assisted Activities
and Therapy Provider and Trainer
12046 12th Avenue NE
Seattle, WA 98125
www.siriushealing.com

Wisconsin

Stable Hands Therapeutic Riding Program for the Disabled
3501 Swan Avenue
Wausau, WI 54401
http://webpages.charter.net/stablehands

Canada

Pacific Animal Therapy Society (PATS)
9412 Laurie's Lane
Sidney, British Columbia
Canada V8L 4L2
http://members.shaw.ca/patspets

The Pet Therapy Society of Northern Alberta
330-9768 170 Street
Edmonton, Alberta
Canada T5T 5L4
http://paws.shopalberta.com

Appendix B

Sample Policy and Procedure

ANIMAL-ASSISTED ACTIVIES/THERAPY

The Jefferson County Department of Health and Environment (JCDHE) Substance Abuse Counseling Program (SACP) may utilize Animal-Assisted Activities (AAA) or Animal-Assisted Therapy (AAT), as described in Appendix A, to enhance the services provided to SACP clients and their family members by improving their mental health via the positive physiological effect of human-animal interaction.

Animal Screening (Health, Skills, and Aptitude):

1. Dogs will be the only animals involved in the AAA/T Program at SACP and must be Delta-registered Pet Partners with current registration.
2. Pet Partners will have completed specific training and passed rigorous screening from Delta-licensed instructors and evaluators, and veterinarians.
3. Dogs must pass a thorough examination by a veterinarian prior to registration.
4. Dogs must be kept on a strict vaccination and parasite prevention schedule, administered, and documented by a licensed veterinarian.
5. Dogs must be clean and well groomed. They must be bathed and/or thoroughly brushed prior to entering JCDHE; nails must be kept clipped, ears clean and free from any odor, eyes clean, and have clean breath/teeth.
6. Dogs will wear a nylon, cloth, or leather buckle collar or a Gentle Leader.
7. Dogs will be on a leash no more than six feet in length, and will be under control at all times.
8. Dogs must wear the proper uniform (Delta vest or scarf) and ID badge (issued by Human Resources) at all times within the facility.

AAA/T may be administered through the use of "resident" and/or "visiting" Pet Partners. Upon receiving permission of the Executive Director, the Director of Health Promotion and Lifestyle Management, and the SACP Program Manager, a clinical SACP employee and his or her pet who are Delta-registered Pet Partners and, as such, agree to the Delta Society Policies and Procedures for Registered Pet Partners as described in Appendix B, may be deemed "Resident" Pet Partners. As such, the Resident Pet Partners may provide both AAA and AAT services. The Resident Animal will reside with his or her handler and may not be at SACP without the handler present.

AAA/T Resident Pet Partners Administrative Guidelines:

1. Resident Pet Partners are covered by JCDHE liability insurance.
2. As Delta-registered Pet Partners, the SACP employee/handler will have specific training and pass rigorous screening from Delta-licensed instructors and evaluators, and veterinarians. Retesting every two years ensures program quality and consistency.
3. Current documentation of Pet Partners and dog credentials will be maintained in the Program Manager's office and will be available for review upon request.
4. The SACP employee/Pet Partner will be the sole handler of the dog during all client interactions. The dog will remain on-leash during all client interactions and will only be allowed off-leash within the confines of a designated office and only when no clients are present (a child gate may be used to secure an office to confine the Resident Animal). The Resident Animal may not be left unattended for lengthy periods of time or if he or she is disruptive to the professional atmosphere (e.g., whining). A designated SACP staff member may voluntarily oversee the Resident Animal for the Handler when the animal is confined, yet only for the purpose of alerting the handler if intervention is necessary.
5. The Resident Animal may attend meetings at the Lakewood JCDHE location with the employee/Pet Partner with other JCDHE employees or outside visitors at the discretion of the SACP Program Manager. The Resident Animal may only attend meetings outside of the Lakewood JCDHE location with the approval of the Director of Health Promotion and Lifestyle Management.
6. The SACP employee/Pet Partner will have the sole responsibility for the care of the Resident Animal while at SACP. The Resident Animal will be provided water/food and will be given regular access to the outside for elimination and/or exercise.
7. Animal waste will be promptly disposed of by the SACP employee/Pet Partner and the waste will be placed in a plastic bag and

placed in an outside waste receptacle. The employee will wash his or her hands before returning to work.

8. All SACP employees will complete training on the benefits of AAA/T and will demonstrate necessary knowledge of how to safely interact with the Resident Animal. Employees must also teach clients how to safely interact with the Resident Animal.

9. SACP employees may interact with the animal under the employee/Pet Partner's supervision, yet they may not play aggressive games (e.g., tug games).

10. SACP staff members will be screened for allergies/asthma and the Resident Animal will not be allowed in the office of an employee who has allergies or asthma. Interaction with the Resident Animal will only be allowed upon the staff member's request. Arrangements will be made to ensure that any employee who has allergies/asthma will receive the same level of interaction with the employee/Pet Partner without the Resident Animal present as requested.

11. The office in which the Resident Pet Partners reside and the common areas will be vacuumed on a daily basis by JCDHE housekeeping services.

12. The Resident Animal will not be allowed in the following areas:
    —JCDHE break rooms
    —Any food preparation areas
    —Any area in which Antabuse or other medication is being monitored
    —Areas in which medications, sterile items, or clean laundry items are stored

AAA/T Resident Pet Partners Clinical Guidelines:

1. The Resident Pet Partners may provide AAA services to clients they encounter in the JCDHE hallways and waiting rooms. Children must be accompanied by their parents/legal guardian and give verbal permission for the visit. The visit may be terminated or declined if the parent/guardian does not participate or provide the necessary supervision. The visit may also be declined if time does not allow due to other work obligations.

2. The Resident Pet Partners will always ask permission before approaching anyone, and will ensure that the visits are welcome and nonintrusive. The Pet Partner will verbally screen for allergies or other medical problems associated with animal contact.

3. SACP clients will be formally screened for pet allergies, asthma, and phobias upon admission to SACP. Clients with mild allergies and/or

controlled asthma will be given the choice if they would like to interact with the Pet Partners. Clients with uncontrolled or severe asthma or with current phobias to dogs will not be allowed to interact with the Pet Partners. The Program Manager will be informed of this client population and appropriate precautions will be taken to avoid interaction.

4. SACP clients will be formally screened for conditions that result in immunosuppressed conditions. Any client who is immunosuppressed will be encouraged to consult with his or her medical doctor prior to interacting with the Resident Pet Partners. Should SACP have any concern, the client's case will be staffed with the JCDHE Medical Director for any additional needed precautions prior to interaction with the Pet Partners.

5. The Resident Pet Partners may offer AAA visits to SACP clients before or after substance abuse treatment groups, or during designated breaks. These visits will be coordinated with the SACP employee's/ Pet Partner's other work obligations. Any client who demonstrates continued disrespect toward the animal or who does not respond to redirection will be referred to his or her primary counselor, and an appropriate treatment plan will be developed to address this behavior. The visit may be terminated at the discretion of the employee/Resident Pet Partner.

6. Clients will be encouraged to wash their hands after interaction with the Resident Animal.

7. Clients will not be allowed to engage in any aggressive play (e.g., tug games) and must be respectful of the animal's wishes for space.

8. The Resident Pet Partners may offer AAT services to currently enrolled SACP clients and their families. A treatment plan will be developed for AAT services, sessions will be documented in the clients' files, and treatment progress will be followed and communicated to the clients' primary counselors. Although the clients' primary counselors may participate in AAT services, the sole responsibility for these services will remain with the SACP employee/Pet Partner.

In the event of an injury, the following steps shall be taken:

1. The employee/Pet Partner will secure the animal so that the situation can be managed. The animal is not to be tied to any furniture, but should be put in the car (weather permitting) or an office.

2. If a person is injured, the employee/Pet Partner is to act as per JCDHE guidelines to obtain treatment services.

3. The employee/Pet Partner will immediately inform his or her direct supervisor and complete the JCDHE Incident Report Form.

4. The Resident Pet Partner program will be continued only after consultation with the Director of Health Promotion and Lifestyle Management and/or the Executive Director.

AAA Visiting Pet Partners Guidelines:

1. AAA volunteers must be Delta-registered Pet Partners and, as such, agree to the Delta Society Policies and Procedures for Registered Pet Partners as described in Appendix B.
2. Registered Pet Partner volunteers are covered by Delta Society's $1 million personal liability insurance.
3. As Delta-registered Pet Partners, handlers will have specific training and pass rigorous screening from Delta-licensed instructors and evaluators, and veterinarians. Retesting every two years ensures program quality and consistency.
4. Current documentation of volunteer Pet Partners and animal credentials shall be maintained in the Program Manager's office and will be available for review upon request.
5. Volunteers must adhere to all JCDHE policies and procedures, including the following:
   —Sign in when entering the building
   —Demonstrate full compliance with immunization requirements
   —Sign a confidentiality statement agreeing to comply with state and federal laws that govern SACP (including 42 CFR, Part 2 and HIPAA)
6. Volunteers must be knowledgeable about the SACP Policies and Procedures that govern their behavior and respond according to JCDHE staff instruction.
7. Volunteers must wear/display Delta Society identification at all times when at JCDHE.
8. Volunteers and their animals must shadow twice with a current Delta Pet Partner before beginning their individual volunteer service.
9. Volunteers will be able to explain the program and answer any questions.
10. Volunteers must follow Delta Society protocol (See Appendix B) for reporting any incident that occurs at JCDHE. Should an incident occur, the volunteer program will be suspended until it is fully investigated and permission to resume is obtained from the JCDHE Executive Director.

_____   _____
Outpatient Program Manager   Date

Appendix A (McQuarrie, 2002)

Animal-Assisted Activities (AAA)

The formal definition* of animal-assisted activities is:

"Activities that involve animals visiting people. The same activity can be repeated with different people, unlike a therapy program that is tailored to a particular person or medical condition."

"AAA provides opportunities for motivational, educational, recreational, and/or therapeutic benefits to enhance quality of life. AAA are delivered in a variety of environments by specially trained professionals, paraprofessionals, and/or volunteers in association with animals that meet specific criteria." (From *Standards of Practice for Animal-Assisted Activities and Therapy,* Delta Society, 1996.)

Key Features of AAA

Specific treatment goals are not planned for each visit.

Volunteers and treatment providers are not required to take detailed notes.

Visit content is spontaneous and visits last as long or as short as needed.

Animal-Assisted Therapy (AAT)

The formal definition* of animal-assisted therapy is:

"AAT involves a health or human service professional who uses an animal as part of his/her job. Specific goals for each client have been identified by the professional, and progress is measured and recorded."

"AAT is goal-directed intervention in which an animal that meets specific criteria is an integral part of the treatment process. AAT is directed and/or delivered by a health/human service professional with specialized expertise, and within the scope of practice of his/her profession."

"AAT is designed to promote improvement in human physical, social, emotional, and/or cognitive functioning (cognitive functioning refers to think-

---

*Reprinted courtesy of Delta Society®.

ing and intellectual skills). AAT is provided in a variety of settings and may be group or individual in nature. This process is documented and evaluated." (*Standards of Practice for Animal-Assisted Activities and Therapy, Delta Society,* 1996.)

Key Features of AAT

There are specified goals and objective for each individual.

Progress is measured.

Appendix B (McQuarrie, 2002)

Delta Society Policies and Procedures for Registered Pet Partners

1. Handlers shall visit with only one animal at a time.
2. Handlers shall visit only with animals registered with the Pet Partners Program.
3. Handlers shall ensure that policies and procedures are in place regarding Animal-Assisted Activities or Therapy.
4. Handlers shall abide by all policies, procedures, and precautions of each facility/unit visited.
5. Prior to each visit, handler shall:
   —Assess animal's overall health and attitude
   —Clean and brush the animal according to facility/program requirements
   —Cut and file nails; clean eyes and ears
   —Allow the animal time to exercise and eliminate
6. Handlers shall check in with the staff/supervisor upon arrival for each visit.
7. Handlers shall observe all rules of privacy and confidentiality.
8. Handlers shall be on time for every commitment made.
9. Handlers shall be responsible at all times for the animal, considering the animal's needs and humane care first. Handlers shall always stay with the animal and in control of the situation. For safety, all animals must wear a collar or harness and be on lead at all times. This is true during Pet Partners testing as well as during visits.

   Dogs shall wear a nylon, cloth, or leather buckle collar. Dogs shall be on a cloth, nylon, or leather leash that is no more than six feet long. Dog prong or pinch collars and retractable leads are prohibited during visits.

   Animals such as cats, rabbits, guinea pigs, etc., shall be carried in a basket and/or on a towel and must wear a collar/harness and be on a lead at all times.

Caged birds that leave their cage for visits must be in a harness and on lead at all times. Caged birds that visit in their cage do not require a harness.

10. Handlers shall dress appropriately for the volunteer assignment. Be comfortable, neat, clean, and well groomed.
11. Handlers shall clean up after the animal, both inside and outside the facility.
12. Handlers shall *not* tie animals to people, equipment, or furniture while visiting.
13. Use of drugs and/or alcohol is strictly prohibited on the day of the visit.
14. Handlers shall not routinely give or accept gifts from people they visit.
15. Handlers shall not charge fees for their services.
16. In case of an accident or unusual occurrence, handlers shall:
    —Secure the animal
    —Get help for the injured person
    —Notify your facility contact person in writing so that it can be documented in the person's medical file
    —Fill out all necessary documentation at the facility
    —End the visit
    —Notify the organization sponsoring the visit
    —Notify Delta Society national office for insurance purposes
    —Evaluate the situation for future prevention

Bibliography

Associated Press. (2004, July 12). Iraqi kitten reunites with Fort Carson soldier. Available at: http://9news.com.

Beck, A., & Katcher, A. (1996). *Between pets and people.* West Lafayette, IN: Purdue University.

Berg, I. K. (1994). *Family-based services: A solution-focused approach.* New York: Norton.

Berg, I. K. (1995). Solution-focused brief therapy with substance abusers. In A. Washton (Ed.), *Psychotherapy and substance abuse: A practitioner's handbook* (pp. 223-242). New York: Guilford.

Berg, I. K., & Dolan, Y. (2001). *Tales of solutions: A collection of hope-inspiring stories.* New York: Norton.

Berg, I. K., & Gallagher, D. (1991). Solution focused brief treatment with adolescent substance abusers. In T. C. Todd & M. D. Selekman (Eds.), *Family therapy approaches with adolescent substance abusers* (pp. 93-111). Needham Heights, MA: Allyn and Bacon.

Berg, I. K., & Miller, S. D. (1992). *Working with the problem drinker: A solution-focused approach.* New York: Norton.

Berg, I. K., & Reuss, N. (1998). *Solutions step by step: A substance abuse treatment manual.* New York: Norton.

Berg, I. K., & Steiner, T. (2003). *Children's solution work.* New York: Norton.

Bobele, M., Gardner, G., & Biever, J. (1995). Supervision as social construction. *Journal of Systemic Therapies, 14*(2), 14-25.

Burch, M. R. (1996). *Volunteering with your pet: How to get involved in animal-assisted therapy with any kind of pet.* New York: Howell Book House.

Clothier, S. (2002). *Bones would rain from the sky: Deepening our relationships with dogs.* New York: Warner.

Coren, S. (2000). *How to speak dog: Mastering the art of dog-human communication.* New York: Fireside.

Crawford, J. J., & Pomerinke, K. A. (2003). *Therapy pets: The animal-human healing partnership.* Amherst, NY: Prometheus.

Cusack, O., & Smith, E. (Eds.). (1984). *Pets and the elderly: The therapeutic bond.* Binghamton, NY: Haworth.

Davis, K. D. (2002). *Therapy dogs: Training your dog to reach others* (2nd ed.). Wenatchee, WA: Dogwise.

de Shazer, S. (1985). *Keys to solution in brief therapy.* New York: Norton.

de Shazer, S. (1988). *Clues: Investigating solutions in brief therapy.* New York: Norton.

de Shazer, S. (1991). *Putting difference to work.* New York: Norton.

de Shazer, S. (1994). *Words were originally magic.* New York: Norton.

de Shazer, S., & Isebaert, L. (2003). "A solution-focused approach to the treatment of problematic drinking." *Journal of Family Psychotherapy, 14*(4), 43-52.

DeJong, P., & Berg, I. K. (2002). *Interviewing for solutions* (rev. ed.). Pacific Grove, CA: Brooks/Cole.

Delta Society. (1996). *Standards of practice for animal-assisted activities and therapy* (No. AAT251). Renton, WA: Author.

Delta Society. (1997). *Therapeutic interventions* (No. AAT253). Renton, WA: Author.

Delta Society (May 2003). *Animal-assisted therapy (AAT) applications I student guide.* (No. AAT-711). Renton, WA: Author.

Dibra, B. (1999). *Dog speak: How to learn it, speak it, and use it to have a happy, healthy, well-behaved dog.* New York: Fireside.

Dolan, Y. M. (1985). *A path with a heart: Ericksonian utilization with resistant and chronic clients.* New York: Brunner/Mazel.

Dolan, Y. M. (1991). *Resolving sexual abuse: Solution-focused therapy and Ericksonian hypnosis for adult survivors.* New York: Norton.

Dolan, Y. (1998). *One small step: Moving beyond trauma and therapy to a life of joy.* Watsonville, CA: Papier-Mache.

Donaldson, J. (1996). *The culture clash.* Oakland: James & Kenneth Publishers.

Donley, R. J., Horan, J. J., & DeShong, R. L. (1989). The effect of several self-disclosure permutations on counseling process and outcome. *Journal of Counseling and Development, 67*(7), 408-412.

Dunbar, I. (1979). *Dog behavior.* Neptune, NJ: T.H.F. Publications, Inc.

Dunbar, I. (1991). *How to teach a new dog old tricks.* Oakland: Kenneth & James.

Duncan, B. L., Hubble, M. A., & Miller, S. D. (1997, July/August). Stepping off the throne. *The Family Therapy Networker, 21*(4), 22-33.

Eckholm, E. (2001, March 19). Dog's life in china: Hiding from police dragnets. *The New York Times* (Late Edition, East Coast), p. A4.

Eckholm, E. (2004, April 11). How's china doing? Yardsticks you never thought of. *The New York Times* (Late Edition, East Coast), p. 6.

Fine, A. (Ed.). (2000). *Handbook on animal-assisted therapy: Theoretical foundations and guidelines for practice.* San Diego: Academic Press.

Friedmann, E., Katcher, A. H., Lynch, J. J., & Thomas, S. A. (1980). Animal companions and one-year survival of patients after discharge from a coronary care unit. *Public Health Reports, 95,* 307-312.

Friedmann, E., Katcher, A. H., Thomas, S. A., Lynch, J. J., & Messent, P. R. (1983). Social interaction and blood pressure. *Journal of Nervous and Mental Disease,171,* 461-465.

Gerben, R. (2003). Kids + dogs = combination for paw-rrific reading adventures. *Interactions, 21*(2), 4-8.

Haggerty, C. (2000). *How to teach your dog to talk.* New York: Fireside.

Howie, A. R. (Ed.). (2000). *The pet partners team training course* (5th ed.). Renton, WA: Delta Society.

Intermountain Therapy Animals (2003-2004). *Reading education assistance dogs training manual.* Salt Lake City, UT: Author.

Johnson, C.E., & Webster, D. (2002). *Recrafting a life.* New York: Taylor & Francis.

Maslow, A.H. (1969). *The psychology of science: A reconnaissance.* Chicago: H. Regnery.

McCollum, E., & Trepper, T. S. (2001). *Family solutions for substance abuse.* Binghamton, NY: Haworth.

McNicholas, J., & Collis, G. M. (1995). The end of a relationship: Coping with pet loss. In I. Robinson (Ed.), *The Waltham book of human-animal interaction: Benefits and responsibilities of pet ownership* (pp. 127-143). Oxford: Pergamon.

McQuarrie, D.M. (2002). *Policy and procedure for animal-assisted activities/therapy.* Denver, CO: Denver Pet Partners.

Monks of New Skete. (2002). *How to be your dog's best friend* (2nd ed.). New York: Little Brown.

Monks of New Skete. (2003). *I & dog.* New York: Yorkville Press.

Miller, G. (1997). *Becoming miracle workers: Language and meaning in brief therapy.* New York: Aldine de Gruyter.

Miller, G., & de Shazer, S. (1998). Have you heard the latest rumor about . . .? Solution-focused therapy as a rumor. *Family Process, 37*(3), 363-377.

Miller, S. D., & Berg, I. K. (1995). *The miracle method: A radically new approach to problem drinking.* New York: Norton.

Miller, S. D., Duncan, B. L., & Hubble, M. A. (1997). *Escape from babel: Toward a unifying language for psychotherapy practice.* New York: Norton.

Nightingale, F. (1860). *Notes on nursing: What it is, and what it is not.* New York: Appleton.

Peca-Baker, T. M., & Friedlander, M. L. (1989). Why are self-disclosing counselors attractive? *Journal of Counseling and Development, 67*(5), 279-282.

Pichot, T. (2001). Co-creating solutions for substance abuse. *Journal of Systemic Therapies, 20*(2), 1-23.

Pichot, T. (2001). What's the big deal about solution focused therapy, anyway? *Professional Counselor, 2*(3), 39-41.

Pichot, T. (in press). Discovering the true expert of the therapeutic process. *Professional Counselor.*

Pichot, T., & Dolan, Y. M. (2003). *Solution-focused brief therapy: Its effective use in agency settings.* Binghamton, NY: Haworth.

Pryor, K. (1999). *Don't shoot the dog* (revised). North Bend: Sunshine Books.

Rugaas, T. (1997). *On talking terms with dogs: Calming signals.* Sequim, WA: Legacy Publications.

Saletan, W. (2002, January 16). Wok the dog; What's wrong with eating man's best friend? Available at: http://slate.msn.com/id/2060840/.

Salmansohn, K. (1994). *How to make your man behave in 21 days or less, using the secrets of professional dog trainers.* New York: Workman.

Selekman, M. D. (1997). *Solution-focused therapy with children.* New York: Guilford.

Serpell, J. A. (1996). *In the company of animals* (2nd ed.). Cambridge: Cambridge University Press.

Siegel, J. M. (1990). Stressful life events and use of physician services among the elderly: The moderating role of pet ownership. *Journal of Personality and Social Psychology, 58,* 1081-1086.

Sussman M. B. (Ed.). (1985). *Pets and the family.* Binghamton, NY: Haworth.

Thomas, J. D. (2003). *Messiah.* Nampa, ID: Pacific Press.

Tillman, P. (2000). *Clicking with your dog.* Waltham, MA: Sunshine Books.

Werner-Wilson, R. J. J. (2000). *Developmental systemic family therapy with adolescents.* Binghamton, NY: Haworth.

Wilkes, G. (1995). *The click and treat starter kit* (with video). North Blend: Sunshine Books.

Wilson, C. C., & Turner, D. C. (Eds.). (1998). *Companion animals in human health.* Thousand Oaks, CA: Sage.

Index

Page numbers followed by the letter "f" indicate figures.